Exploring well-being in the early years

Exploring well-being in the early years

Edited by Julia Manning-Morton

Mc
Graw
Hill
Education
Open University Press

Open University Press
McGraw-Hill Education
McGraw-Hill House
Shoppenhangers Road
Maidenhead
Berkshire
England
SL6 2QL

email: enquiries@openup.co.uk
world wide web: www.openup.co.uk

and Two Penn Plaza, New York, NY 10121-2289, USA

First published 2014

Copyright © Julia Manning-Morton, 2014

A catalogue record of this book is available from the British Library

ISBN-13: 978-0-335-24684-7
ISBN-10: 0-335-24684-2
eISBN: 978-0-335-24685-4

Library of Congress Cataloging-in-Publication Data
CIP data applied for

Typeset by Aptara, Inc.
Printed and bound by CPI Group (UK) Ltd, Croydon, CR0 4YY

Praise for this book

"The 'now' of children's experience emerges as a critical factor from the 'Talking about Young Children's Well-being' Project. It is a timely reminder that young children have a right to be listened to. Well-being as a concept is redefined using the voices of children, parents and practitioners. Important questions are raised about the cost to individuals and society if this is not taken seriously. The authors of each chapter use the research findings to reflect on current early years policy and practice. Their conclusions catch us at the crossroads of a deeply political debate."

Dilys Wilson, Senior Lecturer in Early Childhood Studies at
Middlesex University, UK

"At a time of austerity and pressure on family life and early childhood, I consider this book to be both insightful and thought provoking which has both breadth and depth. Dedicating a book to exploring well-being in early childhood demonstrates a commitment by the author and colleagues to delve deeper into the vital issues of well-being and the impact within early childhood. This text brings together research literature, theoretical understanding and practical application. Recognising the practitioners and leaders who work within early childhood and their well-being is a testament to all involved in co-constructing this text. This book captures the essence of early childhood and provides a dialogue and debate of holistically challenging well-being for all. This is a book to be treasured."

Dr Lesley Curtis, Headteacher/Head of Centre,
Everton Nursery School and Family Centre

"This book is an essential discussion and authoritative account of the explorations and research outcomes of the LMU/NCB project 'Talking about well-being in early childhood'.

The strength of the book is that it represents multi-faceted perspectives about children's well-being that underpin the values and principles of inclusion, understanding that children are citizens with personhood and rights. The influences and barriers to children's well-being are raised and challenged throughout each of the chapters, looking through the multiple lenses of policy, contemporary practice and professionalism.

The social, cultural and political chronology is useful for novice researchers, practitioners and policy makers to consider where well-being of young children is positioned in the here and now. The importance of the well-being of the practitioners is addressed for development in early childhood settings, and completes the essential requirement for reflexive and supportive practice as part of supporting children's well-being. This book will be useful for academics, and practitioners working directly with children and families and anyone studying well-being and applications to contemporary practice in cultural contexts."

Estelle Martin, Anglia Ruskin University, UK

"This book really does explore well-being - thoughtfully, actively and practically and from a range of points of view. It is based on a deep and honest respect for young children and the adults who work and play with them and it illustrates with passion and insight the ways in which emotional and physical well-being are built on positive relationships and connections between people."

Helen Moylett, Early Years Consultant and writer

"This is a comprehensively researched book deriving from collaborative work in the early years. It discusses the complex concept of the well-being of young children and how this determines their life opportunities. From an equality perspective it identifies key issues that practitioners, trainers, policy makers and academics should note with serious concern, including the disproportionate impact of inequality on particular groups. Furthermore, and critically, it opens up the way for future analysis of how society can become more at ease with itself so that the unwitting consequences of deeply embedded institutional discrimination, intolerance, negative assumptions, expectations and judgements are removed from young children's lives."

Jane Lane (advocate worker for racial equality in the early years)

Contents

About the editor and contributors

Julia Manning-Morton has worked as an early years practitioner, manager, adviser, and inspector across a range of settings for children aged 0–8 years, and for 13 years was a senior lecturer and Programme Director for Early Childhood taught courses at London Metropolitan University. Julia's research and writing are focused on practice and provision that meet the needs of children from birth to 3 years and on the personal, social, and emotional well-being of children and practitioners. Julia was the lead coordinator of the London Metropolitan University/National Children's Bureau Project 'Talking about Young Children's Well-being', 2009–2011.

Deborah Albon has worked in a variety of early childhood settings as a nursery nurse, teacher, and then senior manager, primarily in West London from the early 1980s. Since 2003 she has worked across a range of early childhood programmes at London Metropolitan University as a senior lecturer in Early Childhood Studies. Deborah's PhD research looked at children's playful participation in 'food events' in four early childhood settings.

Mary Dickins originally trained as a primary school teacher and has worked with young children and families in various capacities for 34 years. Mary is a specialist in special educational needs and equality issues and has worked with a wide range of national and local organizations and published widely on this issue. She is a senior lecturer at London Metropolitan University and also works as an independent consultant and author on all aspects of equality and inclusion for young children. Mary was part of the core team of the London Metropolitan University/National Children's Bureau Project 'Talking about Young Children's Well-being', 2009–2011.

Penny Holland worked in a wide range of community education, primary, and early childhood settings as an administrator, development worker, adult educator, teacher, and practitioner before joining London Metropolitan University as a senior lecturer in Early Childhood Studies in 1999. She subsequently held the post of Academic Leader for Early Childhood until March 2012. She is an established author who specializes in gender, creativity, and war, weapon and superhero play and now works as an independent early childhood consultant.

Micky LeVoguer is Senior Lecturer in Early Childhood Studies at London Metropolitan University where she teaches on the undergraduate and postgraduate degree programmes. Before working at the University, Micky worked in early childhood education settings and with organizations attached to children's centres to develop services for children, parents, and carers. During her MA in Early Childhood Education, she researched into children's movement and the conditions that enable it to flourish in settings. This has led to working with performers and dance movement therapists to explore the common ground between dance and early childhood.

Melian Mansfield has had extensive experience of the early childhood field and has a thorough knowledge of all aspects of the UK education system from pre-school to post 16. She has worked extensively on policy issues, promoting and defending early childhood provision at all levels of politics and policy making. She has also worked directly in supporting and developing practitioners through her roles as a trainer, governor, and consultant. She has published reviews and articles on a range of education issues for a variety of newspapers, magazines, and journals and is currently chair of the Early Childhood Forum set up by the National Children's Bureau.

Penny Mukherji is an established author with a background in health and psychology. She has been involved in the training and education of early years practitioners in both further and higher education for nearly 30 years and was part of the core team of the London Metropolitan University/National Children's Bureau Project 'Talking about Young Children's Well-being', 2009–2011.

Jasmine Pasch is an experienced community dance artist, choreographer, and educator with a freelance career spanning 30 years. Trained as a professional dancer, teacher, and counsellor, Jasmine has worked in education, arts, and health settings with babies, toddlers, young children, and their parents. She is now a consultant and trainer for local authorities and a visiting lecturer at London Metropolitan University on the Early Childhood Studies degree programme.

Linda Pound has worked in three universities and was an LEA inspector responsible for the early years for almost 10 years. In addition, she has been head of a nursery school and deputy head of a primary school. In her current role as an education consultant, she provides training for early years practitioners around the country and beyond. Linda writes extensively for a range of audiences on a variety of topics related to early childhood care and education.

Judy Stevenson OBE has worked in London as a nursery teacher, nursery school head teacher, OFSTED Inspector and head of an Early Years Centre, joining London Metropolitan University in 2007 as Programme Manager for both the National Professional Qualification in Early Years Leadership (NPQICL) and Early Years Professional Status. She is currently a principal lecturer for Early Childhood at the University. Judy has a particular interest in leadership and management alongside the development of reflective practice.

Acknowledgements

This book was written during a time of great difficulty for many of the people involved, with external factors such as budget cuts, job losses, and policy changes interacting with personal issues that together often threatened our sense of well-being. So my heartfelt thanks go to the contributors to this book for sticking with it and for the expert knowledge and perceptive understanding you each have brought to the book.

The book could not have been written without the enthusiastic and wise contributions of the children, parents, and practitioners from childminding, playgroup, children's centre, nursery school, and university settings, who were also struggling with difficult times during the project – thank you for your generosity and commitment.

I'd also like to thank Jill whose therapeutic guidance has helped me to understand that experiencing well-being is not only possible but permissible and desirable, even in the face of adverse beginnings and during times of great difficulty, and Cesca, whose yoga teaching ensures I regularly appreciate the holistic nature of well-being as a lived experience.

Julia Manning-Morton

Introduction: talking about well-being in early childhood

Julia Manning-Morton

This book arose from the London Metropolitan University/National Children's Bureau Project 'Talking about Young Children's Well-being' (2009–2011) (LMU/NCB Well-being Project). The project came about through discussions between colleagues at LMU and NCB about the view of well-being set out in a range of contemporary policy and guidance documents.

Anyone concerned and involved with young children could not have failed to notice the flurry of media anxiety about children's and young people's well-being in the UK, where there is a general sense that all is not as well as it could be with children and childhood. As it seems in wider society, so it was in the project discussions, that there is general agreement that the well-being of children should always be paramount and therefore should rightfully be a central focus of policy and practice guidelines. Over the last decade, legislation such as Every Child Matters (DfES 2004) and The Children's Plan (DCSF 2007) have aimed to improve outcomes for children's well-being and to 'make this [the UK] the best place in the world for our children and young people to grow up' (DCSF 2007). Such aims and discussions have filtered through to guidance in the early childhood sector through documents such as 'Promoting emotional health and well-being through the National Healthy School Standard' (DoH/DfES 2004) and 'The Early Years Foundation Stage' (EYFS; DfES 2007) standards and curriculum document, which was current at the time.

However, House and Loewenthal (2010) suggest that, as a society, the UK is far from attaining the child-centred approach set out in these documents, and the LMU/NCB project team wondered about the extent to which this was also true of practice in early childhood settings. So the project discussions also focused on practitioners' views on how the EYFS and other policies supported them in providing for young children's well-being. Ideas arising from these discussions are spread throughout the chapters in this book but in Chapter 2, Melian Mansfield and Linda Pound address some of the more general points made about policy and discuss the wider policy context in which we think about children's well-being in the early years.

The economic imperative for addressing well-being, with its emphasis on human capital and future outcomes, plays a central role in government policies that relate to well-being and in much research and many publications on well-being, such as in the New Economics Foundation/Action for Children report 'Backing the future, why investing in children is good for us all' (Aked et al. 2009). For the LMU/ NCB project team, putting children's well-being at the forefront of our thinking was important not only because children's experiences in their earliest years underpin and highly influence their future development and learning and therefore their future contribution to society, but also because their experiences in the here and now are as important as any later outcomes in development. In this respect, the project shared the view expressed by the Good Childhood Inquiry panel that, 'Children are not "incomplete adults"; their current quality of life is as important as the future adults they will become' (Layard and Dunn 2009: 153).

For parents and practitioners sharing this view, promoting children's well-being is a core concern. Yet it is apparent that 'well-being' is a complex concept that has different emphases according to the different perspectives of different disciplines. The project team were therefore interested in how 'well-being' is interpreted in the early childhood field and in Chapter 1, Julia Manning-Morton gives an overview of concepts of well-being and presents the LMU/NCB Project's view that arose from the contributions of practitioners, parents, and children; exploring both the consensus in understandings expressed by stakeholders about 'what well-being looks like' and also the different emphases given by different stakeholders (most notably between adults and children) on what contributes to a sense of well-being.

Much of the concern about children's and young people's well-being reported in the media in recent years has arisen from research such as the UNICEF (2007) report *Child Poverty in Perspective: An Overview of Child Well-being in Rich Countries*. The UNICEF report compared overall child well-being across 21 rich countries and looked at material well-being, health and safety, education, peer and family relationships, behaviours and risks, and young people's subjective sense of their own well-being in order to present a picture of children's lives. It found, for five out of the six dimensions reviewed, that the UK was in the bottom third of the country rankings. Although the UK ranked higher in the educational well-being dimension, we lagged behind in terms of relative poverty and deprivation, quality of children's relationships with their parents and peers, child health and safety, behaviour and risk-taking, and subjective well-being.

Rees et al. (2010) suggest that it is important to know more about why there is this variation between countries because measures of well-being are useful indicators of a functioning society. On this basis, it seems, there are strong grounds for worrying about the functioning of UK society at this present time and, for the Good Childhood Inquiry (Layard and Dunn 2009), the issue of income inequality is one of the roots of this malfunction, an issue that was raised often in the LMU/NCB Well-being Project discussion groups and so explored further by Mary Dickins in Chapter 3 of this book.

Young children's voices

The LMU/NCB project team were also concerned that the concepts of well-being which were influencing policy and practice in the early years are derived entirely from research with children in late childhood and adolescence. As the Unicef report says about its own data, 'the majority of the available statistics relate to the lives of older children' (UNICEF 2007: 3). Most often, measures of well-being for our youngest children are based on objective proxies such as mortality rates and school immunization rates or family income. Sometimes it is measured through subjective proxies such as from the views of experts or teachers/carers (Camfield et al. 2009). In an adult-centred world though, the tendency is to look at children's issues only as they affect adults rather than through the eyes of the children themselves (House and Loewenthal 2010) and clearly, as Ben-Arieh (2008) points out, such methods cannot give a true picture of how children experience their lives. So, some researchers have developed approaches in which children and young people are involved directly in reporting their views. However, even authors and organizations that are critical of measuring children's well-being through indirect methods and advocate ensuring that children's views are heard, have problems including our youngest children. Camfield et al. (2009: 14), for example, assert that 'Engaging with children's experiences and perspectives is beneficial from an analytical as well as an ethical perspective as children are usually the best source of information on their daily activities'. Yet the youngest children, they suggest, are unable to engage in abstract concepts 'in some contexts' until the age of 7. Thus, key pieces of research on children's well-being do not address the well-being of 0–6 year olds directly. For example, The Children's Society's *Understanding Children's Well-being: A National Survey of Young People's Well-being* (Rees et al. 2010) is focused on 10–15 year olds and the Good Childhood Inquiry involved children between 8 and 15 years (Rees et al. 2012).

The use of subjective indicators of well-being is often regarded as problematic in research. Subjective views are seen as inherently unreliable, given the individual contexts of the respondents and the multiplicity of meanings and interpretations that can be attached to them. In addition, young children's ability to report on how they feel and what they think is perceived as unreliable. For example, Thompson and Aked (2009: 5) state, 'children may not be able to report reliably on their inner feelings. Clearly, for pre-school-aged children, reliability is likely to be a problem.' The result of these concerns is that young children's opinions about their experiences are not sought or recorded in the name of 'objectivity' and 'measurability' and so they become invisible. This issue of reliability was something the LMU/NCB project team kept in mind throughout our analysis of the evidence gathered. For example, we were aware that often the children described the activity they were engaged in at the time as the thing that made them happy, which some adults may interpret as children not really understanding the question or being easily influenced by external factors. But maybe this isn't unreliability, maybe it makes more sense if you consider that the child has chosen that activity in the first place as something they like doing. Also, it seems from the many examples given by adults in the discussion groups that this focus the children had, on being 'in the moment' and therefore feeling content, is a useful lesson adults can learn, as we are told that 'mindfulness' contributes to a sense of well-being. In addition, these responses from children reinforce the message that what is important for children's well-being is attention to their present experiences, not calculating their future outcomes.

This example reinforces the LMU/NCB project team's view that not including young children's voices is potentially more of a problem than their perceived unreliability. Aspects of their experience, such as what they think about their relationships with family, friends, and central persons in settings, which are key to their well-being, will not be adequately represented in policy development or practice if they are not heard. Indeed, it was these aspects of children's well-being and the importance of parents' and practitioners' well-being that were most discussed in the LMU/NCB project discussion groups, and so form a major focus in Chapters 4 and 11 by Julia Manning-Morton and Chapter 10 by Penny Mukherji.

But some researchers such as Rees et al. (2010) do acknowledge the limitations of focusing only on older children, asking, 'What are we missing about the well-being of younger children?' (p. 85). In the LMU/NCB Well-being Project, we thought that possibly quite a lot was being missed. As a consequence, the project set out to examine the concept of well-being in early childhood through enabling debate and discussion within the early childhood field. We aimed to gather views about children's well-being that would support the early years sector in developing clarity in relation to principles and practice and thereby influence early years policy and provision.

As advocates for young children and their families though, this meant not only hearing parents' and practitioners' views but also finding out what our youngest children think about their well-being. So, as well as seminars and focus group discussions for parents, practitioners, academics, and students, we developed opportunities for children's voices to be heard. This involved early years practitioners carrying out small pieces of research in their settings exploring young children's views. The pedagogical emphasis that the project team gives to the importance of close relationships in practice with young children meant that it was clear from the outset that these consultations should be carried out by practitioners who were familiar to the children (usually their key person) rather than an unfamiliar researcher. Underpinning the children's voices strand of the project was the concept of 'listening to children' as defined by the NCB Young Children's Voices Network (Williams 2009), which sees listening to young children as an integral part of understanding what they are feeling and what it is they need from their early years experience. The Network defines listening as an active process of receiving, interpreting, and responding to communication involving all the senses, and asserts that it is a necessary stage in ensuring children's participation. It is work such as this and the ideas of the 'mosaic approach' (Clark and Moss 2011) that open up the possibilities of including young children's views in research through using a range of techniques such as creative activities (photographic tours, art or puppets/persona dolls) as well as conversations and observations.

Research values

In this way, the LMU/NCB Well-being Project was constructed to reflect the values held by the project team. The core group members shared social-constructivist pedagogy and an holistic perspective on children's learning and development, reflecting ecological systems theory. Our approach also aimed to reflect andragogical principles of adults' learning (Knowles 1983), that is, to emphasize that there are different ways of knowing – through theory, research, observation and reflection, and that learning is mutual and life-long. This value base meant we designed the project to research 'with' rather than 'on' people, which is the central tenet of cooperative inquiry (Heron 1996; Reason and Bradbury 2001). Like andragogy, cooperative inquiry also identifies different types of knowledge, including practical knowing (the knowledge that comes with actually doing what you propose) and experiential knowing (the feedback we get in real time about our interaction with the world at large), so the project was planned to be a shared process with an experiential focus.

Our commitment to inclusion and developing a listening culture meant that we conceived of the research as a 'conversation' in which the voices of all early childhood stakeholders would be heard. This meant ensuring that the seminars and focus groups were planned at times and locations that would facilitate the attendance of practitioners and parents as well as academics, students, and strategic managers and that a range of settings in both rural and urban locations were represented. This approach met with some success, as the seminars included over 70 practitioners/ students and an additional 70 representatives of 35 different local authorities and 20 independent organizations from across England. In addition, nine practitioners facilitated a total of 13 focus groups in collaboration with the core project team. The 13 focus groups that contributed data to the project included practitioners and parents from eight children's centres (six in inner London, one in Liverpool, one in Manchester), two independent nursery schools (North London), preschool playgroups (rural North England) and childminders (rural South England), and a range of settings in outer London/Hertfordshire – a total of 19 parents (not including the Parents for Inclusion group discussed below) and 78 practitioners.

The gender composition of the seminar and focus groups reflected the early years workforce as a whole in as much as they were predominantly female, with only four males recorded as attending. (A point for future consideration might be whether holding a focus group discussion solely for male practitioners and parents might yield data with different or similar emphases.) Data on the ethnic background of individual participants was not collected, although focus group facilitators recorded the urban groups as being ethnically diverse, while the rural groups were ethnically homogeneous – white British/European. The project group made repeated attempts to arrange focus groups targeted at specific stakeholders, one of parents with children with disabilities and one of childminders of Bangladeshi origin. Unfortunately, bureaucratic delays in getting permission from the local authority management body to carry out the research in that particular children's centre meant that the Bangladeshi childminders group did not take place. There were also difficulties with convening the group of parents with children with disabilities, given that their time commitments to their children leaves very little for additional things such as sitting in a focus group! However, these parents' commitment to ensuring that their children were represented, perhaps facilitated by the independence of their organization, meant that they found a way to gather their views together into a written submission to the project team, which provided valuable insights as discussed by Mary Dickins in Chapter 9. Such situations give rise to necessary reflections on issues of power, voice, and inequality and so, as issues of equality were also identified in discussions as a key facet of well-being, Mary Dickins explores these issues further in Chapter 3.

The project focused on finding out what participants think and feel; a complicated endeavour, which also reflects what Jean McNiff (1988) calls the messy process of action research. This 'messiness' is at the centre of the project not only because of the complexity of the concept of well-being but also due to the intricacies of interaction between personal and professional experience and values that underpin the views expressed. In this project, this is also reflected in the variability in responses across groups according to the influence of the seminar group leader, the composition of the group (children, parents/practitioners, different professional disciplines, gender, and cultural background), the type of setting, and the geographical location. This variability, plus the numbers of participants involved, may raise questions of the validity of the project in research terms. However, the integrity of the project is in the clarity of values and principles that underpin it and its commitment to creating the opportunity for the views of the Early Childhood Community to be heard, which is why we called it a 'conversation'.

We believe that this 'conversation' has raised important issues regarding babies and young children's well-being and has clarified priorities in the field that should be kept at the forefront of practice and provision. Some of these, such as the fundamental importance of prioritizing children and families' socio-cultural contexts, addressing inequalities, and developing a listening culture are identified above. Others include:

- Children's personal, social, and emotional well-being and the relationships with adults and other children that enable this are a priority – as discussed in Chapter 4 by Julia Manning-Morton.
- Play and creativity and well-being are bi-directional; they feed into each other and must be at the core of provision – as highlighted by Deborah Albon in Chapter 5 and Penny Holland in Chapter 6.

- Children's health and physicality are central to well-being but need to be thought of broadly so as to embrace children's priorities for movement (especially outside) and their social experiences and contexts – as discussed by Micky LeVoguer and Jasmine Pasch in Chapter 7 and Deborah Albon and Penny Mukherji in Chapter 8.

Importantly this 'conversation' has emphasized the dynamic interaction between individual/subjective experiences and the social, cultural, economic, and political contexts of children's lives that impact on well-being. This particularly highlights the inseparability of adults' and children's well-being and therefore the need to consider the policy and practice contexts that enhance or inhibit the potential for parents and practitioners to experience well-being, as discussed by Penny Mukherji in Chapter 10, Julia Manning-Morton in Chapter 11, and Judy Stevenson in Chapter 12.

Above all, the LMU/NCB Well-being Project has shown that it is not only possible but crucial that we listen to what our youngest children themselves have to say. This has proved not only important in terms of adults developing a better understanding of children's concerns and priorities, but also in terms of the beneficial impact of the process of listening to the children in the project. All of the practitioners who participated in the children's voices strand of the project emphasized the value of the one-to-one conversations, the focused observations, and the consultations with children. This was echoed by the children, who explicitly and obviously enjoyed the conversations and being listened to; as one child asked, *When can we have chitter-chatter?*

Hill et al. (1996: 142) also found that being listened to and taken seriously led to the primary aged children in their research project identifying that adults should always:

- Stop – and think about children's point of view.
- Look – for their feelings.
- Listen – to what they say.

This is our wish for children and it seems it is also the wish of parents and practitioners involved in this project. When the LMU/NCB project core team sent an email to early childhood settings and academic colleagues enquiring whether anyone would like to be involved in this non-funded project, we received over 200 responses. This, we thought, was a measure of how seriously the issue of young children's well-being is taken in the early childhood field and of early childhood practitioners' commitment (whatever their role) to enabling the well-being of babies, young children, and their families. This commitment is unwavering, even in the face of the current damaging economic and political climate. At the time of writing, the squeezing of funding for local authority services in England as well as for organizations such as the National Children's Bureau, and the intensification of market principles in early childhood in both the voluntary sector and higher education, is resulting in difficult times for the three key partners in the LMU/NCB Well-being Project. The project argued strongly that the well-being of practitioners and families/carers is interwoven with the well-being of children, so the project team's advice at this time is to:

- Look after yourselves so that you are strong enough to defend your work (have fun, play).
- Know your principles and values so that you are clear what you want to defend and why (reflect, be still).
- Speak out where there is threat to children's, families', and practitioners' well-being (listen, talk, and protest)

We wish you well.

The LMU/NCB Well-being Project Core Team: Julia Manning-Morton, Penny Mukherji, and Mary Dickins, London Metropolitan University; Melian Mansfield and Heather Ransome, The National Children's Bureau; with valuable contributions also from Helen Wheeler and Lucy Williams.

References

Aked, J., Steuer, N., Lawlor, E. and Spratt, S. (2009) *Backing the Future: Why Investing in Children is Good for Us All*. London: New Economics Foundation and Action for Children.

Ben-Arieh, A. (2008) Indicators and indices of children's well-being: towards a more policy-oriented perspective, *European Journal of Education*, 43(1): 37–50.

Camfield, L., Streuli, N. and Woodhead, M. (2009) What's the use of 'well-being' in contexts of child poverty? Approaches to research, monitoring and children's participation, *International Journal of Children's Rights*, 17(1): 65–109.

Clark, A. and Moss, P. (2011) *Listening to Young Children: The Mosaic Approach*. London: National Children's Bureau.

Department for Children, Schools and Families (DCSF) (2007) *The Children's Plan: Building Brighter Futures*. London: TSO.

Department for Education and Skills (DfES) (2004) *Every Child Matters: Change for Children*. London: DfES. Available at: https://www.education.gov.uk/publications [accessed 7 January 2013].

Department for Education and Skills (DfES) (2007) *The Early Years Foundation Stage: Setting the Standards for Learning, Development and Care for Children from Birth to Five*. Nottingham: DfES Publications.

Department of Health/Department for Education and Skills (DoH/DfES) (2004) *Promoting Emotional Health and Wellbeing through the National Healthy School Standard*. Wetherby: Health Development Agency.

Heron, J. (1996) *Co-operative Inquiry: Research into the Human Condition*. London: Sage.

Hill, M., Layboum, A. and Borland, M. (1996) Engaging with primary-aged children about their emotions and well-being: methodological considerations, *Children and Society*, 10: 129–44.

House, R. and Loewenthal, D. (2010) *Childhood Well-being and a Therapeutic Ethos*. London: Karnac.

Knowles, M. (1983) Andragogy: an emerging technology for adult learning, in M. Tight (ed.) *Adult Learning and Education*. London: Croom Helm.

Layard, R. and Dunn, J. (2009) *A Good Childhood: Searching for Values in a Competitive Age. The Landmark Report for The Children's Society*. London: Penguin.

McNiff, J. (1988) *Action Research: Principles and Practice*. London: Routledge.

Reason, P. and Bradbury, H. (2001) *Handbook of Action Research*. London: Sage.

Rees, G., Bradshaw, J., Goswami, H. and Keung, A. (2010) *Understanding Children's Well-being: A National Survey of Young People's Well-being*. London: The Children's Society. Available at: http://www.childrenssociety.org.uk/sites/default/files/tcs/research_docs/Understanding%20children%27s%20wellbeing.pdf [accessed 7 January 2013].

Rees, G., Bradshaw, J., Goswami, H., Keung, A., Pople, L. and Main, G. (2012) *The Good Childhood Report 2012: A Review of Our Children's Well-being*. London: The Children's Society. Available at: http://www.childrenssociety.org.uk/sites/default/files/tcs/good_childhood_report_2012_final_0.pdf [accessed 7 January 2013].

Thompson, S. and Aked, J. (2009) *A Guide to Measuring Children's Well-being. Backing the Future: Practical Guide 2*. London: nef.

United Nations Children's Fund (UNICEF) (2007) *Child Poverty in Perspective: An Overview of Child Well-being in Rich Countries. A Comprehensive Assessment of the Lives and Well-being of Children and Adolescents in the Economically Advanced Nations*. Innocenti Report Card 7. Florence: UNICEF Innocenti Research Centre.

Williams, L. (2009) *Listening as a Way of Life*. London: The Young Children's Voices Network, National Children's Bureau.

Part 1

Young children's well-being in context

1 Thinking about well-being in early childhood

Julia Manning-Morton

The London Metropolitan University/National Children's Bureau Project 'Talking about Young Children's Well-Being': the project's conception of well-being

> Well-being is a state that is dynamic and mutable and for which pre-disposing factors and experiences are necessary. These factors interact, combine and accumulate to enable or preclude experiencing states of well-being. In this way factors that are internal/subjective may be enhanced or exacerbated by external social, economic and policy factors and our interpretation and engagement with social factors are influenced by our inner well-being.

Introduction

This chapter explores some of the ways in which well-being is understood in a wider theoretical context and how those ideas link with the concept of well-being that emerged from the London Metropolitan University/National Children's Bureau Project 'Talking about Young Children's Well-Being' (LMU/NCB Well-being Project). It considers the multi-dimensional and dynamic nature of well-being and locates ideas of well-being in a social as well as a personal context.

The chapter considers the instrumental approach to measuring well-being taken in many pieces of research and discusses the importance of adopting a holistic approach when considering the well-being of young children and infants and the implications of that for practice in early childhood settings.

Why think about concepts of well-being in early childhood?

The primary aim of the LMU/NCB Well-being Project was to enable debate and discussion across the field in order to examine the concept of well-being in early childhood and thereby develop clarity in relation to principles and practice. Initially, this might appear straightforward, as it might be assumed that all those concerned with young children would agree on what is meant by well-being. However, as with any process of examination, not only do different views about a concept arise, the concept itself may be problematized.

This is certainly the case with the concept of well-being. Not only is the term used to mean slightly different things by different groups of people, but it has also been deconstructed and criticized by researchers and writers. One critique is that the multiplicity of definitions and meanings render the overall concept of well-being an 'empty notion' (Seedhouse 1995). In this perspective, it only makes sense to look at specific areas such as health, income or life satisfaction separately, rather than use well-being as an overarching concept. However, rather than an 'all or nothing' (well-being is a generally understood and meaningful term or well-being is an empty signifier) approach, the LMU/NCB Well-being Project accepted that 'well-being' is a contested concept that will have different meanings in different contexts, as Seedhouse (1995) also suggests. This view was evident in the project, with participants frequently identifying that 'well-being means different things to different people' and that there is a socio-cultural dimension to how well-being is conceived and therefore experienced. Taking this perspective means that exploration of those conceptions and experiences becomes even more important and the purpose of discussions is then to explore the borders of different ideas and through so doing reach a broader understanding of well-being.

This is important because if, as professionals, our aim is to 'promote' children's well-being, we need to be clear what it is we are promoting and why. One of the critiques of the idea of well-being is that it can be used to support different political agendas according to the meaning ascribed to it by a particular group, thereby advancing a particular view of an appropriate lifestyle (Camfield et al. 2009). Examples of this might be the promotion of breastfeeding or smoking cessation in children's centre activities. Such policies, while positive in their specific support of good health, when linked to the concept of well-being might be criticized for placing all the responsibility for well-being on the individual, rather than also looking at the social context that might, for example, make breastfeeding a lower priority or stopping smoking difficult. Camfield et al. (2009) suggest that in this way, policies based on a concept of well-being can depoliticize adversity.

Considering objective and subjective factors of well-being

For these reasons and reflecting the project's ecological systems perspective (Bronfenbrenner 1979), participants in the LMU/NCB Well-being Project were asked to consider the wider social factors they thought affected children's well-being. The responses included issues such as community stability, outdoor spaces to be and to play in, affordable childcare, parental leave, quality of housing, wealth and poverty, and affordable activities in the community. Participants commented that 'well-being is underpinned by societal health', thereby applying the concept of well-being not only to individuals but also to social groups and communities. The practitioners/students in the seminars held at London Metropolitan University, drawn as they are from an urban, ethnically diverse population, drew due attention to the importance of social well-being and the effects of direct and indirect discrimination. They developed the notion of 'community esteem', which impacts on and interacts with individual self-esteem, as discussed further in Chapter 4.

The Children's Society report *A Good Childhood* (Layard and Dunn 2009) suggests that low self-esteem (and therefore low community esteem too) is linked to materialism and consumerism, whereby buying the 'right' pram/shoes/television gains you acceptance in a society that sees the having of such material possessions a sign of success. In this perspective, the need to bolster individual/family self-esteem through buying consumer goods can be understood as being particularly acute for families who belong to social groups that are less well accepted in wider society and/ or who have less social capital. Layard and Dunn (2009) suggest that this is more acute in societies such as the UK where there is a larger gap between those who are wealthy and those who are poor and also where individualism is promoted.

Participants in the LMU/NCB Well-being Project expressed concern about the increasing commercialization of childhood and the negative pressure they thought this put on children and families. However, when asked about their 'wishes', the children in the project expressed very modest desires in terms of toys but did name favourite toys that were marketed commercial items related to popular television programmes such as Thomas the Tank Engine and Fireman Sam. The emphasis the children put on sharing an interest in something like this was key, and Layard and Dunn (2009) also point out that children may understand the purchasing and having of goods as important for acceptance into friendship groups. In this way, such consumption can contribute positively to a child's well-being, where having a particular item acts as common ground or shared culture between children. However, pressure to acquire consumer goods and competition between children for them can also serve to highlight material inequality and relative poverty, which would then impact negatively on well-being.

These kinds of issues can be described as 'objective' factors of well-being, located in the child's meso-, exo-, and macro-systems (Bronfenbrenner 1979). They are also the kind of issues that have been used more as indicators of well-being in research, as they are seen to be observable facts and therefore scientific and bias-free and easier to measure. When applied to practice in early childhood settings, this emphasis on measurability privileges an instrumental approach to children's well-being; focusing on what children should know or what skills they need (Waters 2009).

Conversely, well-being factors that are located in the micro-system may, on the whole, be described as 'subjective' indicators; they are self-reported aspects such as positive and negative emotions, life satisfaction, and the quality of social relationships, thereby including children's lived experiences. The identification of subjective indicators of well-being was strong in the LMU/NCB Well-being Project discussions, with emotional and personal well-being and positive relationships being the most frequently noted areas.

There is often a distinction made between these subjective experiences of well-being and objective indicators. However, Camfield et al. (2009) assert that this distinction is not helpful as it overlooks the connections between them. Similarly, it could be argued that in early childhood practice, it is important that these two perspectives are linked. For example, children's factual learning about healthy eating will be inextricably linked with their experiences of mealtimes and the feelings they have about food, so each needs to be considered.

Such connections were inherent to the views expressed in the LMU/NCB Well-being Project, where the reciprocal interchange of individual and social experience was emphasized.

> Some of these things have to come from an internal sense that you develop, but it's important to be recognized and respected in the environment that you're in too.

> There are genetic factors and life experiences that affect well-being.

These views helped define the LMU/ NCB Well-being Project's emergent concept of well-being as 'a dynamic process in which factors that are internal/subjective may be enhanced or exacerbated by external social, economic, and policy factors'. This perspective is shared by other reports on children's well-being, such as The Happiness Counts Project by Action for Children, which states: 'children's well-being can be best thought of as emerging from the interaction between their external circumstances, inner resources and their capabilities and interactions with the world around them' (Aked et al. 2009: 29).

Reflective exercise

Consider a recent experience of well-being. To what extent was this experience engendered by internal or external factors? Was the experience enhanced or inhibited by any social or economic factors or by your personal response?

You could repeat this exercise focusing on an experience of ill-being too and consider which factors contribute to or detract from your resilience.

As you read further, you might want to reflect on how your experience relates to the well-being of babies, young children, and their families.

Key themes in well-being in early childhood

Despite the interactionist perspective indicated above, the influence of developmental psychology on the thinking of early childhood practitioners is noticeable in the tendency to categorize and compartmentalize aspects of well-being in ways that reflect areas of development and learning. In the analysis of the LMU/NCB Well-being Project data, this was especially apparent when participants identified aspects of subjective well-being, such as emotional, physical, and personal well-being. However, the broad range of aspects identified meant that a structure of super-categories and sub-categories of well-being developed; for example, the category of personal well-being included self-esteem, confidence, self-awareness, and respect.

But, as well as separate categories, participants also consistently identified the connections between these aspects of well-being and also between the contributory factors, and so a construct of well-being as a matrix emerged (see Figure 1 below). This allows for the interrelatedness of aspects of well-being to be depicted. For example, the category of 'personal' well-being could have included the category 'belonging'. However 'belonging' also closely links to the categories of 'community/ culture' (a sub-category of 'psychological environment') and 'contribution', so it is placed between and overlapping with these other aspects.

It could be considered that there is a contradiction or tension in the conceiving of well-being in the early childhood field as both separate categories and as a connected whole. Yet allowing the possibility of both these things means that we can explore the way in which different aspects of well-being contribute to or detract from a sense of overall well-being and acknowledge that this may vary across social and cultural groups and between individuals (Rees et al. 2010). It may also be the case that early childhood practitioners, whose practice perspective has to cross different professional boundaries and who are immersed daily in the fluctuating spirals and see-saws of children's development, may be uniquely placed to be able to bear the disequilibrium of holding a more fluid concept in mind.

In the LMU/NCB Well-being Project, it also became very clear which aspects of well-being parents and early childhood professionals believe are a priority and which factors contribute most to young children's well-being. Notes from the discussions revealed twelve themes in all, but most emphasis was given to children's emotional and personal well-being and to the contribution of positive relationships with adults and other children to well-being. There is much consistency between the main issues raised here and other research into children's well-being. Layard and Dunn (2009), for example, identify 'loving families and friends' as important to the children in the Good Childhood Enquiry, and Rees et al. (2010) identify themes of family, friends, leisure, school education and learning, behaviour, the local environment, community, money, attitudes, and health as emerging from their national survey of young people's well-being. All of which chime with the themes and issues illustrated in Figure 1.

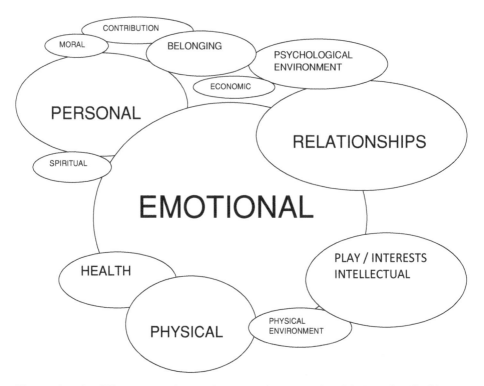

Figure 1 The different contributing factors and aspects of well-being identified by the discussion groups in the adult strand of the LMU/NCB Well-being Project. The emphasis given to each aspect, derived from the number of times each aspect was noted, is represented by the relative size of font and circle. Different aspects have been placed to overlap or put next to each other to represent the links between them made by the group participants.

Differences and similarities in the perspectives of children, parents, and practitioners on well-being in early childhood

Overall, then, there seem to be some common themes and emphases between this and other research on children's well-being. There are, however, some important differences of emphasis as well as useful consistencies between the adults and children and between the different groups of adults in the LMU/NCB Well-being Project.

There was a large degree of consistency between ideas expressed by parents and practitioners about what they thought contributed to or detracted from children's well-being but with different emphases given to some aspects. For example, parents in particular acknowledged the impact of biological traits such as temperament on relationships, as well as discussing the more personal experiences that impact on well-being such as bereavement. In contrast, practitioners more readily identified the impact of factors in children's social contexts on well-being. Perhaps these slight differences reflect each of their particular viewpoints on children's lives, the former being like an intense torchlight and the latter being more akin to diffuse moonlight in what they illuminate. These different perspectives reinforce the importance of the practice issue that was one of the most frequently cited as supporting children's well-being – that is, developing effective, communicative, and reciprocally support-ive relationships between parents and practitioners in early childhood settings.

Sixsmith et al. (2007) also noticed such differences of emphasis in their research that looked at the different perceptions of well-being held by teachers, par-ents, and children (aged 8–12) in primary schools in the Republic of Ireland. In that research, teachers introduced issues of nutrition and spirituality to the categories the children had already identified, whereas parents added emotional expression, festivities, and holidays. In addition, the children in that project had included cat-egories such as 'pets' and excluded others such as 'school', and gave categories such as 'friends' a higher priority than the adults.

These different emphases between the adults' and children's views are also apparent in the LMU/NCB Well-being Project; for example, 'food' emerges as a theme in the children's voices strand but does not appear at all in the adults' discus-sions. Similarly, the importance of intellectual stimulation and learning is noted the most frequently as the aspect that contributes to adults' well-being but only as the fourth most frequent aspect for children's well-being, whereas for the children 'play' was central (Figure 2).

As the Children's Society's Good Childhood Inquiry (Layard and Dunn 2009) has shown, asking children directly about what contributes to their well-being can lead to findings that might not otherwise come to light. In this project, although those who were tuned in to children's thoughts and feelings may have been able to foresee some of their main concerns, without having listened carefully to the children, we would not have identified that young children's concerns are actually sometimes a bit different from our own.

For example, the children who participated in the LMU/NCB Well-being Project emphasized being and playing outdoors as important to their well-being. In contrast, although the adults identified physical exercise and the natural envi-ronment as central to their own well-being, when discussing aspects of practice with children, the adults did not address this area as much. Similarly, although adults did put children's social well-being high on the agenda and identified par-ticular social skills such as empathy, communicating with others, and interacting in groups as important, friendship was mentioned less. However, for the children, social well-being translated into one word – 'friends'; other children were included in the majority of children's responses no matter what the focus of discussion.

This example shows how invoking the voice of the child not only raises sub-tle differences, but also clarifies what is meaningful for children in terms of their

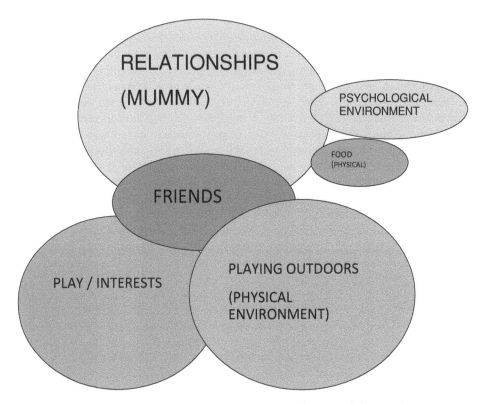

Figure 2 The different aspects of well-being identified by the children who participated in the LMU/NCB Well-being Project. The emphasis given to each aspect, derived from the number of times each aspect was noted, is represented by the relative size of font and circle. Different aspects have been placed to overlap or put next to each other to represent the links that were apparent in the children's comments.

experiences of well-being. Often this process shows that it is the small details of practice and provision that mean the most to children, details that adults are prone to overlook.

There appear to be many similarities between what younger and older children prioritize for their well-being. In the Good Childhood Inquiry (Layard and Dunn 2009), young people identified the importance of stability and security in the family and the huge significance of friends for their well-being. Similarly, the 2–6 year olds in conversations with practitioners for this project placed great emphasis on their relationships with parents, other close adults, and friends as being central to their feelings of happiness.

Children were very clear about the negative as well as the positive impact of these relationships: 'Mummy shouting' and conflict with peers were mentioned as causes of unhappiness. In addition, the high level of children's sensitivity to the well-being of close adults was graphically conveyed in the 'Jelly Cube/Gall Stones' observation described in Chapter 10, clearly showing how personal and social factors that create family stress impact on the well-being of very young children and, importantly, how open-ended play opportunities and sensitive listening by the practitioner enables children's expression of and thinking about their anxieties.

Cross-cutting theme: time and mindfulness, well-being in the here and now

Another important aspect of listening carefully to young children is to tune in to not just what they say but how they say it. This can also help adults to see what perhaps they might otherwise miss about young children's well-being and the connections that exist with their own. An example of this is 'time', which arose as a cross-cutting theme in the LMU/NCB Well-being Project. This theme has two aspects: having well-being over time – that, is across the life span – and having enough time to experience well-being.

The latter aspect was described in terms of the negative impact of too many time pressures on both practitioners' and parents' well-being. This emerged as a key feature in the research and there were many comments about the importance to adults of having 'me time'; quiet time to be reflective and free of others' demands, which would bring 'relaxation and inner peace'. Such ideas are both current and historical. Ideas of meditation and mindfulness as tools that enable subjective well-being stem from ancient philosophical traditions such as Buddhism, and are also gaining currency in the present day as medical research shows their benefits to both physical and mental health (Grossman et al. 2004).

The Leuven Well-being Scales (Laevers 1994) include the capacity for 'being in touch with oneself' as an indicator of children's well-being. Yet the possibility that children might also need 'me time' to develop this capacity for self-reflection did not feature in practitioners' discussions about effective practice. But if we consider the amount of time we expect very young children to be part of large (often noisy) groups, including opportunities for being alone should surely be part of planning practice and provision.

The other aspect of the theme of 'time' introduced above – having well-being across the life span – relates to the idea of developmental connections between childhood and adulthood. Clearly, this idea is integral to our thinking in the early childhood field; the central focus of the developmental sciences is how humans grow and change over the life cycle and what the causal links between one period of development and another might be. But this becomes problematic when conceived of as a linear process with direct causation between early experience and later outcomes applied simplistically to children's lives. Such an approach would emphasize promoting young children's well-being as important for their future outcomes as adults more than for their current experiences. This has been reinforced in recent years by the use of evidence from neuroscience to promote the idea of early childhood as a critical period, the neglect of which has dire consequences for the individual and thereby for wider society and the economy (from the politicians' point of view) in particular. This motivation underpins an outcomes-based focus in policy in the early childhood field, such as early prevention and intervention programmes. This perspective is also apparent in research on well-being, particularly where it focuses solely on measuring objective indicators of well-being, as discussed earlier.

Case study exercise

The Happiness Counts Project indicated that 16–24 year olds in the UK have the lowest overall levels of psychological and social well-being in Europe, with levels of trust and belonging causing particular concern.

These findings not only raise concerns for our older children and young adults, but also raise the question of whether the self-reported unhappiness of young people is related to their negative current circumstances or to their experiences in their early lives, or indeed to innate temperament?

What do you think? To what degree are your feelings of well-being related to your current circumstances, your early experiences or your temperamental approach?

The LMU/NCB Well-being Project's definition of well-being, as set out at the beginning of this chapter, allows for the answer to include each of these possibilities. It suggests that how we respond to and make sense of current difficulties in life is influenced by how those responses were shaped by experiences throughout our early lives and also by our temperamental predispositions to approach life in a particular way. Such a view may reflect a developmental view of well-being, but it also rejects the idea of well-being as a state to be achieved or reached like yet another stepping stone or learning goal in children's early learning and development.

In this way, the LMU/NCB Well-being Project also draws back from the idea of children's well-being as only important as an investment in the future – although we are clear that the future matters, we are concerned that only focusing on the child's future outcomes reduces them to a commodity in the economic market (Dahlberg et al. 2007). This view was expressed in participants' vociferous discontent with the shorthand term 'school readiness', seeing it as insulting to the wealth of learning that goes on in the early years and its disregard for the present experience of our youngest children.

This perspective behoves the early childhood community to consider how best we can identify and support the well-being of children *now*. We need to focus on the journey as well as the destination. The children who contributed to the LMU/NCB Well-being Project frequently identified the activity they were engaged in at the moment as the one they enjoyed the most, which we interpreted as their ability to be focused 'in the moment' rather than always be thinking about earlier or later, yesterday or tomorrow, as adults do. Children's focus on the 'here and now' requires that early childhood practitioners are involved, engaged, and led by children's play interests and scenarios as a key way in which they can both share the moment with the child (when appropriate) and also tune in to the child's interests and concerns effectively.

Cross-cutting theme: holistic perspective

Early childhood practitioners are, it seems, able to cross the boundaries of areas of development and learning inherent in their training and curriculum guidance to see the whole child and in so doing are able to think holistically about well-being:

> Body, mind and soul.
>
> Well nourished – physically, socially, emotionally, and spiritually.
> > (Children's centre practitioners, inner London)
>
> Physical and emotional, mental and physical health; a state of mind and body.
> > (Children's centre practitioner, urban northern England)
>
> All, well-being means many things – emotional, physical, psychological, so it's a huge state of being; they are linked as well.
> > (Parent, independent nursery school, London)
>
> Well-being is the foundation, the building blocks for life. It is holistic, complete.
> > (Parent, children's centre, urban northern England)

It can be seen from these comments that parents and practitioners in the early childhood field take a view of well-being that is complex. For example, it was quite clear that, although emotional aspects were a top priority, well-being is not reducible to being happy only but that happiness is interwoven with other aspects to create a complex tapestry of well-being.

Pollard and Lee's (2003) review of the literature on child well-being identifies five areas: physical, psychological, cognitive, social, and economic. Given the dominance of developmental and educational theory in the professional knowledge base of early childhood practitioners, it might be expected that participants' responses in the LMU/NCB Well-being Project would be confined to these areas too, and indeed this influence can be detected in the data. Yet the group discussions all went beyond identifying the expected areas of physical, cognitive, social, and emotional well-being, including additional aspects such as spiritual well-being, contribution, and belonging.

In addition, even within a more generally discussed area, issues arising in the LMU/NCB Well-being Project show a broader perspective. For example, concepts of physical well-being might be predicted to just focus on physical growth and health, but in the early childhood field it seems our ideas of children's experience of physical well-being is much wider than this, including things such as how children are able to use their bodies, experience physical mastery, and celebrate what their bodies can do. This perhaps reflects a professional knowledge base of the increasing evidence that opportunities for physical movement play support learning and development across all areas.

Camfield et al. (2009) suggest that it is often the case that well-being is used as an umbrella term under which various concepts from education or developmental psychology are loosely gathered. But in the LMU/NCB Well-being Project, rather than just a loose collection, the consistent emphasis on the interconnectedness and interdependence of all aspects of well-being shows a strongly holistic concept of well-being.

Ideas about holism certainly include this notion of close interconnection between the different parts of a whole, but the *Oxford English Dictionary* (2012) states that holism is the 'tendency in nature to form wholes that are *more* than the sum of its parts'. In this definition, not only are the different parts inseparable and the whole inseparable from the parts but, importantly, the whole is somehow different because of the parts coming together.

When applied to the concept of well-being, this could imply not only that 'all the pieces of the jigsaw' need to be in place, as participants described, but that when they are, a state of well-being is achieved that is the pinnacle of all that is positive. Ereaut and Whiting (2008) suggest that this concept of well-being is perhaps the oldest, as it relates to Aristotle's view of well-being as 'an *ideal* – the culmination of a person's idealised journey to "actualise" all their potential' (Ereaut and Whiting 2008: 12).

A drawback of this conceptualization of well-being is that it may imply a hierarchy of states or components of well-being. This was also sometimes reflected in the LMU/NCB Well-being Project group discussions. For example, the importance of providing for children's basic needs for warmth, nutrition, and shelter were often cited as prerequisites for children's well-being, reflecting, perhaps, practitioners' learning about Maslow's (1943) Hierarchy of Needs.

In Maslow's model, physical, emotional, social, intellectual, and spiritual needs are set out in a hierarchical pyramid, with physical needs at the bottom and self-actualization at the top. It could be argued that this perspective reflects 'western' thinking about the self, where the mind is valued over the body, a view that can be traced through attitudes and practices in the early childhood field, such as prioritizing the cognitive skills of early literacy and numeracy and not valuing physical care times or rough and tumble play (Manning-Morton 2006). This perspective, however, is at odds with the clear message from the children in the project that, rather than their physical needs being of a lower priority, running, being outside, and favourite foods are some of the elements they report as being central to their well-being.

The dualist model in 'western' philosophy is also now strongly contested by concepts in developmental psychology such as dynamic systems theory (Schaffer 2006), within which components of a system (such as the body) are mutually inter-dependent, and change (or development) is multi-directional not linear. Neural pathways are an example of a dynamic system and it is evidence from neuroscience that underpins the idea that our physical self is intricately connected to and in con-stant interaction with our emotional and cognitive functioning (Damasio 1999). Examples were raised in the LMU/NCB Well-being Project discussions of how physi-cal well-being and personal/emotional well-being are inextricably linked. These included the idea of how negative body image is a barrier to well-being and, in the same vein, the idea that children's negative emotional experiences create stress that impacts negatively on their immune systems and their physical growth and development.

Ereaut and Whiting (2008: 5) suggest that one of the ways well-being is con-structed is as either 'reducible to components, or an irreducible holistic totality', but from a dynamic systems perspective, reflected in the participants' contributions, this is a false dichotomy since, although the subsystems (in this case the different com-ponents of well-being) have their own function, if one part is affected by a change, then the whole system has to change (Schaffer 2006). Participants in the LMU/ NCB Well-being Project sometimes depicted well-being as a web, and as Friedman (2005: 49) says: 'Touch the web anywhere and the effects are felt throughout'.

The interpretation of 'holistic' offered here, then, is something that is multi-dimensional, with all the different dimensions being interrelated and interdepend-ent: attention should be paid to the whole as well as to each component. This kind of theoretical bringing together of mind, body, and emotion as part of a whole integrated human organism enables us to move away from a dualist perspective on well-being; a necessary undertaking if we are to fully understand children's experi-ence. As Mayes and colleagues (2007: 27) state: 'in early childhood particularly, the academic segregation of mental domains implies the mutilation of reality we expe-rience as clinicians [or practitioners] when faced by a little person'.

The level of holistic thinking displayed by practitioners in the project also shows a remarkable resistance to the compartmentalization of children's develop-ment and learning that is inherent to the Early Years Foundation Stage curriculum framework (DfE 2012) and the focus of much training for early childhood profes-sionals. The Happiness Counts Project suggests that other European countries, which perform better than the UK on child well-being indicators, have a different pedagogical approach. These countries focus on 'positive feelings, social connec-tions and capabilities . . . and the importance of participation', and 'work with the whole child: body, mind, feelings, spirit and creativity' (Aked et al. 2009: 30). It is this approach that the LMU/NCB Well-being Project suggests should be adopted to promote the well-being of babies and young children in the UK.

Reflective exercise

Think about the curriculum in your setting. How much does your daily practice focus on 'positive feelings, social connections and capabilities . . . and the importance of participation', and do you 'work with the whole child: body, mind, feelings, spirit and creativity'?

Conclusion

This chapter puts forward the view of well-being that arose in the LMU/NCB Well-being Project. It suggests that well-being is a complex concept that can be used and understood in different ways. This makes it important for practitioners and parents in the early years field to have the opportunity to learn about and discuss their views of well-being and to consider the implications of their ideas for children's experiences at home and in early childhood settings.

Of particular importance is to look at babies' and young children's well-being holistically and to consider both the personal and the social contexts that impact on children's potential to experience well-being. Parents and practitioners also need to consider what contributes to their own sense of well-being and how those elements might also apply to children's experiences of well-being. To do this, parents, practitioners, and children need time to reflect and to focus on the 'here and now'.

References

Aked, J., Steuer, N., Lawlor, E. and Spratt, S. (2009) *Backing the Future: Why Investing in Children is Good for Us All.* London: New Economics Foundation and Action for Children.

Bronfenbrenner, U. (1979) *The Ecology of Human Development.* Cambridge, MA: Harvard University Press.

Camfield, L., Streuli, N. and Woodhead, M. (2009) What's the use of 'well-being' in contexts of child poverty? Approaches to research, monitoring and children's participation, *International Journal of Children's Rights*, 17(1): 65–109.

Dahlberg, G., Moss, P. and Pence, A. (2007) *Beyond Quality in Early Childhood Education and Care* (2nd edn.). London: Falmer Press.

Damasio, A.R. (1999) *The Feeling of What Happens: Body and Emotion in the Making of Consciousness.* New York: Harcourt.

Department for Education (DfE) (2012) *Statutory Framework for the Early Years Foundation Stage: Setting the Standards for Learning, Development and Care for Children from Birth to Five.* London: DfE.

Ereaut, G. and Whiting, R. (2008) *What do We Mean By 'Wellbeing'? And Why Might it Matter?* Research Report DCSF-RW073. London: Department for Children, Schools and Families.

Friedman, M. (2005) *Trying Hard is Not Good Enough.* Bloomington, IN: Trafford Publishing.

Grossman, P., Niemann, L., Schmidt, S. and Walach, H. (2004) Mindfulness-based stress reduction and health benefits: a meta-analysis, *Journal of Psychosomatic Research*, 57: 35–43.

Laevers, F. (ed.) (1994) *The Leuven Involvement Scale for Young Children.* Leuven: Centre for Experiential Education.

Layard, R. and Dunn, J. (2009) *A Good Childhood: Searching for Values in a Competitive Age. The Landmark Report for The Children's Society.* London: Penguin.

Manning-Morton, J. (2006) The personal is professional: professionalism and the birth to threes practitioner, *Contemporary Issues in Early Childhood*, 7(1): 42–52.

Maslow, H. (1943) A theory of human motivation, *Psychological Review*, 50: 370–96.

Mayes, L., Fonagy, P. and Target, M. (2007) *Developmental Science and Psychoanalysis: Integration and Innovation.* London: Karnac.

Pollard, E.L. and Lee, P.D. (2003) Child well-being: a systematic review of the literature, *Social Indicators Research*, 61(1): 59–78.

Rees, G., Bradshaw, J., Goswami, H. and Keung, A. (2010) *Understanding Children's Well-being: A National Survey of Young People's Well-being.* London: The Children's Society. Available at: http://www.childrenssociety.org.uk/sites/default/files/tcs/research_docs/Understanding%20children%27s%20wellbeing.pdf [accessed 7 January 2013].

Schaffer, H.R. (2006) *Key Concepts in Developmental Psychology.* London: Sage.

Seedhouse, D. (1995) 'Well-being': health promotion's red herring, *Health Promotion International*, 10(1): 61–7.

Sixsmith, J., Nic Gabhainn, S., Fleming, C. and O'Higgins, S. (2007) Children's, parents' and teachers' perceptions of child wellbeing, *Health Education*, 107(6): 511–23.

Waters, J. (2009) Well being, in T. Waller (ed.) *An Introduction to Early Childhood* (2nd edn.). London: Sage.

2   The historical and social policy contexts of well-being

Melian Mansfield and Linda Pound

Introduction

The London Metropolitan University/National Children's Bureau Project 'Talking about Young Children's Well-being' (LMU/NCB Well-being Project) began with a discussion about how various policies that relate directly or indirectly to early childhood provision and practice refer to well-being, but seem to have different emphases and meanings. This chapter explores some of the recent developments in policy in the UK that have had an impact on the well-being of children and families and the historical contexts of these developments. The chapter also describes overarching policy contexts for thinking about well-being, such as the United Nations Convention on the Rights of the Child, and also considers the issue of how children's voices are/are not incorporated into policy. The consequences of changes in government policy are highlighted, particularly the changes to early years curriculum frameworks, aspects of which are discussed in more detail in Part 2 of this book.

An historical background to policy and well-being

Concern for children's well-being has been a long-standing characteristic of developments in early childhood care and education. In the early nineteenth century, the establishment of New Lanark brought with it an early attempt to provide a nurturing environment for the young children of poor families. The mill employed workers, many of whom had been displaced by the Scottish land clearances and provided education both for the young and for workers. Owen directed that within what he called the 'infant school' – although it catered for children from 1 or 2 years of age – young children should not be bothered by books. They should instead have opportunities to sing and dance, and to run in the hills. Teachers were instructed that they should not be threatening or abusive and should seek to develop affection and confidence between children and adults, and among peers. In his view, the best preparation for school and work was the development of a sense of cooperation, respect, and equality. Despite the fact that New Lanark was visited by a good many politicians and heads of state, Owen's views did not immediately influence policy making, since his 'was a lonely voice in an England convulsed with a search for power and quick wealth' (van der Eyken and Turner 1969: 63).

By the beginning of the twentieth century, however, concerns about the well-being of children under 5 were being widely expressed among policy makers. *The Report on Children under Five Years of Age in Public Elementary Schools* (Board of Education 1905) commented on the way in which the discipline of schools appeared to dull children's imagination and independence. The report argued that nursery education should be provided for the young children of the poor, which would offer more sleep, play, conversation, and storytelling. It also indicated that more attention should be paid to physical development.

Throughout the first half of that century, young children's health and well-being was widely seen as having increasing importance both to the individual and to the state. Children were being seen as 'tools for national development' (Pound 2013: 67), and this led the way for the formation of the Welfare State after the Second World War, since children's health and well-being were seen as a national responsibility (Hendrick 1997). In the early part of the twentieth century, the McMillan sisters' pioneering work in developing school meals and school medical services and in recognizing the importance of fresh air, imaginative play, and physical engagement was, for a time, highly influential. The document *Nursery Schools and Nursery Classes* (Board of Education 1936) praised the role of nursery education in nurturing young children. Susan Isaacs, who went on to direct the newly established Department of Child Development (now the Institute of Education at London University), carried a great deal of influence. Trained as she was in psychoanalytic theory, feelings were, for her, paramount in the education of young children. She wrote, 'the thirst of understanding springs from the child's deepest emotional needs' (Isaacs 1933: 113).

In terms of its impact on policy around children's well-being, it is perhaps the work of another psychoanalyst that had the greatest impact in the twentieth century. In 1951, John Bowlby published a report commissioned by the World Health Organization. Its publication led to widespread interest in attachment theory – a theory that held important social consequences at a time when men were leaving the armed forces and seeking employment. The idea that young children needed to stay close to their mothers chimed well with a government seeking to reduce the numbers of women in work and increase the number of nursery places available to cater for the post-war boom in births (Riley 1983). The closure of the wartime day nurseries and the creation of more part-time (rather than full-time) nursery school places for 3–5 year olds, and positive changes in policies relating to parental access to children who were staying in hospital were direct results of official acceptance of Bowlby's theories.

By the last decade of the twentieth century, policies specifically related to young children and their families were becoming more widespread. The short-lived introduction of a nursery voucher scheme in 1995 was accompanied by a set of 'desirable outcomes' (SCAA 1996). The purpose of the voucher scheme was to provide 12.5 hours of free nursery education for all 3–5 year olds. To qualify to accept the vouchers, providers were supposed to show that they were addressing the 'desirable outcomes' outlined in six areas of learning.

When the Labour Party came to power in 1997, Sure Start was introduced, described by Eisenstadt (2011: 3) as 'a case study of policy development'. Norman Glass, a senior Treasury official and architect of Sure Start, had been impressed by findings such as those of HighScope research (Epstein et al. 2011), which indicated the long-term impact of high-quality nursery education. The findings from High/Scope gathered over decades suggested that the real benefits of early education were to be found in improving life chances by lessening the chance of needing educational or other support at a later stage. Reductions in delinquency, drug abuse, numbers of teenage pregnancies, and levels of unemployment were among the measures identified. Cynically, it might be thought that the Treasury's prime interest lay in the much-vaunted claim that for every dollar spent on the education of young children, there might be around an eight-fold saving.

Eisenstadt (2011) indicates that the aims of Sure Start were two-fold. The benefits to children were acknowledged but this was linked to childcare, which would enable parents to work. The aims and aspirations were laudable but from the start there were difficulties that have been fully explored by Eisenstadt (2011). Perhaps the most difficult issue lay in the fact that the government wanted speedy results and therefore pressed ahead without clear pilot procedures. This was particularly inappropriate in an area of work where most change will be generational – changing attitudes to employment and education cannot be achieved in a short space of time. This issue was raised frequently by participants in the LMU/NCB Well-being Project: 'Myriad policies and initiatives that come from Government and Local Authorities that overwhelm adults . . . [there is a] lack of opportunity to embed new initiatives'.

Influential policy contexts for thinking about young children's well-being

An overarching and important context for thinking about young children's well-being is the United Nations *Convention on the Rights of the Child* (United Nations 1989), which was signed by the UK in 1991. The Convention is legally binding and is designed to ensure that:

- decisions are made in the best interests of children
- they are protected from abuse and exploitation
- they are able to enjoy family, cultural, and social life.

Article 12 requires that children's views are heard. The provision of opportunities to play, and to experience the arts and culture are embraced by Article 31. The

Convention also sets standards for health, education, and social care in order to protect children's rights (United Nations 1989). Each of these areas was identified as being important to young children's well-being in the LMU/NCB Well-being Project.

Every five years, governments must report on how they have implemented the Convention and the UNCRC Committee produces a report on each country. Decisions taken by the UK Government have contravened much of the Convention and can be seen as a reason for the low standards of well-being among children in this country. Concerns raised by the Committee in relation to the UK have included the growth in child poverty and inequality, the extent of violence towards children, the use of custody for young offenders, the low age of criminal responsibility, a lack of opportunities for children and young people to express views, the welfare of children in custody, unequal treatment of asylum seekers, and the negative impact of poverty on children's rights (CRAE 2013). In the introduction to *The Good Childhood Report 2012* (Rees et al. 2012), we are reminded that how we fare as a society is dependent on how we treat the most vulnerable, and that of course means children and particularly those who are disabled, poor or suffer abuse. In this context, we are right to be concerned about the well-being of children and young people in the UK.

This concern was raised in the findings of a UNICEF publication (UNICEF 2007), which reported on research into the lives and well-being of children and young people in 21 nations of the industrialized world. It measured and compared children's well-being in relation to six dimensions:

- material well-being
- health and safety
- education
- peer and family relationships
- behaviours and risks
- young people's own subjective sense of well-being.

In all, it draws upon 40 separate indicators relevant to children's lives and children's rights. Under almost all headings, the UK, together with the United States, was at or near the bottom of the table.

Children's voices in policy development

In the *Backing the Future* report, Aked et al. (2009) suggest that there is a gap between policy and the things that young people regard as important. For example, policy focuses on problems such as anti-social behaviour, teenage pregnancy, and crime, while young people connected well-being with ideas such as contentment, curiosity, enthusiasm, and commitment. The project showed that a change of focus on young people's concept of well-being, could have policy implications for issues such as education and crime. It would also identify ways in which services could be joined up to better meet the needs of young people.

However, the need to incorporate children's and young people's views or even to consider their well-being specifically at all does not seem to filter through to other aspects of policy. For example, in the document *Operating Principles for Health and Well-being Boards* (NHS 2011), there is only one statement, which says that there should be a clear focus on children and young people. Yet, according to the Coalition Government (2010–), this is part of the development of the new NHS, giving the community a greater say and improving relationships between health and social care. The purpose of the Health and Well-being Boards set up under the Health and Social Care Act 2012 (DoH 2012) is to improve the health and well-being of local people and reduce inequalities in health; however, with such scant reference to children and no requirement to consult with them, the question of who is considered to be part of a community or not might be asked. This is in complete contrast to the Children's Trusts, set up in 2008 by the Labour Government (1997–2007), which were specifically required to focus on improving the well-being of children and young people. One of their key aims was to listen to children and young people and their parents so as to provide the services they needed, and for professionals to work effectively together.

Twenty-first century policy developments

The first decade of the twenty-first century saw a great deal of interest from policy makers in exploring the impact of well-being. In 2000, the Local Government Act (HM Government 2000) gave powers to local authorities to promote economic, social, and environmental well-being within their boundaries. They had to develop a strategy across health, housing, and environment to improve the well-being of the local community. Participants in the LMU/NCB Well-being Project, particularly parents, identified the need for affordable activities in their communities and for safe (as in free from dog excrement, gangs, and vehicle pollution) community play spaces for their children. The introduction of the National Sustainable Development Strategy (DEFRA 2005: 2) claimed: 'our goals are a strong economy and decent homes in places with clean, safe and green public spaces, where people are able to lead healthy lives, and enjoy the environment around them'. It concluded, perhaps learning from Sure Start's limitations, by saying it was important to have long-term answers instead of short-term fixes and to focus on preventative action.

However, in the UK, the twenty-first century – with its change of government and economic fortunes – has brought with it a great many policy reversals. There is widespread concern about the impact of policies arising from what is seen as economic necessity on our most vulnerable citizens – the young and the poor. However, there is continued political interest in the early years of childhood but the reasons for this are diverse. The interest may spring from concern about the needs of children, the elimination of poverty, and educational disadvantage; many politicians and policy makers recognize the need for high-quality education to support children's well-being. But this may also be identified as going beyond the needs of individuals and interest being more focused on the 'public good' (OECD 2006: 7).

This different emphasis on the individual or the collective interest might then have a bearing on whether policy supports the public funding of services. The Organization for Economic Cooperation and Development (OECD 2006) has demonstrated that countries in which there are affordable high-quality childcare and early years services have far fewer children living in poverty. For example, the Nordic countries spend 2% of their GDP on the early years. This investment contributes not simply to a reduction in poverty but to enhanced well-being and achievement, and should be seen as a sensible investment in the country's future. In the UK, 0.5% of GDP is spent on early years services and although there is now free 'early education' for all 3 and 4 year olds for 15 hours a week, 'childcare' outside of those hours is still funded by parents. And, although there is planned expansion of free places for 'disadvantaged' 2 year olds, the funding for this initiative is to be taken from the Early Intervention Grant from 2013. This is likely to mean cuts in other services; for example, £150 million has been taken from the Grant for adoption.

Policies specifically relating to the well-being of young children

The Children Act 2004 (DfES 2004a) required all local authorities to bring education and social care for children together into a Department for Children and Young People. The aim of this initiative was to focus on the needs of children and provide services that were integrated. To promote more joint working, the Act encouraged early intervention to support children and their families, the integration of different services in one place, and information sharing between services. Clearly, there are huge benefits for families if all services work together and communicate effectively. In many areas this was achieved but in others there were difficulties due to differences in professional language, training, and assessment processes.

A vital element of the Children Act 2004 and a keystone of well-being policy was the Every Child Matters agenda (DfES 2004b), under which local authorities were required to ensure that every child was safe, healthy, could enjoy and achieve, have economic well-being, and make a positive contribution to the community. Early intervention, a shared sense of responsibility, and collaboration between front-line services were essential parts of this policy. The Act asserted that children should be protected from bullying, discrimination and harassment, and be able to develop positive relationships. There was particular recognition of the need for support for children in care, children living in poverty, and children suffering abuse. Every Child Matters became an essential part of all early years and school self-evaluation processes and the focus of Ofsted inspections. As children's well-being was the central focus of Every Child Matters, it is of huge concern that the Coalition Government (2010–) has archived this document, explicitly saying on the current Department for Education website that 'it should not be considered to reflect current policy or guidance' (www.education.gov.uk).

Children's Trusts also focused on services working together to develop a strategy and provide services to improve the lives and well-being of children and young people. Their focus included issues such as improving services for disabled children and their families, addressing the underachievement of young children, and establishing a team around the child – a multi-agency team to identify children who were vulnerable and at risk and to ensure that children would thrive and be safe. In the LMU/NCB Well-being Project, there was much discussion of how the well-being of vulnerable children and families might be supported and it was often considered that the multi-agency approach as adopted in children's centres was effective in this respect: 'Multi-agency approach needed', 'Integrated working – combining perspectives, so more inclusive'. It was also considered that such services needed to be locally available to all to ensure equality of access, particularly in rural areas, and also universal to avoid stigmatization, as it was thought that all families have need of support at some point in their lives.

The requirement to set up children's centres was set out in *The Children's Plan: Building Brighter Futures* (DCSF 2007: 15). This policy represented a commitment to 'secure the health and well-being of children and young people', and achieved considerable improvements in the services to children and their families as the development of children's centres expanded from at first only being in the most deprived areas to every community. However, the recent austerity measures have seen 400 children's centres close to date.

Reflective exercise

There have been numerous initiatives, reports, strategies, and recommendations since 2000, all identifying the importance of high-quality early education and early help and support for children and their families.

- Which of these do you think has been the most effective in supporting babies' and young children's well-being?
- If you could introduce a policy to support children and families in the early years, what would it be?

Curriculum frameworks

The twenty-first century has seen a great deal of change and innovation regarding a curriculum for the early years in the UK. In 2000, the 'desirable learning outcomes'

(SCAA 1996) were renamed 'early learning goals' (QCA 2000) but still only related to 3–5 year olds, so for children up to the age of 3, *Birth to Three Matters* (DfES 2002) was introduced. In the *Curriculum Guidance for the Foundation Stage* (QCA 2000), the concept of well-being was not explicit in the content, while the framework's focus on outcomes and areas of learning can be seen to have set the tone of outcomes-focused practice for subsequent documents. In contrast, *Birth to Three Matters* took 'as its focus the child and steers away from subjects, specific areas of experience and distinct curriculum headings' (DfES 2002: 5). Four aspects of well-being in babies and toddlers were identified, namely: a strong child, a skilful communicator, a competent learner, and a healthy child. Similarly in Scotland the framework for children up to the age of 3 (Scottish Executive 2005) focuses on relationships, responsive care, and respect.

In England, however, the imperative to bring the *Curriculum Guidance for the Foundation Stage* and *Birth to Three Matters* together to develop a consistent framework across the birth to 6 age range brought in six areas of learning and development for all children, babies included, when the Early Years Foundation Stage (EYFS) was introduced (DfES 2007).

In the LMU/NCB Well-being Project, the EYFS principles were seen to be enablers of well-being and some participants were of the view that the framework should only consist of these principles, as the retained focus on areas of learning and early learning goals mitigated against both children's and practitioners' well-being, as they were seen to be target driven and the learning goals are not always well matched to the overall principles. The contrast with other countries, particularly those in Scandinavia, was noted here; however, the adoption of the key person approach, the requirement to observe, the emphasis on partnership with parents, and the focus on a play-based curriculum were all identified as positive support for well-being in the framework.

The children in the LMU/NCB Well-being Project clearly and strongly identified how play, particularly outdoors, is central to their experiences of well-being. The importance of play is explored more fully in Part 2 of this book, but suffice it to say that writers with a worldwide reputation such as Vivian Gussin Paley (see, for example, Paley 2004) underline its impact on children's thinking and understanding, including their insights into social and emotional well-being. Outdoor play is arguably of even greater importance to children's general health and well-being. In his book, Louv (2006) refers to 'nature deficit disorder' and its detrimental effects on the senses and attention. He claims that contact with the natural world has a beneficial effect on both physical and emotional health. Sadly, his concerns are not well addressed by policy makers, since many registered nurseries, for example, have no outdoor space. It is suggested that regular trips outdoors compensate for lack of garden space but in fact a walk to the park or shops does not provide children with the free rein that they need when playing and exploring outdoors.

The EYFS was reviewed by Dame Claire Tickell in 2011 (Tickell 2011) and the revised EYFS (DfE 2012) puts a welcome emphasis on play as the basis of an effective approach to teaching and learning, but has also now separated the areas of learning into three 'prime' areas of learning (Personal Social and Emotional Development, Communication and Language, and Physical Development) and four 'specific' areas (Literacy, Mathematics, Understanding the World, and Expressive Arts and Design). The focus on the three prime areas may be seen as helpful to children's well-being (albeit Creativity is not included), but any benefits may be eroded if an emphasis is placed on children 'growing out of' the prime areas and 'being ready' to focus on the specific areas of learning and development. The status given to literacy, for example, may prevent sufficient focus being given to the social and emotional elements of communication.

This concern was shared by participants in the LMU/NCB Well-being Project, as they strongly argued that the early years is the first stage of life and not a time for preparation for school. Major concerns about policy developments in relation to changes in curricula frameworks were expressed. More training was thought to be needed to ensure that pedagogy does not become over-formalized – leading to a loss of opportunities for extended periods of time and space for playful activity and a loss of fun and spontaneity in learning.

So it seems that the EYFS (DfE 2012) might support children's well-being where it is used:

- creatively
- by adults who are experienced and well trained
- to enable children to explore, share, express, and develop their ideas
- by adults who play alongside and support children and help them follow their interests and imaginations
- to provide a stimulating environment both indoors and outdoors
- by adults who do not allow the assessment system to dominate.

This would all be compromised and put in jeopardy where there are dangers of cuts in funding, staff with inadequate qualifications and experience, a lack of understanding of the needs of young children and their rights, not listening to parents or children, and an over-emphasis on inappropriate assessment such as the phonics reading test (DfE/STA 2012).

Reflective exercise

- How do you use the EYFS to support children's well-being?
- Can you identify any of the negative aspects identified in the paragraph above in your practice or provision?
- If so, what can you do to change this?

As well as frequent and rapid changes to curriculum frameworks, other concerns regarding recent and current policies were raised during the LMU/NCB Well-being Project. These included the impact of the single intake to primary schools, which although already a widespread practice, has become universal with the introduction of the *Early Years Single Funding Formula* (EYSFF) (DfE 2011). This is seen as placing extreme and unnecessary pressure on summer-born children and having a detrimental effect on their well-being – a fact borne out by the gap between these children's achievement and that of older children within the year group throughout their schooling (DfE 2011).

In addition, the LMU/NCB Well-being Project participants shared the current general outrage at the deregulation agenda of the current Coalition Government (2010–) and the threat to impose higher ratios of children to practitioners (DfE 2013). This is seen as a direct threat to the well-being of children, parents, and practitioners in the early years and flies in the face of research into quality provision for babies and young children.

Howes et al. (1992) conducted extensive research in the USA and found that the quality of caregiving is generally lower when more children are being cared for. They found that babies in a group with a ratio of 1:3 or less, toddlers in a group with a ratio of 1:4 or less, and 3 and 4 year olds in a group with a ratio of 1:8 or less are more likely to experience good caregiving and good activities. In the best settings everything will be done to promote children's well-being despite these restrictions or demands of government but this will not be the case everywhere. It is feared that one result of this might be that families with more social capital and financial wealth will be able to buy the better, more costly provision, while more disadvantaged families will only be able to afford the cheaper provision with fewer staff and more children.

Summary and conclusion

This chapter set out to explore the impact of policies on the well-being of young children and their families. An historical context is provided from which it is clear that there have been long-standing understandings of the importance of well-being that have not always been matched in policy terms. Since 2000, there have been a number of twists and turns in policy, some of which have been helpful to those seeking to develop the well-being of society's youngest members. It has not always been easy for practitioners to manage the changes with which they are faced. There is, however, a wealth of evidence from a range of disciplines to support the importance of focusing on children's well-being. This underlines the role of practitioners as advocates – who must continue to bring the needs of young children and the views of early childhood practitioners to the eyes and ears of the public and politicians.

References

Aked, J., Steuer, N., Lawlor, E. and Spratt, S. (2009) *Backing the Future: Why Investing in Children is Good for Us All*. London: New Economics Foundation and Action for Children.

Board of Education (1905) *The Report on Children Under Five Years of Age in Public Elementary Schools*. London: HMSO.

Board of Education (1936) *Nursery Schools and Nursery Classes*. London: HMSO.

Bowlby, J. (1951) *Maternal Care and Mental Health*. World Health Organization Monograph (Series 2). Geneva: WHO.

Children's Rights Alliance England (CRAE) (2013) *State of Children's Rights in England 2012*. London: Children's Rights Alliance. Available at: www.crae.org.uk [accessed 28 February 2013].

Department for Children, Schools and Families (DCSF) (2007) *The Children's Plan: Building Brighter Futures*. Norwich: TSO.

Department for Education (DfE) (2011) *Early Years Single Funding Formula*. London: DfE. Available at: http://www.education.gov.uk/childrenandyoungpeople/earlylearningandchildcare/delivery/funding/a0064843/early-years-single-funding-formula-analysis [accessed 28 February 2013].

Department for Education (DfE) (2012) *Statutory Framework for the Early Years Foundation Stage: Setting the Standards for Learning, Development and Care for Children from Birth to Five*. London: DfE.

Department for Education (DfE) (2013) *More Great Childcare*. London: DfE. Available at: http://www.education.gov.uk/childrenandyoungpeople/earlylearningandchildcare/a00220847/more-great-childcare [accessed 28 February 2013].

Department for Education/Standards and Testing Agency (DfE/STA) (2012) *Assessment Framework for the Development of the Year 1 Phonics Screening Check*. Available at: http://www.education.gov.uk/a00200415/phonics [accessed 28 February 2013].

Department for Education and Skills (DfES) (2002) *Birth to Three Matters: A Framework to Support Children in their Earliest Years*. London: DfES.

Department for Education and Skills (DfES) (2004a) *The Children Act 2004*. London: HMSO. Available at: http://www.legislation.gov.uk/ukpga/2004/31/contents [accessed 28 February 2013].

Department for Education and Skills (DfES) (2004b) *Every Child Matters: Change for Children*. London: DfES. Available at: https://www.education.gov.uk/publications [accessed 28 February 2013].

Department for Education and Skills (DfES) (2007) *The Early Years Foundation Stage: Setting the Standards for Learning, Development and Care for Children from Birth to Five*. Nottingham: DfES Publications. Available at: http://archive.defra.gov.uk/sustainable/government/publications/uk-strategy/ [accessed 28 February 2013].

Department for Environment, Food and Rural Affairs (DEFRA) (2005) *Securing the Future: Delivering UK Sustainable Development Strategy*. London: HMSO.

Department of Health (DoH) (2012) *Health and Social Care Act 2012*. London: TSO. Available at: http://www.legislation.gov.uk/ukpga/2012/7/pdfs [accessed 28 February 2013].

Eisenstadt, N. (2011) *Providing a Sure Start: How Government Discovered Early Childhood*. Bristol: Policy Press.

Epstein, A., Johnson, S. and Lafferty, P. (2011) The High/Scope approach, in L. Miller and L. Pound (eds.) *Theories and Approaches to Learning in the Early Years*. London: Sage.

Hendrick, H. (1997) Constructions and reconstructions of British childhood: an interpretative survey, 1800 to the present, in A. James and A. Prout (eds.) *Constructing and Reconstructing Childhood*. London: Falmer Press.

HM Government (2000) *Local Government Act 2000*. London: HMSO. Available at: http://www.legislation.gov.uk/ukpga/2000/22/contents [accessed 28 February 2013].

Howes, C., Phillips, D.A. and Whitebook, M. (1992) Thresholds of quality: implications for the social development of children in centre-based care, *Child Development*, 63: 449–60.

Isaacs, S. (1933) *Social Development in Young Children*. London: Routledge.

Louv, R. (2006) *Last Child in the Woods*. Chapel Hill, NC: Algonquin Books.

National Health Service (NHS) (2011) *Operating Principles for Health and Well-being Boards*. Available at: http://www.nhsconfed.org/Publications/Documents/Operating_principles_101011.pdf [accessed 28 February 2013].

Organization for Economic Cooperation and Development (OECD) (2006) *Starting Strong II: Early Childhood Education and Care*. Available from: www.oecd.org/dataoecd/14/32/37425999.pdf [accessed 17 April 2012].

Paley, V.G. (2004) *A Child's Work: The Importance of Fantasy Play*. London: The University of Chicago Press.

Pound, L. (2013) Traditions, influences and trends in early years education and care, in F. Veale (ed.) *Early Years for Levels 4 and 5 and the Foundation Degree*. London: Hodder Education.

Qualifications and Curriculum Authority (QCA) (2000) *Curriculum Guidance for the Foundation Stage*. London: QCA/DfEE.

Rees, G., Bradshaw, J., Goswami, H., Keung, A., Pople, L. and Main, G. (2012) *The Good Childhood Report 2012: A Review of Our Children's Well-being*. London: The Children's Society.

Riley, D. (1983) *War in the Nursery*. London: Virago.

School Curriculum and Assessment Authority (SCAA) (1996) *Desirable Learning Outcomes for Children Entering Compulsory Education*. London: SCAA.

Scottish Executive (2005) *Birth to Three: Supporting our Youngest Children*. Edinburgh: Learning and Teaching Scotland. Available at: http://www.educationscotland.gov.uk [accessed 28 February 2013].

Tickell, C. (2011) *The Early Years: Foundations for Life, Health and Learning*. London: DfE.

United Nations (1989) *Convention on the Rights of the Child*. Available at: http://www. unicef.org/crc/ [accessed 28 February 2013].

United Nations Children's Fund (UNICEF) (2007) *Child Poverty in Perspective: An Overview of Child Well-being in Rich Countries. A Comprehensive Assessment of the Lives and Well-being of Children and Adolescents in the Economically Advanced Nations*. Innocenti Report Card 7. Florence: UNICEF Innocenti Research Centre.

Van der Eyken, W. and Turner, B. (1969) *Adventures in Education*. Harmondsworth: Penguin.

3 Young children's well-being in times of austerity

Mary Dickins

Introduction

> Prejudice is nurtured, a product of environments of fear, which is easily stoked up and takes years to quench. One manifestation is that when greater numbers are seen as less deserving . . . a minority can describe their own behavior not as greed but as simply receiving just rewards because they are different kinds of human beings, who deserve to be put on a pedestal above those they view with prejudice.
>
> (Dorling 2010: 22)

The London Metropolitan University/National Children's Bureau Project 'Talking about Young Children's Well-being' (LMU/NCB Well-being Project) identified economic pressures, housing instability, and parental anxieties and conflict as potential barriers to the well-being of young children and their families. This chapter sets out to identify and discuss some of the particular issues that children and their families may face in the economically and socially difficult times that the UK is currently experiencing. It considers how external factors such as poverty, inequality, and discrimination might impact on young children's well-being in environmental, emotional, social, and developmental terms. It also tentatively explores the relationship between prejudice and inequality. This is a vast and complex area to cover representing, as it does, some of the biggest challenges of our time and arguably some of the most urgent. This chapter is guided by Bronfenbrenner's (1979) ecological view of childhood, which graphically illustrates that the individual is deeply connected to the community he or she inhabits.

Owing to the breadth and complexity of the issues in this chapter, it takes as its premise certain 'givens'. The first three are supported by the findings of the LMU/NCB Well-being Project. The case for the latter two will be supported in the course of this chapter. They are, that whatever one's personal or professional and perception of well-being:

- The quality of familial and other relationships is fundamental.
- Family stress and difficulty can impact negatively on young children.

- All children should have the right to live free from discrimination with their individual identities, achievements, and attributes positively reflected and reinforced by their early experiences.
- A lack of collective well-being in families and community is likely to have profound and far-reaching negative consequences.
- Poverty and inequality directly and indirectly create conditions in which prejudice and intolerance of all kinds are more likely to thrive.

Underpinning this chapter is the idea that whatever one's particular view of childhood, a children's rights perspective has the potential to provide us with an opportunity to develop a working consensus about the nature of young children's well-being and about which conditions are necessary for as many children as possible to flourish.

What is poverty and why does it matter?

While it is recognized that child poverty is likely to increase as public spending is reduced (Adamson 2012), the ways in which we assess, understand, and address poverty are increasingly the subject of conflicting debate and analysis. A consensus is developing, however, that the immediate future will be difficult not only for families traditionally thought of as 'deprived', but also for those 'working poor' whose income is becoming increasingly stretched through price rises, loss of tax credits, and pay cuts or freezes (Aldridge et al. 2012). Although wealth by no means guarantees well-being, poverty is often seen as an obstacle that prevents us achieving it. For example, Layard and Dunn (2009) point out a direct correlation between poverty and levels of well-being in the UK.

The Child Poverty Act 2010 identifies four dimensions of poverty, each with a target to be met by 2020. The Act was designed to eliminate child poverty altogether but there is a general consensus that in the current economic climate, these targets are now unlikely to be met. In February 2011, research from Save the Children (2011) used data from a three-year period from 2006 to 2009 to look at the groups of children most at risk in this climate. The report argues that that some children are in 'severe' poverty and are living on low incomes of half or less of the average family income. In addition to tight family budgets for food, clothing, and other necessities, children in severe poverty are most likely to miss out on school trips and hobbies while their parents lack the funds for items like repairs to household appliances and money for emergencies and celebrations. Many of these kinds of issues were raised in the LMU/NCB Well-being Project, with practitioners in children's centres in particular identifying issues such as lack of food and poor housing as impacting negatively on the well-being of children in their care.

Parents and practitioners in the LMU/NCB Well-being Project also frequently noted the high cost of childcare as a problem for families. This is supported by a report from the Institute of Fiscal Studies (Browne 2012), which found that families with children under 5, families with more than two children, and lone parents not in paid work will bear the biggest financial pain in years ahead. In spring 2011, Save the Children and the Daycare Trust surveyed more than 4000 parents to explore their views on access to childcare and the impact of childcare costs on family income and work prospects (Save the Children/Daycare Trust 2011). Key findings included that a quarter of parents in severe poverty have given up work and a third have turned down a job mainly because of high childcare costs and of those parents in severe poverty and currently in paid employment, the majority (80%) agreed with the statement, 'Once I have paid for childcare, I am in a similar position to as if I was not working.' The cost of childcare was also seen as a deterrent to taking up education and training opportunities.

Thus, while the government purports to be interested in the well-being of the population, its policy response to the economic climate is potentially damaging to that well-being, both socially and individually. For example, Maggie Atkinson, the Children's Commissioner for England (OCC 2012), raises the following concerns with regards to the recently introduced benefits cap: a possible increase in child poverty with associated poor health, education, and other outcomes; children losing their home as a result of unaffordability; the breakdown of families and communities and a disproportionate impact on children from some Black and Minority Ethnic (BME) groups; and disabled children and children of disabled parents and children living with kinship carers. The paper also argues that the cap constitutes a contravention of Article 26 of the United Nations Convention on the Rights of the Child (United Nations 1989), which guarantees the right to social security.

In addition to policy that impacts on children's and families' economic well-being, there is a current rhetoric that conveys a particular view of those in poverty. December 2010 saw the publication of a report by Frank Field, *The Foundation Years: Preventing Poor Children Becoming Poor Adults*. The review argued that the UK needs to address the issue of child poverty in a fundamentally different way and that it is family background, parental education, good parenting, and the opportunity for learning and development in those crucial years that together matter more to children than money. Field (2010) cites as the biggest challenge to the well-being of young children, 'The growing indifference from some parents to meeting the most basic needs of children, and particularly younger children, those who are least able to fend for themselves' (Field 2010: 16). This report signifies a significant shift in perspective from a focus on family economics and income as determinants of poverty to a focus on what Peter Moss (2011: 10) describes as: 'A disturbing trend towards viewing the profound problems of an unequal society as individual failings . . . Accounted for by intergenerational cycles of deprivation, each generation passing down dysfunctional ways of living to the next.'

Politicians in the Blair and Brown governments spoke constantly of reforming the system and supporting 'hard-working families', implying other families might be less deserving and that being poor can be a result of personal choice. Current strategies for welfare reform have been criticized as being founded on the moralistic Victorian notion of the 'undeserving' poor, begging the question as to whether children should suffer for their parents' behaviour.

It would appear, then, that a toxic mix exists of economic and social factors such as housing and job insecurity and unemployment plus the negative stereotyping of poor people as feckless and underserving, which may threaten the well-being of many families and children in the UK today.

Reflective exercise

- Who do you think of as poor in today's society?
- Are there any particular groups that are more likely to be economically deprived?
- How do you think views of poverty impact on well-being?

The links between poverty and inequality

Meanwhile, contemporary debate is based more around whether measuring absolute poverty or relative poverty gives the truer picture and therefore which view should underpin policy. These concepts of absolute and relative poverty are central to our current understanding of what poverty is and how it works. In simplistic terms, the concept of absolute poverty is that there are minimum standards below which no one anywhere in the world should ever fall. The concept of relative poverty is that, in a relatively rich country such as the UK, there are higher minimum standards below which no one should fall, and that these standards should rise if the country becomes richer. Thus, while a consideration of poverty allows us to concentrate on the situation of those generally considered to be at the bottom of our society, by exploring *inequality* we can see how resources and wealth are distributed across the whole of society and how unequal some children and families are in relation to others.

It is this idea of relative poverty that has been used in discussions of well-being, as it is the inequality of wealth that is understood to have a negative impact. Generally, countries with high levels of inequality are also likely to have high levels of poverty and therefore less well-being, and those with lower levels of inequality are less likely to have high levels of poverty and therefore higher levels of well-being (Layard and Dunn 2009; Wilkinson and Pickett 2009).

As the Ipsos Mori and Nairn report states:

> A key issue which has been associated with low well-being in the UK is inequality. Amongst wealthy nations, the UK has some of the highest levels

of inequality. Even before the recession, inequality had reached the highest levels in the UK since records began in 1961. This has direct impacts in terms of deprivation and child poverty, with the UK ranking 18th out of 21 in terms of material well-being in UNICEF UK's child well-being league table, despite being one of the wealthiest countries in the OECD.

(Ipsos MORI and Nairn 2011: 7)

Any discussion of the relationship between poverty and inequality is equally likely to provoke a polarized and highly politicized debate. Many argue passionately that a degree of relative poverty and therefore some economic inequality is fundamental to capitalist, market-driven society, and can provide motivation and opportunity for social mobility based on merit. So long as the rich are generating wealth for the economy, then inequality in society can be tolerated. Others such as Wilkinson and Pickett (2009) provide a cogent argument that it is inequality itself that gives rise to many of our social ills and lack of mobility, and that inequality and lack of well-being are inextricably linked. They argue that income inequality is related to deep-seated and self-perpetuating processes of social differentiation and that countries with much bigger income differences tend to have much lower social mobility.

The debate on poverty and inequality is crucial, not least because it determines how individual societies and governments are likely to address their social problems. Although the widespread political recognition of the importance of the early years is to be welcomed, the focus on poor families as failing and dysfunctional and to some degree responsible for their predicament may ring true in a minority of cases but should arguably not form a blueprint for service provision, especially in the current, potentially divisive climate. The danger is that in moving even further away from universal to more targeted provision, services can become more judgemental, narrowly prescriptive and less inclusive, and characterized by a lack of trust and stigma that may ultimately render them less effective.

How do poverty and inequality affect young children and their families?

The effects of poverty and inequality on young children and families are most often explored in terms of the health agenda and the links between economic and health inequalities are well established. The Marmot Review goes further in stating that:

> So close is the link between particular social and economic features of society and the distribution of health across the population, that the magnitude of health inequalities is a good marker of progress towards creating a fairer society.

(Marmot 2010: 10)

It is clear that being poor and unequal can have negative consequences for all aspects of physical and mental health, with serious consequences for overall well-being.

The most comprehensive and holistic recent study incorporating these issues is the Millennium Cohort Study, which follows the story of 19,000 children drawn from the population at large and traces their progress from birth to primary school. Sabates and Dex (2012) draw on the Millennium Cohort Study and use ecological models of child development (Bronfenbrenner 1979) to identify 'multiple risk factors', and to identify the short-term impact of this exposure on developmental outcomes. The analysis uses ecological theory to make a distinction between close *proximal* factors such as the child's relationship with main carers and distant *distal* factors such as socio-economic and demographic circumstances such as a parent's occupation. These proximal and distal factors reflect the 'subjective' and 'objective' perspectives taken in research on well-being but, like the LMU/NCB Well-being Project that clearly identifies a dynamic relationship between these factors, Sabates and Dex are careful to note that this is not a determinant model but that the child and the family are constantly interacting with these factors and influencing outcomes and processes. The proximal factors noted in the Millennium Cohort Study included depression of parent, disability, substance abuse, domestic violence, and lack of basic skills. Distal factors included financial stress and teenage parenthood with overcrowding straddling both categories. The clear implication is that the more problems an individual family is experiencing, the more likely it is that there will be negative consequences for the children.

Reflective exercise

- What indications of poverty and inequality have you observed affecting the lives of babies and young children and their families using your setting?
- What issues might this raise in terms of how you can deliver an effective and equitable service?

Social resilience and young children's well-being

The discussion above clearly reflects the LMU/NCB Well-being Project's emergent concept of well-being as 'a dynamic process in which factors that are internal/ subjective may be enhanced or exacerbated by external social, economic, and policy factors', and allows for personal resilience to be considered as a factor in individuals' experiences of well-being in difficult social and economic circumstances.

The Millennium Cohort Study found that parent–child interactions are central to positive child development and can assist children in developing resilience when the family faces economic hardship. The LMU/NCB Well-being Project also identified the quality of relationships as central to well-being, and evidence from the project suggested that children's sense of well-being and resilience can be enhanced when they are respected members of a community.

The notion of social capital may be useful in considering both community and individual resilience. Although there is no universally agreed definition in this context, social capital can be understood as social relationships and networks based on trust and reciprocity. Putnam (2000) points out that not only are community and equality mutually reinforcing but also that social capital and economic equality have moved in tandem for most of the twentieth century. Importantly, social capital takes time to accrue and as Underdown (2007) points out, there is considerable debate as to whether it is actually an attribute of individuals or communities. However, there is a body of research which indicates that communities that are high in social capital, and thus have dense and complex social relationships, helpful information networks, and community stability, have significantly higher levels of well-being compared with communities that are not high in social capital, which can be characterized by alienation, fragmentation, loneliness, intolerance, and vulnerability (Coleman 1988; Fegan and Bowes 2004; Jack and Jordan 1999). Social capital is the glue that binds members of a community together and gives them a common sense of purpose and values. Studies from the United States have linked high levels of social capital with wide-ranging health, education, and financial benefits (Furstenberg and Hughes 1995; Stone 2001).

The LMU/NCB Well-being Project identified housing issues, such as homelessness, overcrowding, cramped conditions, and the constant upheaval that some families face, as significant barriers to the well-being of young children. There is growing evidence that current housing policy, with its means-tested social housing tenancies, the cap on housing benefits, and the introduction of a universal credit system, is likely to cause significant displacement of families and widespread in-country migration (Lister et al. 2011). This does not bode well for the accrual of social capital and indeed could arguably undermine existing resilience in children, families, and communities.

Poverty, inequality and prejudice

As well as social and economic barriers to well-being, participants in the LMU/NCB Well-being Project identified several factors in the 'psychological environment' as impacting on children's potential well-being, one of which was prejudiced views of children's abilities and behaviours according to their gender, ethnicity, disability, social class, and family form. The growth of such prejudices seems to have some links with poverty and inequality. Wilkinson and Pickett (2009) observe that large inequalities produce the problems associated with social differences and the class prejudices that go with them. This in turn weakens community life, makes trust more difficult, and increases violence. They state that people nearer the bottom of society will nearly always experience downward prejudice and discrimination and observe that:

> Greater inequality seems to heighten people's social evaluation anxieties by increasing the importance of social status. Instead of accepting each other as equals on the basis of our common humanity as we might in more equal settings, getting the measure of each other becomes more important as status differences widen.
>
> (Wilkinson and Pickett 2009: 45)

Similarly, Danny Dorling suggests that elitism fosters prejudice, reinforces differences, and perpetuates social hierarchies. He observes:

> The well-off are ferried around by car, told not to walk down the wrong street – and if they do walk, told that other children are dangerous and not to be mixed with. Poorer children are told they are worth less in comparison with others. They are labelled as failures in a country where we avidly count academic qualifications. Poor children are told that they are poor due to the fault, failure and lack of responsibility of their parents.
>
> (Dorling 2012: 111)

In their 2010 triennial review on well-being, the Equality and Human Rights Commission (EHRC 2010) stresses the pivotal role that negative social attitudes play in undermining the strong sense of self-identity integral to well-being. They report higher levels of stigma, prejudice, and intolerance for older people, lesbian, gay, bisexual, and transgender members of the community and particular religious populations, including Muslims. Gypsies and travellers, refugees and asylum seekers were also found to face similar levels of negative social attitudes and intolerance.

Given the context already explored in this chapter in which identifiable groups are more vulnerable to poverty, it appears that greater inequality is likely to lead to an increase in certain types of prejudice against certain groups. The recent growth of far right groups and ideology in the UK might be an example of this, although a simple correlation between prejudice and inequality is often difficult to prove because of the complex interplay between social, geographical, cultural, and economic factors.

There are, however, firm grounds for concern. Data from the Tellus4 National Report (DCSF 2010) revealed that of over a quarter of a million 6–10 year olds, just under half had been bullied at school and 20 per cent away from school. The increase in cyber-bullying is also a worrying trend (Tarapdar and Kellett 2011). Rifts in friendships, conflicts, and poor peer relationships were identified as significant barriers to child well-being by the LMU/NCB Well-being Project and were found to be of primary importance and significance to young children.

How does prejudice impact on the well-being of young children?

Siraj-Blatchford and Clarke (2000: 3) assert that, 'The way children feel about themselves is not innate or inherited, it is learned.' A body of research exists that indicates that children's self-esteem can be determined by whether or not they feel that others see them as competent and worthwhile (Lawrence 1988; Siraj-Blatchford 1994). Arguably, young children, as they grow, are constantly subjected to overt and subtle messages about who is considered better than whom and who is valued in society at the same time as they are developing an overall sense of identity and self-worth. Prejudice and discrimination within early years settings towards children and their families can mean that rather than being encouraged to grow and develop their full potential and abilities, children are limited by the effects of discrimination arising from the expectations and assumptions of others.

As early as 1980 Louise Derman-Sparks and colleagues argued that not only do young children notice and classify differences but that they also begin to ascribe different values to groups of people according to the responses and behaviour of the adults and children around them. Children as young as 2 years may start asking questions and making comments about differences, such as disabilities, gender, physical characteristics (including skin colour), cultural differences, and family lifestyles (Derman-Sparks et al. 1980). According to MacNaughton (2006), 3 year olds can and do recognize physical differences and can develop prejudices around these. Early years settings, therefore, have a crucial role in helping young children to make sense of their social world and in offsetting negative and divisive influences in communities.

Reflective exercise

At Brook Green Nursery, the children witnessed a heated altercation between two parents in which the abusive terms 'nig-nog', 'Paki', and 'Chav' were used. Some of the children were visibly upset by this incident.

Consider the following questions in relation to this incident. What can the nursery do:

- to mitigate the effects on the children?
- to deal constructively with the parents concerned?
- to promote goodwill and prevent such incidents happening again?

Conclusion

This chapter has raised a number of important questions for consideration at all levels of early years policy, provision, and practice. Not least of these is how the current economic climate and current policy direction of welfare and housing will impact on well-being. If families are subjected to multiple stresses of economic hardship, unemployment, and housing uncertainty, this surely has serious implications for the well-being of their children.

Children themselves are not born prejudiced but learn and develop their attitudes based on the adults around them and their peers. We currently lack a national consensus on the extent and nature of the perceived problems of attitude and prejudice and their interrelatedness with inequality, economic hardship, and social instability. Lane (2006: 5) takes as her premise 'an unequal society is not at ease with itself' and argues for a wide-ranging and coherent strategy to eliminate racial prejudice, but this is equally true for all forms of prejudice and discrimination.

This chapter argues forcefully that it is not helpful just to blame families for their perceived shortcomings but that much wider historical, structural, economic, and social inequalities are a crucial part of the picture and must also be examined and addressed if a more cohesive and cooperative society is to be achieved and sustained. The evidence from the LMU/NCB Well-being Project is that positive attitudes and relationships need to be at the heart of early years practice. If we truly care about the well-being of young children, we ignore these issues at our peril.

References

Adamson, P. (2012) *Measuring Child Poverty*. Innocenti Report Card 10. Florence: UNICEF.

Aldridge, H., Kenway, P., Macinnies, T. and Parekh, A. (2012) *Monitoring Poverty and Social Exclusion*. York: Joseph Rowntree Foundation.

Bronfenbrenner, U. (1979) *The Ecology of Human Development: Experiments by Nature and Design*. Cambridge, MA: Harvard University Press.

Browne, J. (2012) *The Impact of Austerity Measures on Households with Children*. London: Family and Parenting Institute.

Coleman, J. (1988) Social capital in the creation of human capital, *American Journal of Sociology*, 94: 95–120.

Department for Children, Schools and Families (DCSF) (2010) *Tellus4 National Report*. London: DCSF.

Derman-Sparks, L., Tanaka Higa, C. and Sparks, B. (1980) Children, race and racism: how race awareness develops, *Interracial Books for Children Bulletin*, 11(3/4).

Dorling, D. (2010) *Injustice: Why Social Inequality Persists*. Bristol: Policy Press.

Dorling, D. (2012) *Fair Play*. Bristol: Policy Press.

Equality and Human Rights Commission (EHRC) (2010) *Triennial Review: Well-Being*. Available at: http://www.google.co.uk/search?q=EHRC+Triennial+Review+well-being&rls=com.microsoft:en-gb:IE-SearchBox&ie=UTF-8&oe=UTF-8&sourceid=ie7&rlz=1I7GGHP_en-GBGB428&redir_esc=&ei=cNpcT4a8K4q A8wPg66GRAw [accessed 7 April 2011].

Fegan, M. and Bowes, J. (2004) Isolation in rural, remote and urban communities, in J.M. Bowes (ed.) *Children, Families, and Communities: Contexts and Consequences*. Melbourne, VIC: Oxford University Press.

Field, F. (2010) *The Foundation Years: Preventing Poor Children Becoming Poor Adults*. London: HMSO.

Furstenberg, F.F. and Hughes, M.E. (1995) Social capital and successful development among at-risk youth, *Journal of Marriage and the Family*, 57: 580–92.

Great Britain Parliament (2010) *Child Poverty Act 2010*. London: HMSO.

Ipsos MORI Research Institute in partnership with Dr. Agnes Nairn (2011) *Children's Well-being in the UK, Sweden and Spain: The Role of Inequality and Materialism: A Qualitative Study*. London: Ipsos MORI.

Jack, G. and Jordan, B. (1999) Social capital and child welfare, *Children and Society*, 13: 242–56.

Lane, J. (2006) *Right from the Start*. Trowbridge: Focus First.

Lawrence, D. (1988) *Enhancing Self-esteem in the Classroom*. London: Paul Chapman.

Layard, R. and Dunn, J. (2009) *A Good Childhood: Searching for Values in a Competitive Age*. London: Penguin.

Lister, S., Reynolds, L. and Webb, K. (2011) *The Impact of the Welfare Reform Bill on Affordability for Low Income Private Renting Families*. London: Shelter.

MacNaughton, G. (2006) *Respect for Diversity: International Overview*. BVLF Working Papers in Early Childhood Development #40. The Hague: Bernard Van Leer Foundation.

Marmot, M. (2010) *Fair Society, Healthy Lives: Strategic Review of Health Inequalities post 2010. Executive Summary*. London: The Marmot Review.

Moss, P. (2011) Progress or pitfalls, *Nursery World*, 3 March, p. 10.

Office of the Children's Commissioner for England (OCC) (2012) *A Child Rights Impact Assessment of the Welfare Reform Bill*. London: OCC.

Putnam, R.D. (2000) *Bowling Alone: The Collapse and Revival of American Community*. New York: Simon & Schuster.

Sabates, R. and Dex, S. (2012) *Multiple Risk Factors in Young Children's Development*. London: Centre for Longitudinal Studies, Institute of Education.

Save the Children (2011) *Severe Child Poverty: An Update*. London: Save the Children.

Save the Children/Daycare Trust (2011) *Making Work Pay: The Childcare Trap*. London: Save the Children.

Siraj-Blatchford, I. (1994) *Laying the Foundations for Racial Equality*. Stoke-on-Trent: Trentham.

Siraj-Blatchford, I. and Clarke, P. (2000) *Supporting Identity, Diversity and Language in the Early Years*. Maidenhead: Open University Press.

Stone, W. (2001) *Measuring Social Capital*. Research Paper #24, February. Melbourne, VIC: Australian Institute of Family Studies.

Tarapdar, S. and Kellett, M. (2011) *Young People's Voices on Cyber Bullying*. London: Diana Trust.

Underdown, A. (2007) *Young Children's Health and Well-being*. Maidenhead: Open University Press.

United Nations (1989) *Convention on the Rights of the Child*. Available at: http://www.unicef.org/crc/.

Wilkinson, R. and Pickett, K. (2009) *The Spirit Level: Why More Equal Societies Almost Always Do Better*. London: Penguin.

Part 2

Supporting young children's well-being in provision and practice

4 Feeling good: emotional well-being and social relationships

Julia Manning-Morton

Introduction

Throughout all the discussions held during the London Metropolitan University/ National Children's Bureau Project 'Talking about Young Children's Well-being' (LMU/NCB Well-being Project), the strongest emphasis was on the importance of young children's personal, social, and emotional well-being; participants identified emotional expression and regulation, a positive sense of self, confidence, and friendships as central issues. The discussions also focused a lot on the importance of secure, nurturing relationships in children's early lives with a broad acceptance that the presence of such relationships is the primary enabler of well-being, as they promote resilience, emotional literacy, positive self-esteem, pro-social behaviour, and positive dispositions to learning. This chapter explores these ideas by examining some of the research that addresses children's well-being and how it links with a range of theoretical perspectives on babies' and young children's personal, social, and emotional development and effective practice in early childhood settings.

Young children's personal, social, and emotional development and well-being research

The aspects of personal, social, and emotional well-being that we are familiar with in the early childhood field are not usually specified as such in the general literature on well-being, where they are usually grouped together under psychological well-being or mental health. Research on well-being has historically seen the study or inclusion of these subjective experiences as unreliable, so aspects of emotional and personal well-being have often not been included, as they are thought of as being difficult to measure. As the neurologist Antonio Damasio (1999: 39) points out: 'Throughout most of the 20th century, emotion was not trusted in the laboratory. Emotion was too elusive and vague . . . in the end, not only was emotion not rational, even study-ing it was probably not rational.'

Unfortunately, research that has looked at the subjective experiences of older children and adolescents identifies that these aspects of well-being are areas of con-cern in the UK. UNICEF reported that compared with other rich countries, the UK lags behind in terms of the quality of children's relationships with their parents and peers and their subjective well-being (UNICEF 2007). Similarly, the Happiness Counts project (Aked et al. 2009) also indicated that 16–24 year olds in the UK have the lowest overall levels of psychological and social well-being in Europe, with levels of trust and belonging of particular concern. This infers that paying atten-tion to the emotional, personal, and social well-being of children from birth and throughout their childhoods is of paramount importance.

Certainly, in the LMU/NCB Well-being Project, both the children's and the parents' and practitioners' responses clearly identified emotional states and social relationships as central to well-being:

> Asked how she feels today Ellie (3.5 years) replies 'good'. She says that play-ing makes her feel happy and makes her smile but she gets cross when her brother or sister hurt her; this also makes her sad.

The responses of parents and practitioners were in a similar vein:

> If love, trust and security are at the core of each person, that then enables confidence and self-esteem in relationships and positive interactions in the environment.

Emotional well-being and emotional expression

It seems that happiness is the feeling we most frequently think of when considering emotional well-being in early childhood, along with a sense of ease and content-ment in what overall could be described as experiencing emotional equilibrium. However, although we might see emotional balance as a desirable state to be in, the purpose of feelings is to unsettle us, to make us notice when things are dangerous or safe, new and interesting, or familiar and comforting. So learning about these feel-ings and how to express them in culturally acceptable ways is a core focus of early life and is an aspect of learning that continues into adulthood.

It has been suggested that humans have an innate ability to express the pri-mary feelings of sadness, anger, surprise, fear, disgust, and joy from birth (Darwin 1872, cited in Harris 1989). Although the degree to which the expression of these basic emotions is universal is still debated, it is clear that they are then built on through socio-cultural experience to develop a range of secondary emotions so that contentment, for example, is a secondary emotion that has a basic ingredient of happiness but which also includes a sense of satisfaction and tranquillity. However, the cultural variation in different secondary emotions means that through growing up in a particular culture, children will acquire different emotional expressions of contentment and other secondary feelings (Fiske et al. 2010).

But whatever the feeling, being confident enough to openly express emotion is an indicator of well-being identified in the LMU/NCB Well-being Project, and the importance of this is explained by Sue Gerhardt when she says:

> . . . if feelings remain unsymbolised, then emotional arousal cannot be managed in a more conscious, verbal fashion – such as 'talking oneself out of it' in a low mood. Instead, states will be processed through the old non-verbal channels, and will not get updated by new feedback and reflection. This means that the child's sense of self will also remain rather undifferentiated.
>
> (Gerhardt 2004: 51)

This underlines the role that practitioners have in helping children to talk about their feelings in order to support their emotional literacy (Sharp 2001). But when exploring this with practitioners, it often becomes apparent that although the importance of expanding children's language to support cognitive understanding is well established, doing the same to support emotional meaning making is not given adequate focus in practice. Thus practitioners need to be able to name and discuss a wide range of emotions in children as an integral part of their daily practice. As Gerhardt (2004: 51) also says: 'If caregivers don't talk about feelings, or if they represent them inaccurately, it will be much more difficult for the child to express feelings and to negotiate around feelings with others.'

However, practitioners also need to consider that for very young children, especially babies, toddlers, and 2 year olds, emotional feelings are closely intertwined with physical sensations and emotional arousal is often overwhelming, so although verbal expression should be encouraged, the instruction to 'use your words' often heard in settings may not always be possible for the child to achieve. Thus practitioners also need to think about how they can best give physical support to children through cuddles, gentle holding, stroking or staying nearby to a distressed child, according to the child's needs and preferences (Manning-Morton and Thorp 2003, 2006). In cases of distress or conflict, practitioners also require highly developed empathetic skills in containing children's difficult feelings and to provide words for troubling feelings, calmly and gently offering explanations and reassurances, which support children's learning about regulating their emotions.

The interconnectedness of physical and emotional feelings, suggested above, is also emphasized by the neurologist Antonio Damasio (2003) when he describes how the neural patterns that make up a feeling cause biological changes to both our physical state and our cognitive state. He says that feelings and emotions are integral to our basic bodily processes such as metabolic regulation as well as our more complex thought processes and behaviours. By telling us which experiences are pleasurable or painful, feelings coordinate and prepare our brains and our bodies for necessary action, helping us to make choices because they prompt us to move towards pleasure or away from pain. Daniel Goleman's (1996) explanations of the hormones and chemicals produced by the brain and the body at times of fear, anger, happiness, and sadness can help us to understand the physical components of feelings. For example, when we feel happy, there is increased activity in brain circuits that inhibit negative feelings and increase energy, while sadness brings a drop in energy and slows the body's metabolism.

Emotional intelligence and regulation

The concern of practitioners and theorists alike is how children come to be able to manage such feelings. Participants in the LMU/NCB Well-being Project frequently cited self-regulation as an important aspect of emotional well-being and identified the important role that adults have in providing the kind of consistent emotional boundaries that support young children in developing inner control.

These boundaries will be most effective where practitioners have appropriate expectations arising from a good understanding of children's social and cultural contexts and of emotional development. Babies and young children feel their emotions very intensely and immediately and their feelings fluctuate greatly. Neurologically this can be understood through the millions of connections that are being made in these first years and also through considering that the neural pathways that govern non-emergency emotional reactions by sending chemical inhibitors only start to be made at about 18 months old and are not fully firmed up until late adolescence (Eliot 1999). While these are developing, young children are more likely to be responding to raw, spontaneous feelings that we would usually associate with the 'fight or flight' response (Goleman 1996). This will be especially the case when children are constantly faced with situations that are unfamiliar and out of their control, prompting feelings of fear, anger, and sadness. But excitement and elation may also sometimes feel overwhelming, prompting the need to run around!

Being able to self-regulate emotional expression is seen as important in research into children's well-being because it is related to their ability to control impulses and tolerate frustration and thereby contributes to their social competence (Mayr and Ulich 2009); in this way, self-regulation is also part of what Goleman (1996) calls 'emotional intelligence'. He says, 'Self-regulation, which is like an ongoing inner conversation, is the component of emotional intelligence that frees us from being prisoners of our feelings' (Goleman 1998: 98). For Goleman, emotional intelligence is the foundation of success in life and, as well as emotional regulation, includes emotional self-awareness. This relates to what Gardner (1999) refers to as 'intrapersonal intelligence'.

The seeds of emotional self-awareness and regulation are planted early in the furrow that the caring adult ploughs with their responses to an infant's intense feelings and needs. When babies' needs are generally responded to promptly and lovingly, they learn that uncomfortable feelings are manageable because their parent or practitioner manages it for them. In contrast, if babies' needs are not responded to or are responded to inconsistently, their anxiety increases because they feel as if the discomfort will go on forever. If this is a regular experience, babies cannot find a causal connection between needing and receiving and their internal understanding of feelings and how to manage them is compromised (Gerhardt 2004; Lieberman 1993; Robinson 2003).

Reflective exercise

Identify three ways in which you support babies' and young children's emotional well-being, through both your physical interactions and your verbal interactions.

Developing emotional understanding in relationships

'Well-being is like a jigsaw puzzle; you need the strong corners and edges of love, trust, confidence, self-esteem and security so that the middle pieces are able to fall into place.'

The kind of loving responsiveness referred to above was identified in the LMU/NCB Well-being Project as a key component in relationships that are integral to supporting young children's well-being. This loving responsiveness is manifested in the adult's ability to tune in to children's sometimes subtle communications of their needs. The idea of being 'tuned in' derives from the concept of 'affect attunement' (Stern 1998), which is the process whereby an adult is able to pick up the child's cues and align their state of mind with the child's to engage with them in the way they need. The child experiences this as 'feeling felt' and 'being understood', which Siegel (1999) emphasizes as important in supporting a child's self-regulation.

Alongside the capacity for attunement, the LMU/NCB Well-being Project also identified the requirement for caring adults to be able to 'hold children in mind', 'be there, not always on top of them, but available'. These phrases, together with images of well-being as a set of Russian Dolls or the edges of a jigsaw puzzle that hold the frame for the other pieces, very much reflect Bion's concept of 'container-contained' (Bion 1962). In Bion's perspective, the caring adult not only tunes in to the child's experience but also transforms it as they process it through their own mind and actions, thereby mentally and emotionally 'holding' a baby's or young child's distressed and uncomfortable feelings, which would otherwise threaten to overwhelm the child leading to a fragmentation of their sense of self (Miller et al. 1989).

So, the impact of relationships on how well the 'jigsaw pieces' fit together was seen as central in the LMU/NCB Well-being Project. Elements of nurturing relationships were identified as 'being understanding and reassuring', 'showing warmth', 'caring', and 'cuddles', which together offer children 'emotional and physical security', 'safety and protection', all of which relate to the features of secure attachment relationships identified by John Bowlby (1969), thus reflecting the strong influence of attachment theory on our thinking in the early childhood field. In attachment theory, the child's need for this kind of security is important because it is through the interactions in those relationships that the child creates an 'internal working model' upon which they will build relationships in the future (Holmes 1993). At the same time, the child internalizes concepts of themselves as lovable or unlovable, worthwhile or not valued, according to the overt and covert messages they receive from adults' behaviours towards them.

Practitioners and parents also described emotional well-being as being at the core of one's sense of self; a bit like the 'Ready-brek' glow, which may shine bright or waiver and be dimmed, according to the messages received. The negative impact of the absence of nurturing relationships was thus noted and identified as the main barrier to well-being. The Mental Health Foundation (1999) identifies relationships within the family as one of the key factors associated with levels of risk or resilience in children's mental health.

The idea that resilience is a key component of well-being was raised by participants in the LMU/NCB Well-being Project. However, there are two issues to consider here: First, it is clear that resilience is understood to be the ability to rely on others when necessary, not the 'compulsive self-reliance' (Bowlby 1979: 138) that comes from insecure attachment relationships. It is about the ability to be flexible and to take on others' viewpoints, and to be able to recover from setbacks and persevere in the face of difficulties. Second, it is clear that resilience might enable the possibility of experiencing well-being but it does not itself equal well-being. Resilience, even when understood in a positive way as defined above, still has an element of surviving difficulty. In contrast, well-being means thriving and flourishing; being able to move beyond difficulty, to leave past trauma behind you as you move into your own future.

The Mental Health Foundation (1999) also notes that having the ability to thrive against the odds seems to arise from having someone at some point in your life who believes in you and acts as an advocate for you. This has clear implications for the quality of relationships developed between key persons and children in early years settings, as the impact then of the presence or absence of a responsive relationship with a caring adult on children's emotional well-being and self-esteem is well established.

The psychological environment

In the LMU/NCB Well-being Project, a theme of the 'psychological environment' and its impact on children's well-being emerged. This theme included the caring interactions in relationships discussed above but also focused a lot on ideas of 'boundaries' and 'consistency'. Commonly, the term 'boundaries' is used in early childhood practice to refer to rules about children's behaviour, but it might be useful to think of practice in this area as more of a continuum. This would span from the 'holding' boundaries provided in the process of 'attunement' and 'container-contained' important for emotional self-awareness, through the consistency of physical care, daily routines, and adults' responses required for children to develop an integrated sense of self, to the clear identification of acceptable behaviour and group values that are important for social harmony.

The importance of this kind of consistency for children's personal, social, and emotional well-being is clear. Children, who are not in control of most of their lives, can gain a sense of emotional security (and also cognitive understanding) from the regularity and predictability of response and routine. But for the outer control of the adult to become the child's inner control, there also needs to be flexibility and compromise of response and routine, so that there is enough room for the child to practise making choices and decisions and to feel the edges of their autonomous/ interdependent, self/other boundary.

The theme of the psychological environment also included the idea that 'praise' is a key practice in supporting children's well-being, but again, this warrants some examination. Although praise may be believed to help children feel good about themselves, too much non-specific or empty praise such as 'good work' can result in children being over-reliant on others' opinions as a motivating factor rather than intrinsic self-belief (Henderlong and Lepper 2002). This can lead to children being anxious about their abilities and engender an atmosphere of comparison and competition rather than cooperation and teamwork, especially where only final products are noticed and not the amount of effort put into a task. This doesn't mean that adults shouldn't show appreciation of children's behaviour and creations, but often it is sufficient for a child to know that you have noticed them, and being involved in children's play activities is the best kind of attention you can give to creative thinking and pro-social behaviour.

Personal well-being, self-esteem, and self-confidence

It is these kinds of interactions in the child's psychological environment that will support the positive self-concept that early childhood practitioners and parents identify as being fundamental to being more able to experience well-being. This is apparent in children who show pride in themselves and their achievements, are able to express their individuality, and have a view of themselves as being important, with high self-esteem. These children are assertive, optimistic, and adaptable and can recover from setbacks and mistakes. When in a state of well-being, they were described as 'vibrant': 'Their feeling of well-being can be contagious, it radiates off them.'

Many of the characteristics suggested in the LMU/NCB Well-being Project are similar to Mayr and Ulich's (2009) research into children's well-being and resilience. Their personality factors of resilient children include all of the above and both pieces of research reflect the signs of well-being identified by Ferre Laevers and his colleagues. Laevers et al. (1997: 17–19) also include the capacity for 'being in touch with oneself' as well as 'self-confidence and self-esteem' as signals that indicate well-being.

'Being in touch with oneself' relates to what Dowling (2000) calls self-knowledge. She writes: 'As young children develop they start to learn about themselves and what they can do; they begin to recognise those things that they find easy and where they need help and support' (Dowling 2000: 9). Having confidence in their abilities but a real sense of their limitations in any one situation, means that a child has what Winnicott (1960) would describe as just the right amount of 'self-doubt'. Such children will have a positive attitude to the everyday challenges of life, while those with too little self-doubt may assume they can do everything and be unprepared to deal with failure and setbacks, while children with too much self-doubt may be withdrawn and reluctant to take risks.

Having too much or too little self-doubt arises from the kind of self-concept a child develops from the images of themselves conveyed by significant people in their lives. Where these messages or 'scripts' (Berne 1970) convey an idealized image that is very different to the child's internal self-awareness, the child may blame themselves for not living up to expectations and then feel lacking or unworthy, resulting in low self-esteem (Lawrence 1988). However, there will usually be some discrepancy between how one sees oneself and how others see us and this can be useful in terms of both extending self-awareness and also motivating change or development of an aspect of our personality.

So what was seen as important in the LMU/NCB Well-being Project in this regard is that children are recognized and respected for who they are by adults: 'Acknowledging every child is different and unique'. This is particularly important when combating bias and stereotyping of children according to their social identity. Biased expectations of children according to social class, sexual orientation, gender, disability, and ethnicity will have a negative impact on all children's self-concept and self-esteem. The children who are seen as part of the 'ideal' group may gain a false sense of themselves as much as the children who are seen as 'other' or 'different', who may have to struggle with the discrepancy between their internal self-awareness and the stereotyped images presented to them.

Thus in the same way as well-being is multi-faceted, so is identity formation (Siraj-Blatchford and Clarke 2000). In a dynamic systems view of development, the different systems of gender, class, ethnicity, disability, and sexual orientation overlap and interact with each other, resulting in a complex personality that cannot be confined to a stereotype. In addition, an interactionist perspective would suggest that the bi-directionality of development means that children are active in the process of identity development, so also develop a self-concept that is at odds with the structural prejudice in society. Both these theoretical perspectives of development underpin the view of well-being put forward in this book.

To develop positive practice in this area, practitioners need to be aware of their own childhood experiences and cultural values that will influence the personal characteristics that they value and therefore encourage in children's development. Western European culture, for example, places a strong emphasis on independence and the unique individual, whereas in other majority world cultures children may be encouraged more to develop interdependence, emphasizing the individual more as part of the whole social group (Cole 1998).

Practitioners and parents could also usefully reflect on the degree to which they believe that children's capacities and personalities are biologically determined or socially learned, as this can impact on their expectations of children's efforts and achievements. Some participants in the LMU/NCB Well-being Project, mainly parents, raised the influence of a child's innate temperament on their personality development and their experience of well-being. Mayr and Ulich (2009) identify an easy temperament and friendliness as personality traits of resilient children, implying a nativist view of subjective well-being. However, overall, the views expressed in the LMU/NCB Well-being Project very much reflected an interactionist view wherein the child's inborn characteristics and the environment play an equal role in shaping personality. In this view, there may be genetic pre-dispositions but temperament is shaped, strengthened or counteracted through relationships and experiences.

Reflective exercise

- How do you support babies' and young children's self-awareness and self-esteem in your setting?
- Identify practices in relation to adult–child interactions, the physical environment, and connecting with families and communities.
- How does your understanding and beliefs about personality development impact on these practices?

Self-esteem and community esteem

Discussions in the LMU/NCB Well-being Project groups raised many pertinent concerns about external factors that impact negatively on young children's personal, social, and emotional well-being. Many of these focused on direct personal experiences such as bereavement, abuse and neglect, and negative family relationships, while other factors raised, such as the commercialization of childhood in the media and a lack of affordable activities and safe play spaces in the local community, demonstrate a clear understanding in the field of the wider social context of young children's well-being: 'How the community feels affects the individual'; 'The community can affect them if it is not safe.'

The issue of community stability – especially where this is negatively affected by levels of disruption caused by changes in housing allocation, involuntary displacement, migration, and resettlement – was one example of the awareness among participants of the impact of negative social contexts on children's well-being. This awareness extended to understanding the lack of community esteem that can arise from such circumstances and how it links to an individual's personal, social, and emotional well-being. In the same way that individual self-esteem is negatively impacted on by images of an 'ideal self' that is not congruent with one's 'inner' self, a dissonance between the values promoted by wider society and one's family and community values may compromise social well-being. In consideration of these issues, the LMU/NCB Well-being Project highlighted that a sense of belonging would buffer the impact of this dissonance of values, so connectedness to family and community was seen as being important for well-being.

Belonging and contribution

The idea of a reciprocal flow between the internal and the external, the individual and the community is inherent in the concepts of belonging and contribution that are at the heart of the New Zealand Early Childhood Curriculum, Te Whāriki, where they are seen as essential to children's positive disposition to learning. It states: 'This curriculum is founded on the following aspirations for children: *to grow up as competent and confident learners and communicators, healthy in mind, body, and spirit, secure in their sense of belonging and in the knowledge that they make a valued contribution to society*' (NZ Ministry of Education 1996: 9).

Belonging and contribution are seen to arise from relationships in the family, community, and early childhood setting, and are seen to enhance the child's well-being in ways similar to those already explored in this chapter by contributing to 'inner well-being, security and identity'. For the 'belonging' strand, this is brought about by providing an environment in which links between setting, family, and community are strong and children feel comfortable and 'know they have a place'. Each of these reflects the ideas raised in the LMU/NCB Well-being Project group discussions:

> A setting where they can feel they are themselves.

> Sense of belonging, a 'second home'.

> It's about feeling connected, give and take.

> Children need to feel valued/accepted.

The last point echoes the 'contribution' strand, which requires that: 'Opportunities for learning are equitable, and each child's contribution is valued' (NZ Ministry of Education 1996: 16).

In Te Whāriki, 'contribution' is also seen as 'playing a part in a common effort' (NZ Ministry of Education 1996: 99). In the LMU/NCB Well-being Project discussions, participants also identified the benefits for children's personal well-being when they 'took on being in charge of something', though there was some tension identified between children being given too much responsibility versus being infantilized by their ability to contribute being denied. So although children's involvement in 'real-life experiences' is seen to enhance their well-being, as some parents pointed out, where those experiences include having to take on extensive family responsibilities because their parents are not able to, then the impact on well-being is potentially negative.

Social well-being, communication, and friendships

Te Whāriki also states that, 'Belonging builds opportunities for social interaction with adults and other children' (NZ Ministry of Education 1996: 54). In this way, it places a focus on social relationships as fundamental to children's learning and development. A focus on communicating with others was also evident in the LMU/NCB Well-being Project. Participants considered a willingness to communicate with adults and peers as an indicator of well-being, while children learning English as an additional or second language who are not given adequate support in their transition into a setting were considered at greater risk of having their well-being compromised.

However, non-verbal communications can equally indicate well-being, as communicating through crying, smiling, and other facial and bodily expressions conveys our state of mind very strongly. Therefore, social well-being is not just about the child's open communication; very importantly it is about the adult's willingness to listen. Engaging in active listening, in which we understand all behaviour as a communication that has meaning, means that all aspects of communication will be heard, even those we may find uncomfortable such as hitting out. Ensuring that our communications with children are also authentic, interested, interesting, and sustained is a key way in which we can facilitate children's well-being.

This kind of focused, active listening and responding is important from day one. Colwyn Trevarthen (1998) views babies as social beings from birth: an 'innate companion and co-operator'. Babies' early abilities show a pre-disposition to be part of a social world and children gradually develop the skills they need to successfully interact with others, such as understanding other people's feelings, becoming aware of other people's ideas, thoughts, and beliefs, and using non-verbal skills such as smiling and nodding to engage in communications with others, and thereby enter into interactions, play, and friendships.

The development of 'theory of mind' or 'mind sight' (Siegel 1999) is fundamental to social competence. Using 'social referencing' (Schaffer 2006) to interpret events, understanding that other people have needs and desires which are different to one's own, and the ability to delay or inhibit the gratification of one's own wishes and desires in favour of another's, are all seen as indicators of positive social adaptation in developmental psychology.

In writings about well-being, social competence and pro-social behaviours are also seen as crucial indicators (Mayr and Ulich 2009) and are identified as important for 'school readiness'. However, the kind of skills identified as necessary for this, such as initiating interactions with peers, cooperating with children and adults, sharing, showing concern for others, resolving conflicts without aggression, and cooperating with adults, all rely on children having a good level of linguistic competence and a pre-existing broad range of positive social experiences. For children starting school at the young age of 4 years, such as we have in the UK, these skills are likely to be less well developed. In addition, where children may have learning difficulties that are yet to be identified at such a young age or are in the process of developing proficiency in more than one language, it has to be asked whether UK schools, with their large class sizes and a focus on testing and league tables, are ready to support the well-being of all our children.

Layard and Dunn (2009) set out the importance of schools adopting practices that support the personal, social, and emotional well-being of children and cite evidence from programmes adopted in the USA that have raised the emotional well-being of pupils by at least 10 per cent, thereby also reducing negative behaviour and improving academic performance. This illustrates the clear links between social and cognitive development. As children interact with others, their minds are opened up to new ways of thinking and different perspectives, but it remains that being open to new experiences and learning is highly influenced by having a positive sense of self and sufficient social competence. This perspective endorses the focus given to supporting young children's social well-being in the LMU/NCB Well-being Project, where 'caring for each other, empathy and the ability to balance their desires with others' were identified repeatedly as indicators of social abilities necessary for the well-being of the group as well as the individual.

Friendships

Well-developed social skills such as the ability to sustain an interaction and high levels of cooperation are also identified as characteristics of 'popular' children who are more liked by their peers (Schaffer 2006). This is a key factor in children's well-being, as friendships are known to influence children's development in a range of ways. It is in these horizontal relationships where interactions are reciprocal that situations of cooperation and competition are explored. Friendships also give children emotional support and contribute to self-knowledge as well as knowledge about others. In this way, they provide experiences of balancing intimacy and autonomy in relationships that are beyond the parent–child relationship and so anticipate relationships later in life.

The children in the LMU/NCB Well-being Project consistently identified other children as being central to their sense of well-being, as they mentioned peers and friends in most of their responses. Some also showed a sophisticated understanding of the pleasures and the challenges of these relationships and how they impact on their well-being:

Adult: Who is this? Why did you take a picture of them?

Child: I love this girl, but not when she bosses me around because when I say no she says, 'Come then, come then, come then.'

Adult: How does that make you feel?

Child: Sad, of course.

The children in the project identified a friend as someone with whom they played but importantly, someone who liked the same kind of play activities and shared the same interests as them. This information should give practitioners a clear message about where they place the emphasis in their planning of the play environment, routine times, and how they set up play opportunities, because although the adults in the project clearly identified children's friendships as important for their well-being, this aspect was not so readily noted when discussing practice that supports children's well-being. This may be partly as a result of the emphasis in the UK early childhood curriculum on the 'unique child', which, as identified earlier, is vital in supporting children's self-knowledge and self-esteem. However, a primary wish of parents for their children's learning in an early childhood setting is that they learn how to be part of a group, and Layard and Dunn (2009) identify 'excessive individualism' as the leading social evil that causes children the biggest problem in being able to experience well-being. Therefore, if we want children to be able to locate themselves as part of a bigger whole and have a sense of belonging and contribution as well as a positive sense of self, practitioners need to develop practices that give children messages that they *are* unique individuals but that they are also an important part of a group.

Reflective exercise

Think of a child in your care and identify three ways in which you support their unique self and three ways you encourage them to see themselves as part of a group.

Is there any contradiction in these practices or do they complement each other?

Conclusion

This chapter has emphasized the importance of young children's personal, social, and emotional well-being to their overall well-being. It has suggested that secure, loving relationships at home and in early childhood settings are primary enablers of well-being in young children, as they support emotional literacy, positive self-esteem, and social competence. This indicates the fundamental importance of positive key person relationships in settings and of the skills practitioners need in supporting individual children's self-awareness and also their belonging and contribution to the group.

The reciprocal flow between the individual child's subjective well-being and their wider social context has been identified and the impact of the psychological environment and the social environment on a child's potential for well-being has been discussed. These suggest that practitioners need to pay good attention to 'strong connection and consistency among all the aspects of the child's world' (NZ Ministry of Education 1996: 42) in order to support their well-being.

References

Aked, J., Steuer, N., Lawlor, E. and Spratt, S. (2009) *Backing the Future: Why Investing in Children is Good for Us All.* London: New Economics Foundation and Action for Children.

Berne, E. (1970) *Transactional Analysis in Psychotherapy.* New York: Ballantine.

Bion, W.R. (1962) *Learning from Experience.* London: Karnac.

Bowlby, J. (1969) *Attachment and Loss Vol. 1: Attachment.* London: Hogarth Press.

Bowlby, J. (1979) *The Making and Breaking of Affectional Bonds.* London: Tavistock/Routledge.

Cole, M. (1998) Culture in development, in M. Woodhead, D. Faulkner and K. Littleton, K. (eds.) *Cultural Worlds of Early Childhood.* London: Routledge.

Damasio, A.R. (1999) *The Feeling of What Happens: Body and Emotion in the Making of Consciousness.* New York: Harcourt.

Damasio, A.R. (2003) *Looking for Spinoza: Joy, Sorrow, and the Feeling Brain.* New York: Harcourt.

Dowling, M. (2000) *Young Children's Personal, Social and Emotional Development.* London: Paul Chapman.

Eliot, L. (1999) *Early Intelligence: How the Brain and Mind Develop in the First Five Years of Life.* London: Penguin.

Fiske, S.T., Gilbert, D.T. and Gardner, L. (2010) *Handbook of Social Psychology, Vol. 2* (5th edn.). New York: Wiley.

Gardner, H. (1999) *Intelligence Reframed: Multiple Intelligences for the 21st Century.* New York: Basic Books.

Gerhardt, S. (2004) *Why Love Matters: How Affection Shapes a Baby's Brain.* Hove: Brunner-Routledge.

Goleman, D. (1996) *Emotional Intelligence: Why It Can Matter More Than IQ.* London: Bloomsbury.

Goleman, D. (1998) What makes a leader?, *Harvard Business Review*, November/December, pp. 93–102.

Harris, P. (1989) *Children and Emotion: The Development of Psychological Understanding.* Oxford: Blackwell.

Henderlong, J. and Lepper, M.R. (2002) The effects of praise on children's intrinsic motivation: a review and synthesis, *Stanford University Psychological Bulletin*, 128(5): 774–95.

Holmes, J. (1993) *John Bowlby and Attachment Theory.* London: Routledge.

Laevers, F., Vandenbussche, E., Kog, M. and Depondt, L. (1997) *A Process Oriented Child Monitoring System for Young Children.* Leuven: Centre for Experiential Education.

Lawrence, D. (1988) *Enhancing Self Esteem in the Classroom.* London: Paul Chapman.

Layard, R. and Dunn, J. (2009) *A Good Childhood: Searching for Values in a Competitive Age.* London: Penguin.

Lieberman, A.F. (1993) *The Emotional Life of a Toddler.* New York: Free Press.

Manning-Morton, J. and Thorp, M. (2003) *Key Times for Play: The First Three Years.* Maidenhead: Open University Press.

Manning-Morton, J. and Thorp, M. (2006) *Key Times: A Framework for Developing High Quality Provision for Children from Birth to Three Years.* Maidenhead: Open University Press.

Mayr, T. and Ulich, M. (2009) Social-emotional well-being and resilience of children in early childhood settings – PERIK: an empirically based observation scale for practitioners, *Early Years*, 29(1): 45–57.

Mental Health Foundation (1999) *Bright Futures: Promoting Children and Young People's Mental Health.* London: Mental Health Foundation.

Miller, L., Rustin, M. and Shuttleworth, J. (eds.) (1989) *Closely Observed Infants.* London: Duckworth.

New Zealand Ministry of Education (1996) *Te Whāriki/He Whàriki Màtauranga mò ngà Mokopuna o Aotearoa: Early Childhood Curriculum.* New Zealand: Ministry of Education/Learning Media Ltd.

Robinson, M. (2003) *From Birth to One: The Year of Opportunity.* Buckingham: Open University Press.

Schaffer, H.R. (2006) *Key Concepts in Developmental Psychology.* London: Sage.

Sharp, P. (2001) *Nurturing Emotional Literacy.* London: Fulton.

Siegel, D.J. (1999) *The Developing Mind.* New York: Guilford Press.

Siraj-Blatchford, I. and Clarke, P. (2000) *Supporting Identity, Diversity and Language in the Early Years.* Maidenhead: Open University Press.

Stern, D. (1998) *The Interpersonal World of the Infant.* London: Karnac.

Trevarthen, C. (1998) The child's need to learn a culture, in M. Woodhead, D. Faulkner and K. Littleton (eds.) *Cultural Worlds of Early Childhood.* London: Routledge.

United Nations Children's Fund (UNICEF) (2007) *Child Poverty in Perspective: An Overview of Child Well-being in Rich Countries. A Comprehensive Assessment of the Lives and Well-being of Children and Adolescents in the Economically Advanced Nations.* Innocenti Report Card 7. Florence: UNICEF Innocenti Research Centre.

Winnicott, D. (1960) The theory of the parent–child relationship, *International Journal of Psychoanalysis*, 41: 585–95.

5 Play, playfulness, and young children's well-being

Deborah Albon

Introduction

At the present time, play in early childhood tends to be cast in instrumental terms, valuable primarily for the role it plays in young children's learning and future academic success. This has been described by some commentators as a pervasive discourse of play in many contemporary minority world societies and can be seen strongly in the (English) Early Years Foundation Stage documentation. Participants in the London Metropolitan University/National Children's Bureau Project 'Talking about Young Children's Well-being' (LMU/NCB Well-being Project) resisted such an instrumental, future-oriented view of play, and the children in particular pointed to the importance of peer relationships and friendships formed through play as well the outdoor environment as offering the possibility for more exuberant physical and imaginative play. This chapter, therefore, focuses on the contribution of play and playfulness to young children's well-being and, in exploring this, reflects on the possible tensions between valuing and supporting the often mercurial, spontaneous play of young children and the insidious drive towards planning, measurability, and target setting. The chapter concludes that there is a need to treasure play and playfulness in early childhood settings, but that alongside this, there is a need for practitioners to acknowledge a less romantic reality of play: the unfairness and inequity it may engender. This suggests the need for a reflective, critical (but also *playful!*) approach to play from practitioners in early childhood settings.

Play and well-being research

It would be surprising to have any discussion of young children's well-being without reference to play, especially in the UK context – or so I thought! However, a review of some recent reports on well-being shows a lack of explicit and detailed reference to play (e.g. The Children's Society 2011; UNICEF 2007). This perhaps reflects the tendency to ask children and young people in their late primary and secondary school years (as opposed to younger children, who perhaps have greater opportunity to play at nursery or school) about their well-being, as well as a tendency to measure educational well-being in terms of academic success. When play is mentioned explicitly with respect to well-being, discussion tends to confine itself to the outdoor area and 'natural' spaces (e.g. London Play 2010). Yet play is regarded as important in all human lives and is also considered to be a significant part of the early childhood curriculum (Moyles 1989), although the idea that 'free' play can perform an important role in young children's learning is not necessarily shared across the world (for a discussion of the Indian context, see Gupta 2011).

Play and its contribution to well-being

Defining 'play' has been shown to be difficult by many commentators (e.g. Bennett et al. 1997; Bruce 1991). In attempting to determine what activities constitute 'play', coming to any *certain* and *universal* understandings poses further difficulty. There is a sense that, at the present time, everything is coming to be regarded as 'play' in early childhood settings because to suggest otherwise is antithetical to perceived wisdom on how children learn and develop. In the LMU/NCB Well-being Project, one practitioner stated there needed to be 'training on play and child development/how children learn', as if play and learning were inextricably entwined or even synonymous. This is not to say that I think play is unimportant in children's learning (and for adults too) – indeed, I think it is incredibly important – but I wish to emphasize that it is one vehicle of many through which children learn. Activities such as helping prepare food for tea, nappy changing, sleeping, learning how to use a drill at the woodwork table, and many other activities, I suggest, are not play but are nonetheless important for children's learning. Thus, all activities undertaken by young children may *not* be considered as play and play is not the *only* means through which young children learn. This, I believe, is a vital point to hold on to, not least because I think it enables us to envision play *beyond* learning and to consider its importance to well-being in a broad sense. Yet many activities might be approached playfully. Following Bruner, play can be considered as an approach to action (Moyles 1989), and as such, playful dispositions towards activities such as mealtimes are, of course, possible and, I would suggest, important.

Play contributes to well-being in a range of ways. For example, some theories of play emphasize its therapeutic and healing qualities (Axline 1974); others emphasize its role in providing a pleasurable release of surplus energy (Schiller, cited in Saracho and Spodek 2003). In terms of future well-being, some theorists view play as significant as a vehicle for the rehearsal of activities that children may perform in their adult lives (Groos 1901). But while these are important perspectives on play and well-being, my intention is to focus on more instrumental views of play for the purposes of this chapter.

Play is often regarded as something that is self-chosen, spontaneous, often unpredictable and, therefore, something that cannot be tightly regulated by adults (Bruce 1991; Kalliala 2006). This view permeates romantic or nostalgic discourses of play (Ailwood 2003). But by far the most pervasive discourse on play at the current time relates to play as synonymous with learning. This has become what Lyotard (1979) has described as a 'metanarrative' or over-arching 'truth' that governs thinking about play in many contemporary minority world societies, although the powerful hold it has over particular groups at particular historical junctures often remains unrecognized (Albon 2011). The LMU/NCB Well-being Project, as we will now see, highlighted the concern many adults have about such instrumental views of play.

Targeting play

A dominant theme that emerged from the LMU/NCB Well-being Project was the idea that children's spontaneous play and opportunity to be 'in the moment' were being compromised by the pressures placed on practitioners to ensure children meet a myriad of targets. Many practitioners in the seminar sessions were critical of the direction of education policy in England and argued that to meet targets, they were under pressure to introduce a more formal, didactic curriculum – one seemingly at odds with a more spontaneous, play-based curriculum. Typical responses included:

Didactic practice.

Take targets off childhood.

Top down pressure.

Can lead to children sitting down too much: fun and spontaneity lost.

On examining the narratives from the LMU/NCB Well-being Project, a romantic discourse of play seems to emerge: one of play as a special site of childhood, one that should remain unfettered by the pressures of later life (Ailwood 2003). However, another reading might be that there was strong resistance among participants in the project to the idea of the child as 'futurity' (a term coined by Jenks 1996) or human 'becoming' as opposed to human being (Qvortrup 1994). And it is this second reading of the data that I now wish to explore in more detail.

Childhood is sometimes characterized as a period of social investment – a human capital argument for early childhood provision – in which the present needs of children (and I do not present 'needs' here as necessarily synonymous for all children) are subordinated to the needs of the future economy (Dahlberg and Moss 2005). As Dahlberg and Moss (2005: 3) note, the responsibility of early childhood practitioners too often gets framed within 'a technical question: how effective are pre-schools/schools/school-age childcare in producing certain outcomes?' And in considering the proliferation of targets in relation to young children, it has been suggested by Bialostok and Kamberelis (2010: 299) that 'childhood is, arguably, the most intensively governed sector of personal existence'.

One such area of government is play. In many early childhood settings, young children's play is carefully documented and as such brings into being what Jones et al. (2010) have called the 'paper child': a child who is classified, assessed, and 'normalized'. And as a consequence of this activity, opportunities for early childhood practitioners to participate directly in children's play are reduced (Gulløv 2012). Moreover, play is positioned in instrumental terms, as needing to be 'well-planned' and 'purposeful' rather than treasured for its own sake (Kjørholt and Qvortrup 2012), which Rogers (2010) has described as the 'pedagogization' of play. As Wood (2010) observes, the vision of play in the Early Years Foundation Stage (in England) is one in which play is viewed as the prime vehicle through which the curriculum is 'delivered' and, as a consequence of this, play becomes judged as 'good play' or 'bad play' according to whether it meets with adult-derived, institutional, and political imperatives (Rogers 2010).

The work of practitioners is similarly governed through play, as their assessments of children derived through observing their play coupled with their ability to deliver a well-planned 'play-based curriculum' are subject to external scrutiny (in England: the Office for Standards in Education). For many practitioners in the LMU/NCB Well-being Project, the time spent on paperwork 'required' for the purposes of external scrutiny was regarded as damaging to their opportunities to play with young children for long and sustained periods. There was a strong sense in which participants in the project baulked against this trend for ever more regulation and target setting for young children and the resultant lessening of focus on their spontaneous, playful activity. As one participant noted, 'pressure to meet targets takes us away from physically working with children'. Another suggested that opportunities be provided so children can be 'absorbed in the moment'. Thus, while play offers an important context for 'wallowing' (Bruce 1991), exploration, and experimentation (Moyles 1989), this pre-supposes that children have the time to do so and also pre-supposes that adults are available to respond accordingly.

Reflective exercise

Reflect upon the play experiences of children in a setting within which you work or have contact with.

To what extent do the demands of paperwork impinge on your ability to spend time playing with young children, attending to their present concerns?

The physical environment, play, and well-being

Another key theme to emerge from the LMU/NCB Well-being Project relates to the environment in which children play. As Robson (1996) reminds us, the physical environment in early childhood settings encompasses not only the way space and resources are organized, but also how time and people intersect with that space. However, early childhood settings are not the only places where young children play: there are many different spaces for their play, including the home, local parks, the homes of friends, and – particularly as they get older – virtual spaces and the street. For young children growing up in the contemporary minority world, their freedom to play away from the gaze of adults outside of the home or outside of 'official' or 'designated' spaces is likely to be severely curtailed (James et al. 1998). Moreover, within the home, children's play and the artefacts they use for their play are increasingly located in bedrooms (Mitchell and Reid-Walsh 2002), as homes have become demarcated into 'adult' and 'child' areas, with this demarcation intersected by conceptualizations of time. Thus, play in the main living space – 'front room' or 'sitting room' – may be permitted at certain times of the day only.

In early childhood settings, the opportunities for children to engage freely in play at different times of the day vary according to the extent that children are able to move freely between different spaces and play for long periods of time. This is sometimes known as 'free-flow' play (Bruce 1991), albeit that this is becoming a term that encompasses a vast array of different practices. 'Interrupting children's activities' was regarded as a poor play environment by some practitioners in the LMU/NCB Well-being Project and could be interpreted as reflecting the idea that children should be allowed to 'naturally' engage in play as if the 'naturalness' of play for all children is a given (Grieshaber and McArdle 2010).

The outdoor space was cited time and again as important to the children in the LMU/NCB Well-being Project, and was strongly linked to the opportunity it affords for being physically active. Andrea pointed to enjoying playing on a bouncy castle outdoors and Hamid stated he relished playing with a 'big bouncy ball' when outside. While being physically active is important in terms of one's health and well-being (Van Zandvoort et al. 2010), for the purpose of this chapter I wish to posit that the outdoor area is emblematic of other persistent ideas in early childhood education and care, which link to previous discussion about the worrying trend towards the 'pedagogization' of play.

Stephenson's (2002) work shows that children emphasize what they can *do* when outside as opposed to what they have *made* (indoors). The open-endedness that the outdoor area affords offers exciting possibilities as a play environment because – aside from fixed structures such as climbing frames – it usually needs setting up each day and each day is subject to the vagaries of the weather (to name but two examples). Although some people shy away from spending periods of time outdoors when cold or wet, others enjoy the possibilities this affords. In the LMU/NCB

Well-being Project, Molly (2 years 11 months) stated that she liked being outside at nursery because 'It's all freezing and frosty'. This suggests that it is the very unpredictability of the outside environment that makes it attractive, which, ironically, sits uneasily with the idea of a tightly pre-planned curriculum noted earlier. After all, in England who could plan with certainty for particular weather conditions to prevail at a certain time on a certain day?

The outdoor environment also affords children opportunities for exuberant or 'gleeful' play (Tovey 2007), such as spinning around or laughing and shrieking aloud. In contrast, the indoor environment is a space where quiet and calm are often prized by adults, and the space is sometimes deemed to be more conducive to purposeful, adult-directed learning. When outdoors, then, children's play themes can often involve more movement and greater noise and this may be especially significant in imaginative play. Jake (5½ and in Year 1 of primary education) talked about the kinds of superhero play he engaged in outdoors in the school playground such as playing 'Halo men' and 'Baby raptors' with groups of his peers. He was keen to emphasize how the play involved seeking and capturing 'baddies'.

When asked about activities he enjoys doing indoors, Jake declared that he liked 'playing games' but found it difficult to think of many – finally putting the game 'Snakes and Ladders' (a formal board game) forward as an example. His response is suggestive of the way that Year 1 classrooms are likely to offer a more formal curriculum than that in many early years settings. Moreover, a key opportunity for children to engage in the kind of spontaneous play with friends they enjoy is playtimes: a period that is often less regulated by the managing hands of adults. However, it is important to add the caveat here that the freedom afforded during such play opportunities does not mean that children will play 'nicely'. For example, children who are physically bigger can use their size to obtain the play equipment of their choice. As Grieshaber and McArdle (2010) observe, romantic ideas about the play of children as 'natural' and 'innocent' mask the inequities that are reproduced and enacted through play. And this in turn is problematic if adults persist with the idea that 'interrupting' play should be avoided. As we will see when I discuss the importance of friendships for well-being, children do need adults to help to provide an environment in which positive and socially just relationships are fostered.

As well as the importance placed on the outdoor environment, the data from the focus groups in the LMU/NCB Well-being Project show that practitioners regard 'poor resources' or 'no open-ended materials' as indicative of a poor play environment. 'Being mentally stimulated' was generally regarded as vital for children's well-being, but resources were seen as not needing to be costly. As one practitioner in the focus groups noted, 'you can be really rich and get them loads of toys but do nothing (by way of interacting with children)'. Similarly, in a seminar discussion, one participant noted 'let kids be: children don't need expensive toys'.

A UNICEF report (Ipsos MORI and Nairn 2011), however, concludes that the issue is more complex. For instance, low levels of well-being of adults and children have been linked to the desire for consumer goods and it seems unfair to expect children to remain outside of such desires by virtue of being children as opposed to adults. Perhaps young children do not 'need' expensive toys but this same argument can be put to adults in relation to the money that they spend on electronic gadgets, for instance. Moreover, this aspiration is not necessarily linked to greed; the products may serve other needs, such as a longing to participate in shared activities with other children and it is this desire for relationships that I return to later in this chapter.

But in concluding this section, it is important to note the wider context in which resources for play might be conceptualized. The opportunity for children to make choices among play materials and activities was considered important for many participants in the focus group sessions. This is indicative of the neoliberal context in which the LMU/NCB Well-being Project was carried out, as 'choice' tends to be prized more highly in contemporary minority world societies compared with other parts of the world. As an individual 'consumer', through play the child is expected to exercise choice over their play activities and materials (Tobin et al. 2009), which mirrors the 'choices' exercised by people in a market. But while children in the project did prize their favourite toys and possessions, they also emphasized their relationships with others, notably peers.

Friendships, play, and well-being

The most important plaything(s) identified by the children in the LMU/NCB Well-being Project was other children. However, the data show that adults tended to talk about adult–child relationships – notably the key person approach and the importance of adult family members – as central to children's well-being. Although friendships were mentioned by adults, there was a distinct difference in emphasis between the adult-generated data and that generated with the children. Perhaps there is a tendency to valorize caregiver–child relationships over child–peer relationships despite evidence that the latter are of huge significance to young children (Degotardi and Pearson 2009). Overwhelmingly, the children stressed the importance of friendships and were able to name their friends – sometimes calling them 'special friends' or 'buddies'; saying whether they knew them through their setting or from outside the setting they attend.

Play is an important vehicle for forming and cementing friendships, and for many children discussion of friendship was interwoven with their discussion about play. The work of Corsaro (1985) has shown that in play, children generate their own peer cultures and that this is important in forging a shared sense of community.

Friendship also emerged as of central importance in Langsted's (1994) Children as Citizens study, which in part examined 'quality' from children's perspectives in the Danish context. A key finding in this study was that children considered other children to be the key determinant of quality in their settings. She states:

> This conclusion underlines the importance of a factor which experts, parents and centre staff are all aware of but may tend to forget from time to time, i.e. that children are important for children's development. The conclusion also underlines the fact that it is important for children to have a world in which there is room for contact with other children.
>
> (Langsted 1994: 40)

Significantly, many children in the LMU/NCB Well-being Project talked about the difficulties they encounter with their peers. Maisie talked of a particular child being overly 'bossy'. Likewise, Pearl stated:

> I do like Hema, but not when she bosses me around. I love Pauline because she doesn't boss me around. Shaquille – I hate him because he bosses me but he doesn't do that anymore . . . He's [Shaquille] a friend from Fulham. He fights a lot with me and Fenella but he doesn't do that anymore.

When thinking about what made him sad, Jake talked of 'friends not playing with me' as being the most significant factor. Earlier in the chapter, I highlighted how play often reproduces inequities and in 'free' play especially, children can be marginalized and isolated. This means that practitioners need to take responsibility for teaching about how to play fairly and about diversity and difference, which may require a re-orientation of understandings of childhood play as inherently 'innocent' and 'fair' (Grieshaber and McArdle 2010). And this further suggests the need to re-appraise relationships between practitioners and children.

Play-based, child-centred pedagogies can result in a distancing of relationships between practitioners and children as the adult's role is confined to that of facilitator and observer (Langford 2010). Yet, on occasions, children in the LMU/NCB Well-being Project discussed their relationships with peers as interwoven with their relationships with adults; indeed, in some instances, the children emphasized the role of adults in supporting their relationships with children. By way of example, Angelo stated:

> Playing with mummy makes me happy . . . I like playing games with her . . . My brother keeps fighting with me it makes me sad . . . he hits and smacks me when I sit next to him but then mummy gives me nice cuddles and says, 'Stop fighting'.

Reflective exercise

The evidence from the LMU/NCB Well-being Project and from studies which have elicited children's perspectives on the quality of their provision has shown that friendships are considered highly significant by young children in relation to their feelings of well-being.

- To what extent do you support the development of friendships in children's play and how do you help them to resolve any difficulties they have with their peers?
- Do you teach children how to play fairly – if so, how?

Langford (2010) is critical of the tendency of practitioners towards seeing and responding to children as if individual units in isolation from one another. As Von der Assan and Kernan (2011) assert, adults should try to ensure that their provision fosters friendships between children such as through keeping friends together in groups and further argue that adults can play an active role in providing inclusive play opportunities for disabled and non-disabled children to play together. Von der Assan and Kernan (2011: 109) also emphasize how practitioners should reflect on the play space in terms of how it fosters small group and large group interactions, 'allowing noisy, silly, active play so that children can have fun and experience the togetherness that comes from shared laughter'. And it is this sense of fun and camaraderie that I wish to stress as I conclude this section.

When reflecting on the process of the LMU/NCB Well-being Project seminars, I continue to be struck by the significance of playfulness on the part of the participants. Alongside the more 'serious' conversations and presentations about well-being, there were opportunities for those adults involved to have a joke with each other and many seemed to enjoy re-connecting with people they knew in the early childhood community who, perhaps, they had not seen for a while. Adults, like children, need to experience the fun and camaraderie to be had with friends and polarizing play as the preserve of childhood alone negates its importance for adults too. Moreover, children and adults can enjoy moments of playfulness and laughter together, which may have little or nothing to do with meeting prescriptive curricular outcomes (Grace and Tobin 1997) but have everything to do with their present well-being. The Early Years Foundation Stage (DfE 2012) makes little mention of such playfulness in relation to early childhood practice and of course it would be ridiculous to suggest a prescribed target for it.

Reflective exercise

Consider all the different types of opportunities for play in your setting and evaluate the value given to them. For example:

• How do adults respond when children play with the water coming out of the taps in the bathroom or chase each other across the indoor play area?
• What is the longest period of time that children can play without interruption in your setting?

Conclusion

In summary, play is an important factor in children's well-being but at the current time this tends to be framed in relation to children's future academic 'success' as opposed to their present lived experience. Although I would not want to downplay the importance of play in children's learning, there is a need for caution: the data from the LMU/NCB Well-being Project highlight that there is concern among practitioners, especially that play is being framed increasingly in instrumental terms – as a prime vehicle through which children will 'reach' pre-determined curricula outcomes. This was contrasted with a view of play as being valuable for its own sake and for the enjoyment children derive from playing now. This suggests a need for adults to be able to maximize opportunities for being 'in the moment' with children and the ability to respond sensitively to their play.

The data generated from the research with the children suggests two further important avenues for exploration in relation to play and well-being. The environment was seen as a crucial factor in children's play, notably the outdoor environment, which I suggested may relate to the open-endedness the environment affords as well as the opportunity it affords for exuberant, loud, and physically active play compared with the indoor environment. In addition, children in the LMU/NCB Well-being Project highlighted the importance of friendships with other children engendered through play. Thus, there is a need for adults to consider how they foster the development of positive relationships between children at play as well as between adults and children, which includes a re-appraisal of the idea that play is innocent and fair. The data from the children demonstrate how difficulties experienced with peers have a strong impact on children's sense of well-being and this requires far more of practitioners than a mere facilitative or observational role in relation to play.

References

Ailwood, J. (2003) Governing early childhood education through play, *Contemporary Issues in Early Childhood*, 4(3): 286–99.

Albon, D. (2011) Post-modern and post-structuralist perspectives on early child-hood education, in L. Miller and L. Pound (eds.) *Theories and Approaches to Learning in the Early Years*. London: Sage.

Axline, V.M. (1974) *Play Therapy*. New York: Ballentine.

Bennett, N., Wood, L. and Rogers, S. (1997) *Teaching through Play: Teachers' Thinking and Classroom Practice*. Buckingham: Open University Press.

Bialostok, S. and Kamberelis, S. (2010) New capitalism, risk, and subjectification in an early childhood classroom, *Contemporary Issues in Early Childhood*, 11(3): 299–312.

Bruce, T. (1991) *Time to Play in Early Childhood Education*. London: Hodder & Stoughton.

Corsaro, W. (1985) *Friendship and Peer Culture in the Early Years*. Norwood, NJ: Ablex.

Dahlberg, G. and Moss, P. (2005) *Ethics and Politics in Early Childhood Education*. Abingdon: Routledge/Falmer.

Degotardi, S. and Pearson, E. (2009) Relationship theory in the nursery: attachment and beyond, *Contemporary Issues in Early Childhood*, 10(2): 144–55.

Department for Education (DfE) (2012) *Statutory Framework for the Early Years Foundation Stage*. London: DfE. Available at: https://www.education.gov.uk/publications/standard/AllPublicationsNoRsg/Page1/DFE-00023-2012 [accessed 30 January 2013].

Grace, D. and Tobin, J. (1997) Carnival in the classroom: elementary students making videos, in J. Tobin (ed.) *Making a Place for Pleasure in Early Childhood Education*. New Haven, CT: Yale University Press.

Grieshaber, S. and McArdle, F. (2010) *The Trouble with Play*. Maidenhead: Open University Press.

Groos, K. (1901) *The Play of Man*. New York: Appleton.

Gulløv, E. (2012) Kindergartens in Denmark: reflections on continuity and change', in A.T. Kjorholt and J. Quortrup (eds.) *The Modern Child and the Flexible Labour Market*. London: Palgrave Macmillan.

Gupta, A. (2011) Play and pedagogy framed within India's historical, socio-cultural and pedagogical context, in S. Rogers (ed.) *Rethinking Play and Pedagogy in Early Childhood Education: Concepts, Contexts and Cultures*. Abingdon: Routledge.

Ipsos MORI Research Institute in partnership with Dr. Agnes Nairn (2011) *Children's Well-being in the UK, Sweden and Spain: The Role of Inequality and Materialism: A Qualitative Study*. London: Ipsos MORI.

James, A., Jenks, C. and Prout, A. (1998) *Theorizing Childhood*. Cambridge: Polity Press.

Jenks, C. (1996) The postmodern child, in J. Brannen and M. O'Brien (eds.) *Children in Families: Research and Policy*. London: Falmer Press.

Jones, L., Holmes, R., MacRae, C. and MacLure, M. (2010) Critical politics of play, in G.S. Cannella and L. Diaz Soto (eds.) *Childhoods: A Handbook*. New York: Peter Lang.

Kalliala, M. (2006) *Play Culture in a Changing World*. Maidenhead: Open University Press.

Kjørholt, A.T. and Qvortrup, J. (2012) *The Modern Child and the Flexible Labour Market: Early Childhood Education and Care*. London: Palgrave Macmillan.

Langford, R. (2010) Critiquing child-centred pedagogy to bring children and early childhood educators into the centre of a democratic pedagogy, *Contemporary Issues in Early Childhood*, 11(1): 113–27.

Langsted, O. (1994) Looking at quality from the child's perspective, in P. Moss and A. Pence (eds.) *Valuing Quality in Early Childhood Services: New Approaches to Defining Quality*. London: Paul Chapman.

London Play (2010) *The Importance of the Natural Environment for Play*. London Play Briefing, December.

Lyotard, J.F. (1979) *The Postmodern Condition: A Report on Knowledge* (translated by G. Bennington and B. Massumi). Manchester: Manchester University Press.

Mitchell, C. and Reid-Walsh, J. (2002) *Researching Children's Popular Culture: The Cultural Spaces of Childhood*. London: Routledge.

Moyles, J.R. (1989) *Just Playing? The Role and Status of Play in Early Childhood Education*. Buckingham: Open University Press.

Qvortrup, J. (1994) Childhood matters: an introduction, in J. Qvortrup, M. Bardy, G. Sgritta and H. Wintersberger (eds.) *Childhood Matters: Social Theory, Practice and Politics*. Aldershot: Avebury.

Robson, S. (1996) The physical environment', in S. Robson and S. Smedley (eds.) *Education in Early Childhood: First Things First*. London: David Fulton.

Rogers, S. (2010) Powerful pedagogies and playful resistance: role play in the early childhood classroom, in L. Brooker and S. Edwards (eds.) *Engaging Play*. Maidenhead: Open University Press.

Saracho, O. and Spodek, B. (2003) Understanding play and its theories, in O. Saracho and B. Spodek (eds.) *Contemporary Perspectives on Play in Early Childhood Education*. Greenwich: Information Age Publishing.

Stephenson, A. (2002) Opening up the outdoors: exploring the relationship between the indoor and outdoor environment of a centre, *Early Childhood Education Research*, 10: 29–38.

The Children's Society (2011) *How Happy are Our Children: Measuring Children's Well-being and Exploring Economic Factors*. London: The Children's Society.

Tobin, J., Hseuh, Y. and Karasawa, M. (2009) *Pre-School in Three Cultures Revisited: China, Japan and the United States*. Chicago, IL: University of Chicago Press.

Tovey, H. (2007) *Playing Outdoors: Spaces and Places, Risk and Challenge*. Maidenhead: Open University Press.

United Nations Children's Fund (UNICEF) (2007) *Child Poverty in Perspective: An Overview of Child Well-being in Rich Countries. A Comprehensive Assessment of the Lives and Well-being of Children and Adolescents in the Economically Advanced Nations*. Innocenti Report Card 7. Florence: UNICEF Innocenti Research Centre.

Van Zandvoort, M., Tucker, P., Irwin, J.D. and Burke, S.M. (2010) Physical activity at daycare: issues, challenges and perspectives, *Early Years*, 30(2): 175–88.

Von der Assan, N. and Kernan, M. (2011) Including children with disabilities: promoting peer relationships and friendships, in M. Kernan and E. Singer (eds.) *Peer Relationships in Early Childhood Education and Care*. Abingdon: Routledge.

Wood, E. (2010) Reconceptualising the play–pedagogy relationship: from control to complexity, in L. Brooker and S. Edwards (eds.) *Engaging Play*. Maidenhead: Open University Press.

6 Creativity, imagination, and well-being

Penny Holland

Introduction

> The concept of 'what might be' – being able to move in perception and thought away from the concrete given, or 'what is', to 'what was, what could have been, what one can try for, what might happen' and, ultimately, to the purest realms of fantasy – is a touchstone of that miracle of human experience, the imagination.
>
> (Singer and Singer 1990: 19)

I have always introduced the subject of creativity and imagination to students and practitioners as being about 'life, the universe, and everything' in order to emphasize creative and imaginative development as underpinning a range of human capacities that are not just confined to the artistic realm. That emphasis applies equally to this chapter, whose purpose is not to offer certainty in claiming links between creativity, imagination, and well-being, but rather to offer practitioners ways of exploring creativity and imagination as concepts rather than activities and to consider ways in which young children's imaginative and creative engagement may support their individual well-being and in turn their active and critical engagement with society.

Creativity, imagination, and well-being are broad terms and initially this chapter will explore some of the ways in which the terms are understood and applied in early childhood practice. This will be followed by a discussion of the ways in which creativity and imagination underpin the development of empathy, flexibility, tolerance, and the ability to consider a range of possibilities, which relate to our scientific, mathematic, artistic, political, and emotional endeavours. This includes a consideration of how this critical area of development allows us to understand that there can be more than one answer to a question. Drawing on these discussions, the following section outlines a range of ways in which the development of creativity and imagination may support children's well-being and then moves towards a more general discussion of how practitioners can effectively support and enable the development of creativity and imagination.

In the London Metropolitan University/National Children's Bureau Project 'Talking about Young Children's Well-being' (LMU/NCB Well-being Project), adult participants in focus groups and seminars referred frequently to the importance of freedom of choice, open-ended activities, imaginative play, and opportunities to be creative as helping to make sense of experience and develop young children's imagination. This connection was further reinforced when participants were asked to consider practice that inhibits well-being. Responses include references to 'having no freedom to use your imagination and having no open-ended materials, inhibiting exploration, messiness and risk-taking'. In the consultations with children, they most often mentioned free flow imaginary play as making them 'happy'. The relationship between happiness and imaginative functioning is a strand that will be explored and questioned later in this chapter.

What do we mean by creativity?

Although the focus of this chapter is on the relationship between creativity, imagination, and well-being, it is necessary to first spend some time looking at what is understood by these terms in early childhood and identify some key perspectives before considering the connections.

Reflective exercise

Before reading on, take time to reflect on the ways in which you see yourself as being a creative person. Make some notes so that you can review what you have said at the end of the chapter.

Many of you, in response to the reflective exercise above, may have noted that you do not see yourselves as creative because you do not see yourself as artistic or musical. While creativity is intrinsically connected to those endeavours and to those who create works of art and music, there has been a significant shift towards understanding creativity more as a process and underlying disposition. Anna Craft (2002: 51–2) proposes that we distinguish between 'big C creativity', which she links to 'the sort of publicly acclaimed creativity, which fundamentally changes knowledge and/or our perspective on the world', and 'little c creativity', or 'ordinary, everyday creativity'. Tina Bruce (2004) also explores this distinction when she talks about 'everyday creativity' and clearly emphasizes the importance of process: 'Creativity is hugely about process, and only sometimes carries through into a product' (Bruce 2004: 15). This focus on process has two significant implications for practice: first, that we need to see creativity as a disposition rather than a talent, and second, that we need to identify creativity in all children's activity and behaviours across all areas of development, play, and learning rather than just in artistically creative products.

This might mean that you recognize the creative thinking involved in children's problem-solving strategies; for example, the child playing with the hollow blocks who uses a chair to help them construct a bridge when they have run out of blocks of the right size for the job. It also means tuning in to the stories that children might be composing as they chase each other around the garden hiding from imagined baddies, the multiple symbolic transformations that another child might make to a stick ('is it a bird, is it a plane . . .'), or the responses a child might be able to offer when you ask 'how do you think Hakim felt when you laughed at him for falling over?' These are all examples of the developing flexibility of young children's thinking and while problem-solving processes do not just relate to imagined situations, I would argue that all these examples draw on children's experiences of imaginative symbolic play, where children learn that language, ideas, and objects can be flexible. An object is not defined by its name and what it does; ideas can encompass what could be, as well as what is or what has been. Vygotsky argues this point in relation to symbolic play and abstraction when he describes a child moving beyond the point where 'things dictate to the child what he must do' towards a point where 'thought is separated from objects and action arises from ideas rather than from things: a piece of wood begins to be a doll and a stick becomes a horse' (Vygotsky 1978: 96). Craft (2007: 1) describes this as 'possibility thinking': 'Possibility thinking, then, essentially involves a transition in understanding; in other words, the shift from "what is this?" to exploration – i.e. "what can I/we do with this?"' And "what could it be?"'

In starting to outline some central perspectives on creativity, it is clear that it is virtually impossible not to mention imagination, and while there are a range of perspectives on the detailed relationship between the two (for a helpful discussion of this relationship, see Craft 2002: 79–97), there is a consensus that creativity and imagination are intrinsically linked and this perspective will be applied throughout the chapter.

Reflective exercise

Spend some time thinking about and recording notes on how you see the relationship between creativity and imagination.

- Can you be creative without using your imagination?
- Can you imagine without being creative?

Reflections on imaginative and creative processes

The next section will consider a range of ways in which young children's engagement with imagination and creativity might support their well-being, and to help illustrate this I will use an example from my own research and practice in relation to war, weapon, and superhero play (Holland 2003). One of the initial triggers for my interest in this area of children's imaginative and creative play was coming to realize that applying a negative approach to this area of play (i.e. stopping the play in its tracks) was having a damaging effect on the well-being of the children with a persistent interest in these themes. This was evident in a number of ways: the children would not engage with other activities offered to them; they were not developing positive relationships with other children, and did not display a sense of belonging and they could often display challenging behaviour in response to our attempts to distract them from their chosen form of play. Overall, we felt that they were displaying low self-esteem. I came to understand that one of the major implications of banning their pursuit of this play interest was that they were effectively being prevented from engaging with any form of creative or imaginative play because war, weapon, and superhero play was their chosen point of access.

Clearly, if we accept the perspective outlined above, which places creativity and imagination at the heart of learning, development, and well-being, the implications of inhibiting these children from engaging in this area of play are of great concern. In response to these concerns, it was decided to pursue a more relaxed approach to war, weapon, and superhero play and to observe, analyse, and support children engaged in this area of play in the same way that we do with any other area of play and in tune with the principle that we start with the child's interest. There were many challenges for the team involved with making this shift of approach, which related to their moral concerns about allowing children to play out violent themes and to their anxieties about the spiralling impact of noisy and physically active play. However, the positive outcomes recorded in settings that altered their approach in this way, turned our fears aside. These included an enhanced sense of belonging and self-esteem alongside improved social skills and friendship. This is illustrated in an observation undertaken for the LMU/NCB Well-being Project of two 4 year old boys playing together:

> Ben and Frank pulled small chairs into a circle shape and put cushions and blankets in the middle. They then walked around the chairs and jumped on to the cushions, laughing. After 8 minutes they moved to a table under which they remained quietly talking together for 3 minutes. Then they came out and moved the small chairs into a shape around the table and went back under. When asked what they were doing, they both said it was their rocket and they were flying 'in space'. When asked what they could see in space, Ben replied: 'Planets – stars – lots'.

Singer and Singer's (1990: 68) longitudinal study was conceived specifically to 'look at the patterning of emotions during a child's spontaneous play and to determine whether positive emotions related in any systematic way to imaginative play'. The positive outcomes of their study are outlined below:

> Our research studies of 3–4 year old children followed for one year indicate that those who played more often at make believe or who developed imaginary playmates were also reported by observers to be more likely to smile and laugh during the play school situation, to be more persistent and less likely to be angry, aggressive or sad. In studies of imaginative older children we find them to be less unwarrantedly aggressive, less impulsive and better able to discriminate reality from fantasy.
>
> (Singer 1994: 12)

It is important to point out that it is not enough to simply assume that these findings point to a simplistic and direct connection between young children's engagement in creative and imaginative play and external expressions of happiness on the basis that we assume them to be having fun or indeed that having fun is the goal. Nor should it be assumed that children playing quietly alone without any external sign of happiness are neither engaged in creative and imaginative processes nor that they are unhappy. Humes (2011: 10) reminds us that 'Happiness, confidence and well-being are likely to be by-products of other activities rather than qualities which are themselves the object being pursued.' Similarly, Tina Bruce (2004) refers to fulfilment rather than happiness or enjoyment. The work of Laevers et al. (1997), which emphasizes both well-being and involvement as preconditions for deep level learning and offers practitioners two interlinked scales of well-being and involvement as tools for observing and assessment, is also relevant to the connections between well-being and creativity and imagination that are being considered here.

In writing about creativity with a focus on adult experiences, Csikszentmihalyi (1996) writes about the state of 'flow', which has echoes of Laevers' 'deep involvement' and which we might commonly relate to the idea of 'being in the zone' or deeply absorbed to the point of not hearing the doorbell ring or realizing how much time has passed. Csikszentmihalyi reminds us that creativity is hard work and helpfully refers to two sides of the well-being coin, which will be all too familiar to readers. On the one hand, he identifies 'entropy' (p. 119), which 'gives us pleasure when we are comfortable, when we relax, when we can get away with feeling good without expending energy', and on the other, the satisfaction we feel after committing ourselves to deep involvement in a challenging artistic or academic creative process. He suggests that 'It is only after we get out of flow, at the end of a session or in moments of distraction within it that we might indulge in feeling happy. And then there is the rush of well-being, of satisfaction that comes when the poem is completed or the theorem is proved' (p. 123). Although Csikszentmihalyi is writing about adults, it is helpful to reflect on the difficulties, challenges, efforts, and depth of discoveries that young children also experience while engaged in creative and imaginative play.

Reflective exercise

In the spirit of criticality, this might be a good moment to ask the question of what comes first, that is: do children experience well-being because they are creatively and imaginatively engaged or do they need to have a high level of well-being before they can function well imaginatively or creatively?

What do you think? And remember the statement at the beginning of the chapter; there can be more than one answer to a question.

Creativity, imagination, and well-being

The challenge now is to explore and analyse the possible connections beneath the surface of what we can observe and to ask why observers might be noticing a relationship between young children's creative and imaginative engagement and their well-being. To provide a framework for this, I will return to the war, weapon, and superhero play example that was described earlier in the chapter, which indicated that benefits had been observed to the self-esteem, engagement, sense of belonging, and social skills of the children with a persistent interest in this area of play following the relaxation of a negative approach to this interest. The enhancement of self-esteem is perhaps the most readily explainable of these effects. The children concerned had been receiving a significant degree of negative feedback from practitioners in relation to their play interests and while it could be argued that the feedback was being directed at the play and not the children, it would be naïve to claim that a 3–4 year old child could grasp that distinction. It is not surprising, then, that a shift to an acceptance of and positive support towards the child's play interest would enhance their self-esteem.

The connection becomes more complex when considering why a child's sense of belonging and social skills should benefit from this change of approach. This connection can partly be explained by the overt sanctioning and legitimization of the child's play interest, and the fact that the child is no longer marginalized as a result of that interest. Here it is important to acknowledge the extent to which other children receive and respond to the signals of approval and disapproval that practitioners communicate. However, this is only part of the picture and the focus needs to shift towards the internal processes that connect imagination and creativity with social understandings, and the key concepts that are helpful here are those of theory of mind and empathy. In relation to theory of mind, I have previously noted that:

> I view imagination as the thread that enables us to connect with other human minds . . . I referred to the perspective held by neuroscientists concerning the plasticity of the human brain and how experience will sculpt

each individual's brain differently. It is this individuation in brain development that underpins the theory of mind (Lewis and Mitchell 1994) by which we come to understand that no other individual can precisely share our thoughts, memories and understanding of the world. Developing a theory of mind is one of the conceptual leaps that young children have to make in their early years: understanding that communication is not mind to mind . . .

(Holland 2003: 31)

Developing theory of mind is a crucial first step in the journey to being able to empathize – that is, we cannot imagine ourselves in 'someone else's shoes' if we do not first understand that we all wear different shoes. It can be argued that without developing theory of mind and, subsequently, empathy, we will not be able to achieve tolerance and respect for difference, which depends on being able to see a situation from different perspectives and understand that there at least two sides to every story. The latter capacity is also essential for children's growing ability to resolve conflict effectively. Crucial for the growth of these abstract understandings is playing with objects in a transformatory and flexible way. This supports the development of symbolic representation and the ability to use symbolic systems including language, which require that we can use a sound, mark, gesture or image to represent an object or experience. It should not take a huge leap of thought to recognize that the context in which young children are honing, stretching, and gaining mastery of these capacities is imaginative and creative play. Indeed, it is impossible to conceive of how one could possibly understand the complexities of someone else's feelings and behaviours without a well-developed imagination. To summarize, then, the argument that has been made in this section is that one aspect of well-being is the experience of a sense of belonging and positive social relationships, which for young children depends on their developing capacity to understand that we are all different, will respond in a variety of ways to situations, and will not all feel the same at the same moment and cannot communicate from mind to mind. Imaginative play and creative activities are seen as providing the soil, sun, and rain in which these capacities can flourish.

Spiritual and symbolic narratives

There is a further layer of interpretation of some aspects of children's imaginative and creative behaviours, which draws on psychodynamic perspectives (Bowlby 1969; Erikson 1967; Fromm 1951) and is offered here as a taster of another tool that we can use in our efforts to observe, analyse, and support children's creativity and imaginative play in an open and respectful way. To illustrate, I will again draw on an example from my own research into children's war, weapon, and superhero play. During the course of my research, I was struck by the commonness of death and resurrection as a theme enacted during this form of imaginative play and felt that it warranted further thought and analysis. I was fascinated by scenarios that emphasized the healing or restorative process, with the child taking on the role of medical or magical healer. This included those scenarios where a child pretends to shoot and kill another and then makes them better so that they can rejoin the play.

This theme of death and resurrection is ubiquitous in traditional tales such as Red Riding Hood, Snow White, and Sleeping Beauty, and is regularly found in contemporary children's popular culture, for example Power Rangers and Transformers. But observing children's re-enactment of these scenarios also led me to explore the long path of cultural resurrection narratives in the stories, films, and beliefs of adult life. The world's major religions all offer accounts of life beyond death, whether via reincarnation or entry into parallel universes of the living dead or spiritual worlds, which often build on pagan and Wicca folk traditions that are concerned with the cycle of life and the cycle of the year. And alongside children's stories are contemporary fantasy and science fiction related adult narratives that restate and expand the central themes of parallel worlds and transformations; all reflecting a desire to transcend mortality both materially and conceptually.

Faced with this weight of diverse but related narratives, it strikes me that the questions we should be asking are why does this concern emerge so early in childhood and why do related narratives persist throughout our lives? It would seem rather than popular texts introducing this theme inappropriately to young children that, conversely, they embody deeper human concerns and are of interest to children for that reason. I am not suggesting that children's interest arises from conscious pondering of the mystery of what happens after death, although for some children, who have experienced bereavement directly, this may be true. Rather, I am looking at a connecting strand that could offer meaning to the persistence of revival narratives across the human life span.

If we accept, then, that even very young children may be drawn to a theme because it has symbolic resonance with significant feelings and events, we can start to move beyond literal interpretations of revival scenarios in play. The most resounding connection that I have been able to make with common childhood experience is with attachment and separation (Bowlby 1969), as all children entering early childhood settings will be experiencing either their first extended separation from their primary carers or a major change in their pattern of care. It is not then a huge leap to recognize death and revival as a possible metaphor for the anxiety experienced when a carer leaves and returns. Nor does it seem unreasonable to speculate that this primary anxiety continues to seek expression in narratives of resurrection, immortality, and parallel spirit worlds throughout our lives in relation to the ultimate separation of death.

> As Freud was writing about this he became aware . . . of the fact that the frequency of the main theme (something or somebody disappears and

comes back) corresponded to the intensity of the life experience reflected – namely, the mother's leaving in the morning and her return at night. This dramatization takes place in the play sphere. Utilizing his mastery over objects, the child can arrange them in such a way that they permit him to imagine that he is master of his predicament as well . . . He has, as Freud put it, turned passivity into activity; he plays out doing something that was in reality done to him.

(Erikson 1967: 209–10)

It would be wrong to assume that the revival theme has a common meaning for all children and Fromm's (1951) framework of 'conventional, accidental, and universal' levels of symbolism helps us to understand this. Within this framework I am suggesting that separation relates to the universal level of symbolism, which may have resonance for all children, while popular culture provides access to the theme at the conventional level and direct personal experience of bereavement, or possibly other loss and rejection related experiences, at the accidental level.

To summarize, it is clear that for practitioners, it is as essential as it is for young children to develop an understanding that there may be many different ways to interpret a situation.

Implications for practice

What, then, are the implications for practice? How do practitioners ensure that young children are supported in their imaginative and creative development, which relates so centrally to social aspects of their well-being? Much has been written elsewhere about the detail of how we can prepare the environment and plan experiences based on observation to support children's imaginative and creative development (Bruce 2004; Holland 2003; Manning-Morton and Thorp 2003; Wright 2010) and this cannot be covered within the limits of this chapter. However, it is important to consider some of the underlying principles of good practice in this area. Singer and Singer again provide us with some food for thought:

> What we have discovered, however, is that there are certain essential ingredients that are conducive to fostering this willingness to explore the possible. There must be a key person in a child's life who inspires and sanctions play and accepts the child's inventions with respect and delight. There must be a place for play, a 'sacred space' (no matter how small), and time, open-ended and unstructured. And there must be simple objects or props to help inspire the adventure . . .

(Singer and Singer 1990: 4)

Reflective exercise

Using the above quote as a framework, relate the ingredients listed by Singer and Singer to examples of practice in your setting and identify areas that you might need to develop.

In carrying out this task did you consider the ways in which you match up to the description of the 'key person . . . who inspires and sanctions play and accepts the child's inventions with respect and delight'? This is not necessarily as easy as it sounds and can present us with some challenges. An example of this from my own practice is the huge shift in attitude that I had to undergo to come to understand, respect, and become fascinated by children's war, weapon, and superhero play, of which I had previously held extremely negative views and had definitely not 'sanctioned'. As I came to identify the limitations and negative impact of a zero tolerance approach to this area of play and to understand the importance of relaxing that approach to ensure access to those crucial experiences of imaginative and creative play for children with a consuming interest in these play themes, I realized that I had to suspend my own moral judgements and feelings. Within a short time the positive impact of this change of approach on the well-being and social and cognitive growth of the children concerned helped me to fully understand the extent of the influence of practitioners' attitudes on the experience of the children in their care. While I am sure that there are many great practitioners delivering excellent practice in this area, I offer this example to encourage them to be honest in their reflections and analysis of their own practice.

Supporting young children's creativity and imaginative play can present us with many challenges: it can often (though not always) be noisy, lively, and messy and children often need to mix resources from across areas of learning. As practitioners, we can often inhibit the flow by seeking to control children's exuberance and interrupt them to tidy up, for example, rather than allowing them 'open-ended and unstructured' time. In some settings, your personal good practice might be limited by the demands and routines of the setting that you work in. This might be, for example, an insistence on activities being cleared at the end of a session while children are expected to participate in a whole-class activity. A recent piece of research in Greece (Gregoriadis et al. 2011) looking at perceptions of creativity in young children's education found a discrepancy between practitioners' recognition of the importance of creativity and understanding how to support it. They cite the earlier work of Westby and Dawson (1995), who 'noted the inconsistencies in teachers' self-reports, according to which they value creativity but dislike personality traits related with creativity – such as impulsivity, autonomy, risk-taking, etc. These two researchers attributed this "gap" to the fact that teachers' main pursuit is to maintain the order and management of the classroom.' This may resonate with the pressure some of you may feel in relation to increasing formal elements of learning to supposedly ensure school readiness. Inconsistencies in practitioners' reports of creative pursuits that support their own well-being and practices that support children's well-being were also noted in the LMU/NCB Well-being Project. For example, adults frequently identified music – listening to it, dancing to it, playing an instrument or singing in a choir – as activities that contributed to a sense of well-being but did not identify these as practices that would support children's well-being.

This brings us to the final focus of this chapter, which briefly considers the guidance offered to practitioners to support the dual development of children's creativity and imagination as an essential and complex support to their experience of well-being. In comparing the statutory frameworks for the Early Years Foundation Stage from 2008 (QCA 2008) and 2012 (DfE 2012), it is evident that the centrality of creativity has been understated in the current document. In the 2008 framework, creative development was identified as one of six areas of learning, each of equal importance, whereas in the 2012 framework, seven areas are identified, with 'expressive arts and design' replacing 'creative development' and this is relegated to the secondary ranks rather than being one of the three prime areas. This 2012 framework in placing Personal, Social and Emotional Development and Expressive Arts in unrelated categories clearly fails to make the link between creativity, imagination, and children's well-being that has been explored in this chapter.

Conclusion

This leads us to the conclusion of the chapter, which puts the ball back in the practitioners' court, as it is your challenge, yet again, to develop practice that meets both the requirements of official government policy and the needs of the babies and young children in your care according to your academic and professional knowledge and conscience. I wish you well.

References

Bowlby, J. (1969) *Attachment and Loss*, Vol.1. London: Pimlico.

Bruce, T. (2004) *Cultivating Creativity in Babies, Toddlers and Young Children*. London: Hodder & Stoughton.

Craft, A. (2002) *Creativity and Early Years Education: A Lifewide Foundation*. London: Continuum.

Craft. A (2007) *Creativity and Possibility in the Early Years*. Available at: http://www.tactyc.org.uk/pdfs/Reflection-craft.pdf [accessed 8 August 2012].

Csikszentmihalyi, M. (1996) *Creativity: Flow and the Psychology of Discovery and Invention*. New York: HarperCollins.

Department for Education (DfE) (2012) *Statutory Framework for the Early Years Foundation Stage: Setting the Standards for Learning, Development and Care for Children from Birth to Five*. London: DfE.

Erikson, E. (1967) *Childhood and Society* (2nd edn.). London: Penguin.

Fromm, E. (1951) *The Forgotten Language: An Introduction to the Understanding of Dreams, Fairytales and Myths*. New York: Grove Weidenfeld.

Gregoriadis, A., Zachopoulou, E. and Konstantinidou, E. (2011) *Early childhood educators' perceptions of creativity in education*, in Conference Proceedings of OMEP European Conference 'Perspectives of Creativity and Learning in Early Childhood' (pp. 120–8), Nicosia, Cyprus.

Holland, P. (2003) *We Don't Play with Guns Here: War, Weapon and Superhero Play in the Early Years*. Maidenhead: Open University Press.

Humes, W. (2011) Creativity and wellbeing in education: possibilities, tensions and personal journeys, *TEAN Journal*, 2(1) [Creativity Issue]. Available at: http://bit.ly/tmkJYf [accessed 27 August 2012].

Laevers, F., Vandenbussche, E., Kog, M. and Depondt, L. (1997) *A Process Oriented Child Monitoring System for Young Children*. Leuven: Centre for Experiential Education.

Manning-Morton, J. and Thorp, M. (2003) *Key Times for Play: The First Three Years*. Maidenhead: Open University Press.

Qualifications and Curriculum Authority (QCA) (2008) *The Early Years Foundation Stage Profile Handbook*. London: QCA.

Singer, D. and Singer, J.L. (1990) *The House of Make Believe: Children's Play and the Developing Imagination*. Cambridge, MA: Harvard University Press.

Singer, J.L. (1994) Imaginative play and adaptive development, in J.H. Goldstein (ed.) *Toys, Play and Child Development*. Cambridge: Cambridge University Press.

Vygotsky, L. (1978) *Mind in Society*. Cambridge, MA: Harvard University Press.

Westby, E.L. and Dawson, V.L. (1995) Creativity: asset or burden in the classroom?, *Creativity Research Journal*, 8(1): 1–10.

Wright, S. (2010) *Understanding Creativity in Early Childhood*. London: Sage.

7 Physical well-being: autonomy, exploration, and risk taking

Micky LeVoguer and Jasmine Pasch

Introduction

Data from the London Metropolitan University/National Children's Bureau Project 'Talking about Young Children's Well-being' (LMU/NCB Well-being Project) revealed that children wanted to experience exuberant physical movement, often outside. This matched comments from adult participants who mourned the loss of space and time for outdoor play for children, recalling their own joy in childhood outdoor risky play. Children also highlighted the need for close companionship from mums, from dads, with carers, and with friends. Data from the project found that many children and some adults linked physical play with ideas of well-being. Adult participants highlighted the holistic nature of physical and emotional well-being as interconnected states.

This chapter explores the way movement supports young children's health and well-being. The first part will focus on the specific types of movement in early childhood that encourage a child's brain to develop patterns that support learning and emotional development. Robust physical movement can be thrilling and joyful, so the second part of this chapter will explore elements of well-being resulting from these experiences. It will also consider how children learn about social rules through shared risk taking and the give and take and boundary setting of rough and tumble play. The third section will explore the way touch and movement is used to communicate within companionable relationships offering pleasure and reassurance between babies and carers. Throughout the chapter there are reflections on what adults and environments need to provide to promote well-being through movement.

The relationship of movement to well-being

From the beginning of life, body movement stimulates the growth of brain circuitry – the 'wiring'. This is then insulated by myelin, which is a white, fatty substance that forms a protective sheath around nerve fibres and allows for more efficient transmission of impulses. Through movement and play, neural networks are formed and strengthened to support emotional and cognitive functioning (Goddard Blythe 2008). Babies and young children, therefore, need plenty of opportunity for unrestricted movement to make those vital connections, and enough space to move around in so that they can practise over and over again, strengthening the connections as they move, play, and actively explore the world around them. Lamont (2009) likens this to young children having all the 'programmes' available in their brain architecture, while movement provides the 'double click' to open the programmes.

The significance of creeping and crawling

Two significant early patterns will be discussed in detail here: the belly crawl, and creeping on hands and knees.

The young infant placed on the tummy will squirm and wriggle in a seemingly random way but, given the opportunity, will find a pattern of movement that will lead to the belly crawl. Belly crawling is the culmination of lots of practice of reaching, pulling, and pushing. Babies initially push their head into the floor, then push from their bottom (tail) and then push their arms into the floor, which Bainbridge Cohen (1993) refers to as homologous movement. As they develop muscle strength and ease of movement through practice, they can push and pull their body along with contralateral sequences – that is, reaching with the right elbow with the left leg bent at the same time, then repeating this with left arm and elbow and right leg (Goddard Blythe 2004).

The belly crawl is a top to toe workout, and very hard work. It may be a brief phase, but is a critical and distinct phase that puts many specific and necessary pieces into place. According to Bette Lamont:

> Many people allow, or encourage children to skip it because when they put them down they hear grunting and fussing that sounds like distress. In many cases this is simply the infant trying to sort out breathing from moving, so the grunts are understandable . . . and necessary.
>
> (B. Lamont 2006, personal communication)

It can be difficult to watch babies and toddlers struggling to gain mastery over their body movements because it is hard work for them and they become frustrated. However, with plenty of time and practice they will solve the problems, particularly if they have adult support and attentiveness. Lamont advises that the fussing and crying is borne of frustration and is 'a bit like salt. A little is fine, but a lot is harmful, so the youngster needs comfort and reassurance if they get too stressed' (B. Lamont 2010, personal communication).

In the LMU/NCB Well-being Project, many adult participants identified reassuring companionship as an essential factor in enabling well-being for children. However, they also pointed to resilience, autonomy, and self-assurance as being valuable components. According to Walsh (2004), autonomy, assurance, and resilience are experienced through repeated opportunities for children to wrestle with problem solving and to independently follow their own desires. Roberts (2006) states that a parent who learns to accept a range of emotions from their baby can support the baby's self-esteem. Similarly, parents and practitioners who can accept that babies will sometimes struggle to integrate new movement patterns are supporting children to develop a feeling of competence as well as smooth neurological functioning. One participant in the project explicitly referred to the importance of balancing children's developing autonomy with the experience of being helped. It is important not to rush youngsters through a developmental sequence, instead, adults should join babies and young children as they play on the floor and take pleasure in their discoveries and achievements as these unfold in the moment.

Case study exercise

The following experiences occurred during a drop-in movement and play session in a children's centre for babies and toddlers and their parents.

One tiny girl just sat still in the middle of the room under a small tent, and her mother told me, 'She does not move. We only have a small flat so she cannot move much. She is either in her buggy, or in her bed.' Her mother pulled her up to standing and held her there saying, 'She will walk soon?'

We got the little girl on her tummy lifting up her head and supporting herself on her hands, then a bit of pushing from the left foot, then the right. Taking off her socks and shoes helped her feet to get a grip on the firm surface. There was a bit of protest, as this was not a familiar place for the child, so she needed a cuddle and some reassurance from her mother before trying again.

We gave the child lots of encouragement down on the floor with her. I asked her mother to do some 'homework' between sessions; putting the girl on her tummy as well as trying out various holds in her arms, on her body or across her legs with the child in a tummy down or prone position.

The soft play roll was helpful in getting a bit of hip extension with support on the front of her body. A rolled up towel would do the same thing in the home environment.

One month later:
The girl's mother was very excited to tell me all about how her daughter was moving, and set her down on the floor to show me. What a difference! She was creeping on all fours, and moving about to change direction.

I also noticed her pulling herself up to stand against one side of the soft play block. This is very different to being pulled up to stand by someone else, as observed at the beginning of the sessions.

- If you are a practitioner, can you identify children who have been 'walked' round the room by adults before they can walk independently? How is this different from a child's self-propelled movement?
- Reflect on the ways that you encourage children to persevere with tummy time. Do you provide opportunities for this kind of movement or not? How might you encourage this sort of movement in older children?

Towards the second half of the first year, a baby may push up onto hands and knees and, after a bit of rocking back and forth and going backwards instead of forwards, the infant begins to creep on all fours. Creeping on all fours builds on many of the movement experiences during tummy time and floor play (Lamont 2009). ['Creeping' is an American term that is equivalent to the UK crawling on hands and knees, and it is used here to differentiate the action from belly crawling.] Contralateral creeping on hands and knees, where a child moves in a sequence of right leg, left hand and then left leg, right hand, offers experiences that can help the left and right hemispheres of the brain to integrate as neuronal connections are strengthened through the repetition of movement (Goddard Blythe 2008). This fires connections between the two hemispheres of the brain supporting learning and memory tasks such as retrieval, filtering, sorting, sifting, and sequencing information. Without these connections, children may have difficulties knowing right from left and may later confuse some letters, numbers, and words.

This experience of being on hands and knees affords the child lots of new opportunities. Strength can be developed in the head and neck, which helps with later walking (Lamont 2009). In this position, a child's eyes are able to practise focusing and converging, which supports the tracking movement needed for reading and writing (Goddard Blythe 2004). Bainbridge Cohen (1993) discusses the different perspectives offered by this change in position. She stresses that crawling forward is initiated by a reach and pull of the head propelled by an inner desire for a new awareness of the environment. This self-generated reaching activates a curiosity for learning that can bring a sense of well-being. As noted above, children who are rushed through these movement sequences by adults may not develop a grounded and embodied sense of perspective that is integral to certain bodily positions.

Bainbridge Cohen (1984: 25) suggests that in the first year of life: 'The relation of the perceptual process (the way one sees) and the motor process (the way one moves or acts in the world) is established. This is the baseline for how you will be processing activity, either in receiving or expressing, throughout your life.' This view of movement explicitly links the physical and emotional processes of movement. Lamont (2009) also emphasizes that physical balance, for example, is entwined with an emotional sense of balance throughout life. In a similar way, adult participants in the LMU/NCB Well-being Project expressed an understanding of how these are linked: 'emotions and physical states – you can't separate these'.

Connecting the vestibular system through joyful movement

In addition to the familiar senses of sight, hearing, taste, smell, and touch, there are three other sensory systems that strengthen a child's sense of self in the world: the vestibular, proprioceptive, and tactile senses.

The vestibular sense is a balance mechanism, which processes information about movement, gravity, and balance. It is the first system to become myelinated in the brain and is dedicated to posture, equilibrium, muscle tone, and spatial orientation. It works closely with the cerebellum, which is the principal neural organ regulating the coordination of muscular activity (Goddard Blythe 2004). Balance is also supported when the hemispheres of the brain are connected, as the vestibular, proprioceptive, and visual systems can connect and operate together to help a child recognize space and depth perception (Field 1995).

There are connections between balance and the eyes, balance and the ears, and balance and body movement, and the young child spends much time practising and playing the systems into good working order. The baby is rocked gently, bounced on the knee, twirled around, and thrown high in the air. The young child swings, spins, tips, twirls, rocks, and rolls over and over, stimulating the vestibular system, then hops, skips, climbs, jumps, and runs, improving coordination between the vestibular and motor systems. Children in the LMU/NCB Well-being Project expressed desire for such exuberant movement:

> . . . jumping on the bouncy castle.

> . . . being tickled and spinning around really fast.

> . . . going 'bump'.

> . . . climbing on the climbing frame.

Adult participants identified physical well-being in children who:

- arrive at the setting and 'bounce in the door'
- are keen to be physical
- are always moving about happily running, jumping, dancing, clapping hands.

It would seem that there is some agreement between adults and children in the project about how well-being is expressed physically. What may be less readily apparent is the relationship between this exuberance and the way brain connections are formulated that underpin many information-processing skills in the growing child.

The most advanced level of movement is the ability to stay totally still (Goddard Blythe 2002). This requires muscle groups to operate together in perfect synchrony with the balance mechanism, and is dependent on a certain level of maturity in the nervous system (Goddard Blythe et al. 2009). The typically developing child wriggles and fidgets and dashes about as the system is still immature. Like a coin spinning on its axis, 'balance is only initially maintained by moving fast, and wobble sets in as the movement slows down, stops or starts. As control over balance improves, the amount of movement required to remain upright can be reduced' (Goddard Blythe 2002: 105). This has implications for provision and practice in early childhood settings and the first years of school. It is important to note that children cannot learn to be still through being still; fast and excitable movement precedes this ability to be still.

The role of robust and risky play in well-being

The second 'hidden' sense is the proprioceptive sense, which processes information about body position, and body parts through muscles, ligaments, and joints. It enables a child to know where parts of his or her body are at any time, and to make the appropriate postural adjustments. The proprioceptor nervous system consists of sensory neurons and stretch receptors in muscles. Information from them continuously updates a dynamic sensory-motor map of the body either at rest or in motion, and helps children to feel at home in their bodies.

The young baby stretches out its spine, wiggles around, and touches its hands and feet together through the action of the proprioceptive sense. Young children will continue to build a more three-dimensional sense of proprioception as they experience their body moving in space.

Some activities that will help the proprioceptive system to develop include climbing, pushing or pulling heavy objects, jumping, walking uphill, wearing a backpack, crunching vegetables with a firm texture, weight bearing on hands or arms, hanging by the arms or legs, tug of war games, and rough and tumble play.

Rough and tumble play may be a universal human experience that children and adults share. Panksepp says that rough and tumble play in young mammals is characterized by moments of chasing, bowling each other, pivoting round, leading and following, pouncing on each other's backs, wrestling and pinning down, all carried out with a 'flurry of dynamic, carefree rambunctiousness' (Panksepp 1998: 284). It is a very important type of movement play that can help animals and humans develop body and cognitive skills, assimilate into groups, learn to problem solve creatively, manage aggression, and accept defeat graciously. It is distinguished from aggressive fighting because there are positive rewards for all participants, the action moves quickly with role reversals, and there is no overall winner. Rough and tumble play involves different neurochemical systems than aggressive fighting and promotes more joyous feelings (Panksepp 1998).

During rough and tumble play, children develop an 'everyday morality' that is crucial for understanding social rules (Gill 2007: 43) – literally knowing how far to push at a particular time. The acquisition of social skills was articulated as a contributory factor for experiencing well-being by participants in the LMU/NCB Well-being Project: children need to be able to join in groups, know when to stop, self-regulate, and have the ability to balance their desires with others. Rough and tumble play is one way to develop these skills and attitudes (Lamont 2009).

Reflective exercise

However, risky, joyful, exuberant play fighting may be viewed as aberrant behaviour rather than revelry. Gill (2007: 43) says: 'Two linked anxieties lie behind adult reactions to play fighting: fear of being blamed if any children are hurt or upset, and a sense that allowing such play is somehow bad practice.'

- If you are an early childhood practitioner or in a managerial position in a setting or local authority, what is your reaction to Gill's statement and the children's experiences above?
- How could you provide opportunities for rough and tumble play that are safe?

Adult participants in the LMU/NCB Well-being Project also identified risky play as part of well-being: 'taking risks and having challenge' and desired an environment where children 'are encouraged to run free and climb up trees'. Some participants railed against a 'risk averse culture' that left children with a 'lack of freedom to take risks'. Children in the LMU/NCB Well-being Project cited being 'outside, always outside', 'in the big playground', 'nowhere 'cept the big playground' as favourite places to be, perhaps because of the physical challenges and opportunities the outdoors can present.

Lindon (1999) differentiates between risks and hazards: a hazard is a situation that has the potential to cause harm; a risk is a measurement of how likely or unlikely that harm will be caused by the particular hazard. Different situations and different children will alter the probability of harm occurring as a result of a hazard. This means that risk assessments cannot easily be applied as a 'one size fits all' policy. Tovey (2007) cautions against an environment that irons out all risk, as a degree of risk is necessary if children are to learn how to problem solve and to be safe. Walsh introduces the Japanese concept of *Genki*, which is to be 'aware and confident in their physical capabilities' (2004: 103). He marvelled at the daring of young Japanese children and realized that 'the daring moment masked the gradual process of becoming daring . . . begun when they were toddlers' (2004: 102). This was possible because robust physical play and risk taking are encouraged from an early age within settings in Japanese culture.

Many factors inhibit early childhood practitioners from encouraging children to take risks. The Japanese notion of *Genki* (Walsh 2004), which pictures young children as physically capable, can only be successfully nurtured because it is a shared cultural value. There is, as yet, no equivalent shared concept in the UK, although there have been some positive changes to early childhood provision as a result of research like Holland's (2003) study of war, weapon, and superhero play and government guidance about boys' creativity in the early year (DCSF 2007). Also, many local authorities have organized training and projects that promote children's movement play (e.g. Lamont 2009). These initiatives have sown the seeds of a cultural shift in relation to movement in early childhood settings.

But this shift is not as easy as it might appear. As Gill (2007) suggests, in allowing children to take risks, early childhood practitioners themselves take a risk that they will be seen to indulge children in play that should be discouraged – or worse, that will cause hurt; this pressure is not easy to withstand. However, the other side to this picture is that not allowing this play could be as harmful to children as going too far. Vygotsky (1978) advocated that learning for children occurs when they are able to experience moving to the edge of their current knowledge, a concept he termed being in the zone of proximal development. Inhabiting the edge of physical experience includes taking a risk and facing the unknown. Children who shy away from going to this edge miss out on learning experiences and risk not developing the 'active body language' that participants of the LMU/NCB Well-being Project recognized as signalling high well-being in young children.

Case study exercise

One of the authors worked in a setting that installed a zip wire for children to whiz along on. Over time, as children gained confidence, it became a sort of rite of passage of daring-ness. Children built up their courage to have a go and then to introduce more and more challenges. They brought over hollow blocks and learnt that the higher the stack the more of a swing and speed built up, resulting in a bigger challenge and a bigger thrill. Whoops and yells accompanied these exploits. Children performed their own sort of risk assessment and gave each other advice. In time, practitioners gained confidence in children's ability to manage this activity for themselves.

If you are a practitioner or visit settings as a student, consider some of the attitudes you have experienced towards risk taking in adults and children.

- Is there a culture of risk taking or is it left to one member of the team?
- What sorts of things are said about taking risks?
- How do you feel when you watch children taking risks?

Companionable movement, touch, and well-being

The third 'hidden' sense to be discussed here is the tactile sense, which processes information about touch through the entire surface of the skin, the largest organ. Touch receptors cover the entire body from top to toe, and the area in the brain that perceives touch is called the somatosensory cortex. It registers heat, cold, pain, pressure, and body position, and the most sensitive parts of the body have a correspondingly large representation in the somatosensory cortex, for example, the hands and mouth.

Touch is a direct way in which children gain a perception of the world. Bainbridge Cohen (1984: 25) differentiates between the touch that underpins 'mechanical stimulation' and the touch of 'playful dialogue'. The former will help the infant position herself in relation to gravity and provide tactile feedback, which helps her to develop movement patterns. The latter type of touch, however, offers 'tactile stimulations [that] organises the baby's attention so that it is able to exercise intention' (ibid.). In this view, a baby is gaining a sense of self and agency through the touch of loving caretakers. In early life, touch is associated with feeding, security, warmth and comfort, and giving and receiving affection. Touch helps to establish strong emotional attachments, relate to how others are feeling, and develop empathy (Gerhardt 2004).

A well-regulated tactile sense is, therefore, fundamental to getting along well with others, and building relationships. Some activities that will help children to grow and develop tactile awareness include being rolled up inside a blanket and unrolled, being massaged, being squashed, eating textured food, walking on different surfaces, and receiving big bear hugs.

The LMU/NCB Well-being Project linked this companionship with touch saying that well-being occurs 'where the need for physical touch is recognized'. But touch was more often explicitly mentioned by participants in relation to barriers to well-being. They identified practitioners or settings who had a 'no touch policy' or a 'fear of physical closeness' in this respect. This recalls the idea of the moral panic of touch (Johnson 1997), which may have been generated to protect children from sexual abuse. However, Lindon (2008) reminds early childhood practitioners of children's needs and rights to experience positive touch in order to build bodily and emotional well-being. She acknowledges the perceived risk of touch for practitioners and weighs this against the risk of children not getting enough loving touch.

Phelan explains some practitioners' unease with touch because 'bodies in proximity to other bodies (in early childhood settings) pose a menace to order' (Phelan 1997: 82). This order can refer to two interrelated aspects. First, the hierarchy of adults and children in a setting can be challenged because when an adult and child are in bodily contact they may be feeling the same physiological states (Schore 2003). There is also the aspect of pleasure, which may be physiologically and psychologically experienced by the adult as well as the child. Phelan argues that this is a taboo subject for early childhood practitioners lest it be seen as abusive towards the child. She also thinks that the price paid for containing their physical pleasure around children is the loss of a 'capacity for feeling' (Phelan 1997: 89), which is both a personal loss and the loss of a useful disposition for working with children.

Case study exercise

One of us recalls a 2 year old child she used to work with. This girl required a lot of tactile contact from adults when she was upset or going to sleep or when she was separating from her parent in the morning. The girl liked to snuggle one hand onto her carer's warm soft belly skin or she would settle for their neck. She would knead the adult's skin softly until she fell asleep or was soothed. This looked to be an obviously pleasurable experience for her. It was something that practitioners allowed and laughed indulgently about. However, it was not something that was openly acknowledged as being pleasurable for them.

- What is your reaction to this story or to Phelan's ideas?
- Can you recall similar instances in your practice?
- How are these aspects of adult–child relationships discussed within your setting?

Conclusion

In this chapter, we have discussed ideas about the ways movement and well-being are interrelated. Movement and touch are the primary sources of perception for babies and remain important throughout early childhood and beyond. Certain types of movement patterns are very important for babies and young children to practise so that they can organize sensory information in ways that support their emotional and cognitive functioning. We also saw the benefits of exuberant and risky play in allowing children to strengthen neuronal brain connections, experience autonomy, and come to understand social rules.

While these ideas are gaining legitimacy in early childhood settings, some opportunities for these ranges of movement are curtailed perhaps due to lack of knowledge of their importance or fears around the potential disorder and hazards involved. We suggest that early childhood practice needs to understand and acknowledge the primacy of movement and touch for children's well-being and to consider that there are very real risks to children's emotional, social, and cognitive development if movement and touch are disregarded.

References

Bainbridge Cohen, B. (1984) Perceiving in action, the developmental process underlying perceptual-motor integration, *Contact Quarterly*, Spring/Summer.

Bainbridge Cohen, B. (1993) *Sensing, Feeling and Action: The Experiential Anatomy of
Body–Mind Centering*. Northampton, MA: Contact Editions.

Department for Children, Schools and Families (DCSF) (2007) *Confident, Capable and
Creative: Supporting Boys' Achievements*. London: DCSF Publications. Available at:
http://dera.ioe.ac.uk/6621/2/DCSF-00682-2007.pdf [accessed 20 December 2012].

Field, J. (1995) *The role of the corpus callosum in the acquisition of the 3 R's*. Paper presented at the 7th European Conference of Neuro-Developmental Delay in Children with Specific Learning Difficulties, Chester.

Gerhardt, S. (2004) *Why Love Matters: How Affection Shapes a Baby's Brain*. London:
Routledge.

Gill, T. (2007) *No Fear: Growing Up in a Risk Averse Society*. London: Calouste Gulben-
kian Foundation.

Goddard Blythe, S. (2002) *Reflexes, Learning and Behaviour*. Eugene, OR: Fern Ridge
Press.

Goddard Blythe, S. (2004) *The Well Balanced Child*. Stroud: Hawthorn Press.

Goddard Blythe, S. (2008) *What Babies and Children Really Need*. Stroud: Hawthorn
Press.

Goddard Blythe, S., Beuret, L.J. and Blythe, P. (2009) *Attention, Balance and Coordination: The A.B.C. of Learning Success*. Chichester: Wiley-Blackwell.

Holland, P. (2003) *We Don't Play with Guns Here: War, Weapon and Superhero Play in
the Early Years*. Maidenhead: Open University Press.

Johnson, R. (1997) The 'no touch' policy, in J. Tobin (ed.) *Making a Place for Pleasure
in Early Childhood Education*. New Haven, CT: Yale University Press.

Lamont, B. (2009) *Moving, Learning, Growing*. Available at: http://vimeo.com/
19610498.

Lindon, J. (1999) *Too Safe for Their Own Good?* London: National Early Years
Network.

Lindon, J. (2008) A touchy subject, *Developmental Movement Play Journal*, 5: 18–19.

Panksepp, J. (1998) *Affective Neuroscience: The Foundations of Human and Animal
Emotions*. Oxford: Oxford University Press.

Phelan, A. (1997) Classroom management and the erasure of teacher desire, in
J. Tobin (ed.) *Making a Place for Pleasure in Early Childhood Education*. New Haven,
CT: Yale University Press.

Roberts, R. (2006) *Self Esteem and Early Learning: Key People from Birth to School*.
London: Paul Chapman.

Schore, A. (2003) *Affect Dysregulation and Disorders of the Self*. New York: Norton.

Tovey, H. (2007) *Playing Outdoors: Spaces and Places, Risks and Challenge*. Maidenhead: Open University Press.

Vygotsky, L. (1978) *Mind in Society: Development of Higher Psychological Processes.* Cambridge, MA: Harvard University Press.

Walsh, D.J. (2004) Frog boy and the American monkey: the body in Japanese early schooling, in L. Bresler (ed.) *Knowing Bodies, Moving Minds: Towards Embodied Teaching and Learning.* Dordrecht: Kluwer Academic.

Films that may be of interest

www.thenext25years.com: see *Baby Liv*, a montage of the first year of life in movement.

Babies, Brains and Balance: made by Harborough Sure Start.

8 Health and well-being: food and mealtimes

Deborah Albon and Penny Mukherji

Introduction

This chapter focuses on the way food and mealtimes contribute to young children's health and well-being. This is a vital area to consider in early childhood practice, as many young children receive their breakfast, lunch, tea, and snacks while attending an early childhood setting. Drawing on data from the London Metropolitan University/National Children's Bureau Project 'Talking about Young Children's Well-being' (LMU/NCB Well-being Project), this chapter will begin by highlighting the importance of physical health for children's well-being. It will then focus on the importance of food and drink provisioning in terms of nutrition. The issue of young children's health is explored in relation to health inequalities with the focus on providing children with optimum levels of nutrition for growth and development.

The second part of the chapter will highlight the socio-cultural significance of food and mealtimes. Not only does food provide us with our nutritional needs, which is vital for our present and future health, it is also inextricably linked to our sense of personal identity. Moreover, events such as mealtimes are significant as occasions for collective activity, which engender a sense of group identity and community. The sociality associated with food, cross-culturally (Shilling 2005), points to its importance, especially as relationships are generally regarded as of central importance to subjective definitions of well-being. In this way, the chapter embraces a holistic as well as an instrumental view of well-being (Waters 2009).

The relationship between health and well-being

In the LMU/NCB Well-being Project, the parents and practitioners viewed the concept of well-being as complex and holistic in nature. Participants used words such as 'net' and 'mesh' to explain the connectedness of aspects of well-being. Furthermore, the concept was seen to be mutable (in that an individual's state of well-being can fluctuate over time), and that the experience of well-being may be subjective. One early childhood practitioner attending a seminar put it this way; 'everyone's ideas of well-being are different, but there may be common themes'.

There have been many attempts to define health and well-being. Some approaches see well-being as an aspect of being healthy, whereas other definitions see health as an aspect of well-being. In 1948, the World Health Organization (WHO) defined health as 'a state of complete physical, mental and social well-being and not merely the absence of disease or infirmity'. This definition appears to equate health with well-being, in that to be healthy one has to be in a state of well-being. Since 1948, others have added emotional, spiritual, and social aspects of health to the concept, so that now 'health' is defined in holistic terms. In 1986, the WHO extended its definition to include the idea that health is a resource related to how well an individual can adapt to change. Health is now defined as:

> the extent to which an individual or group is able, on the one hand, to real-
> ize aspirations and satisfy needs; and on the other hand, to change or cope
> with the environment. Health is, therefore, seen as a resource for everyday
> life, not the objective for living; it is a positive concept emphasizing social
> and personal resources as well as physical capacities.
>
> (WHO 1986)

Case study exercise

In the LMU/NCB Well-being Project, participants in the seminars and focus groups saw health as being an aspect of well-being, but not synonymous with it. Health was seen as a prerequisite for an individual's well-being; as one participant said, the 'way in [is] through health'. However, it was acknowledged that good health on its own was not a guarantee of well-being.

That health was seen to be the basis of well-being was evidenced by the frequent references made by the participants to Maslow's (1943) theory of the hierarchy of needs. In this theory, the highest levels of self-fulfilment and realization of one's full potential can only be achieved if one's basic physiological needs for air, food and drink, shelter from the elements, and safety are met. For the participants, 'healthy food' was seen an important aspect of well-being.

- If you are an early childhood practitioner, reflect upon how much thought goes into planning to provide for babies' and young children's basic needs. How much care is taken to ensure that children receive a healthy diet?
- Ask children what they think being 'healthy' means. When students at LMU undertook this exercise, they found that children as young as 3 years could articulate what they understood health to mean to them and that, for younger children, this usually involved eating healthy food, while older children were able to give more complex replies, involving exercise and not being ill.

Health, food, and early childhood

> A vital and productive society with a prosperous and sustainable future is built on a foundation of healthy child development. Health in the earliest years – actually beginning with the future mother's health before she becomes pregnant – lays the groundwork for a lifetime of well-being.
>
> (Center on the Developing Child 2010: 2)

Blair (2008) outlines why it is so important that resources are allocated to maximizing the health of children in the first five years of life:

- It is a basic human right: Article 24 of the United Nations Rights of the Child requires us to work towards achieving the best health for all children.
- Neurobiological evidence indicates that the first few years of life are influential in terms of future physical and emotional health.
- Children and families are at particular risk of negative economic and societal forces such as economic inequality. Allocating resources to support families in a holistic way will increase family resilience to these threats.
- If resources are used to support families and children in the early years then there is a cost benefit to the nation as children will be less likely to need hospital services, will be less likely to be involved in criminal activity and will be more likely to continue in education and become productive members of society.

(Blair 2008: 3)

In England, the Healthy Child Programme is in place to protect and promote the health of children (DoH 2010). One of the aims of the programme is that children (and families) should eat healthily, with the acknowledgement that good nutrition, starting from preconception onwards, is one of the foundations of children's health.

The Children's Food Trust (2012) guidelines for early years settings outline that a healthy diet has a positive effect both on development and learning. Being breastfed and eating healthily protects against obesity and can help prevent diabetes, heart disease, and strokes in later life. Good nutrition means that children receive sufficient calories to be active and to grow; it also encourages children to eat a wide variety of foods and to get into the habit of eating healthily, which will help them eat healthily as adults and avoid obesity.

In addition to the health risks associated with poor nutrition, there are well-documented links between children's nutrition and learning. In a review of the literature, Sorhaindo and Feinstein (2006) concluded that there was a complex interaction between nutritional factors and socio-economic factors, but that there were some clearly identified links between poor nutrition and learning. These relate to the adverse effects of lack of key nutrients in infancy on cognitive development in adolescence and the finding that poorly nourished children show improvement in cognitive functioning and behaviour if they are given vitamin supplements. Glucose fluctuations during the day, due to irregular patterns of eating (skipping breakfast, for example) have also been shown to have adverse effects on cognition. The Children's Food Trust (2012: 7) concludes 'that healthy eating habits in the years before school are very important because they influence growth, development and academic achievement in later life'. They have produced guidelines for early childhood settings to help them plan meals that will provide young children with the best possible nutrition while at nursery.

Food and health inequality

In the LMU/NCB Well-being Project, participants from the focus groups and seminars agreed that economic and social disadvantage has negative effects on adults' and young children's well-being. In particular, poverty, inequality, and discrimination were singled out for discussion. One participant commented, 'you can't have well-being when there are such profound inequalities'. In this section, the link between social and economic inequality and health will be discussed, focusing on children's nutrition.

Life expectancy is a very good measure of the health of a community. In 1852, for example, life expectancy in England and Wales was 40 years for men and 44 years for women (Newton 2006). Now, a third of babies born in 2012 can expect to live to over 100 years of age (ONS 2012). Albon and Mukherji (2008) identify the factors that have contributed to this dramatic change, which include: improvements in public health (e.g. clean water, efficient sanitation, and efficient refuse disposal), medical advances (e.g. immunizations and the development of antibiotics), the advent of the National Health Service (NHS), and the reduction of absolute poverty by the introduction of the benefits system.

However, although people's health has undoubtedly improved, it has also become evident there are considerable inequalities. In 1980, the report of a research working group identified that there were social class differences in health (Black et al. 1980). This was evident from birth, when infant mortality was found to be higher for babies born to parents of the poorest social class, compared with the infant mortality rate for the richest.

Despite several government initiatives, including the Tackling Health Inequalities Programme (DoH 2003), these health inequalities persist. The Marmot Review, published in 2010, aimed to identify the health inequalities that faced the nation and suggested strategies for closing the gap. Marmot reiterated that health inequalities were the result of social inequalities, commenting that people from the poorest neighbourhoods tend to die seven years earlier and spend a greater part of their old age disabled or chronically ill, than those from the richest neighbourhoods. The Marmot Review suggested six objectives:

- Give every child the best start in life
- Enable all children, young people and adults to maximise their capabilities and have control over their lives
- Create fair employment and good work for all
- Ensure a healthy standard of living for all
- Create and develop healthy and sustainable places and communities
- Strengthen the role and impact of ill health prevention.

(Marmot 2010: 9)

Linking health inequalities with social inequalities demonstrates that Marmot considers that the concept of health is inextricably bound to a holistic view of well-being, an approach that recognizes that physical health both influences and is influenced by the well-being of an individual.

The Marmot Review emphasized the importance of children's earliest years and recommended that resources should be made available to support all children and families, not just those identified as being vulnerable. It recommended that interventions should be universal, but that the scale and intensity of such interventions should be proportionate to the level of disadvantage. This approach is similar to that adopted by the Healthy Child Programme (DoH 2010), where there is a universal programme of health promotion for all children, with children and families who are at particular risk receiving extra, targeted support.

The nutritional status of children is directly linked to poverty and disadvantage, with the poorest children tending to be the most malnourished. Because of the economic downturn, there has been an increase in the numbers of children who have been identified as being hungry in the UK (Action for Children 2012). Hunger is a direct and basic threat to children's health. Participants in the LMU/NCB Well-being Project who work in children's centres have identified that some children in their care are hungry and that lack of food is a huge barrier to young children's well-being.

In a review of the literature, Ruxton and Derbyshire (2011) found that although there had been some improvement in children's diets in the UK, diets were still lacking in fruit, vegetables, oily fish, and fibre and that children from poorer households were much less likely to have adequate intakes of fruit and vegetables than children from wealthier homes. This is not a new finding; in 2004, the National Children's Homes (NCH) undertook a study of 55 poor families and found that nearly a third of children never ate salad or green vegetables and that 10 per cent never ate fruit. The study revealed that parents knew what foods children needed to be healthy but could not afford them.

Nutritional inequalities can also be seen in the rates of dental disease. In a study of children aged 3–11 years in Glasgow, Cameron et al. (2006) found that children having tooth extractions for dental disease were more likely to come from the poorest areas in the city and to eat diets containing high levels of sugar. Nearly 40 per cent of children reported eating a chocolate bar every day and one-third of children consumed sugary drinks after brushing their teeth in the evening. Children with most decay were also significantly thinner, indicating that not only were they eating the wrong types of food for optimum health, but that they were also not eating a diet high enough in calories.

There is a strong relationship between social class and obesity in children. Stamatakis et al. (2010) examined the results of the annual Health Surveys of England and found that levels of childhood obesity appear to be levelling off, findings later confirmed by the Child Measurement Programme (Dinsdale et al. 2012), as discussed earlier. However, these findings mask that over the years the social gradient has been increasing; children from lower social economic groups have not benefited from the general slowing down of rates of childhood obesity.

It is difficult to accept that at the time of writing, young children's health and well-being is being compromised by social and economic inequality but according to the Child Poverty Action Group (CPAG 2012), there are nearly four million children living in poverty in the UK today, almost two-thirds of them in families where at least one of the parents is in employment.

Reflective exercise

How do the foods offered to babies and young children in your setting match up to the Children's Food Trust guidelines (2012)? Undertake a review and discuss with colleagues and parents any changes you might want to make.

So far in this chapter, we have focused primarily on the importance of food for young children's physical health. But as we noted in the Introduction, food has significance for well-being that goes beyond the nutritional health of individuals. In the final two sections of this chapter, we wish to explore the significance of food and mealtimes for children's well-being in terms of their link to a positive sense of identity as well as to collective well-being. After all, mealtimes play an important role in a child's participation in the life of their culture and engender a sense of community and belonging.

Food and identity

Our identities as individuals and as groups are inextricably bound up with what we eat. We are, quite literally, what we eat (Falk 1991), as food is incorporated into the body unlike other aspect of our material culture, for instance the clothes that we wear or the music that we listen to. Food plays an important role in the formation of our identities, as the food we eat, as well as the ways in which we prepare, cook, and share it, is an inextricable part of who we are (Valentine 1999).

The data from the LMU/NCB Well-being Project show that children had an appreciation of food as part of their nursery experience and were able to express clear preferences in relation to their likes and dislikes. For example, Molly (aged 3 years) stated: 'chicken – it's my favourite dinner' in response to being asked what made her happy at nursery. Although young children are often regarded as malleable in relation to their food behaviours, beliefs, and preferences (Lupton 1996), babies and toddlers unable to put their preferences into words are still able to make clear the foods they like and dislike. Indeed, from birth children exercise agency in relation to feeding. For instance, Keenan and Stapleton's (2009) study of babies and the feeding relationship they develop with their mothers highlights how mothers recognize their babies as active in manipulating this feeding relationship. Observation of children's facial expressions, vocalizations, tongue movements, and bodily movements more generally all provide cues to the caregiver as to the infant or young child's preferences (Albon and Mukherji 2008).

Reflective exercise

How do you ensure children's perspectives on the food that they eat are incorporated into the menu planning of your setting? Consider this in relation to: (1) a child with a communication difficulty and (2) a young baby. In addition, if children need their food mashed up to aid eating, how do you know what individual foods they like and dislike?

Food is reflective of one's gender, class, 'green', religious, and ethnic identities (Albon and Mukherji 2008). However, with advances in technology and increasing globalization, which have radically altered the availability and demand for foods, as well as changes in family consumption, such as family members eating at different times, patterns of eating are changing (Bell and Valentine 1997). And children, in moving beyond the family home, may often be at the forefront of extending their families' eating repertoires. An example of this can be found in Bembreck's (2009) work on children from immigrant families in Sweden. In this study, children explore and claim new identities for themselves and their families through encountering different foods beyond the family home.

However, some studies have shown that in migrating to another country, parents are keen that their children hold on to a sense of cultural identity through food. In Jonsson and colleagues' research, which examines the experiences of Somali families living in Sweden, Somalian mothers expressed a longing for foods tasting of the 'cultural identity one longs for in exile' (Jonsson et al. 2002: 102). Taste and smell are incredibly important parts of our sensory experience (Howes 2005), so early childhood practitioners should bear this in mind when reviewing their provision in terms of the opportunities it affords for sensory exploration.

Reflective exercise

Consider which foods you would miss if you moved to another country or region where they were not easily available; perhaps you have had personal experience of this. Now consider the significance of particular foods to your subjective sense of well-being. This might include the feelings you have in preparing certain foods; sharing these foods with family and friends every day or maybe on special occasions; and of course smelling and tasting these foods yourself! Maybe, too, these foods are linked to significant memories such as the person who taught you how to prepare the dish or who, lovingly, cooked it for you.

Now think about this in relation to early childhood practice. To what extent are you aware of the meanings attached to particular foods for children and families with whom you work?

Finally, food dislikes can be amenable to change in all of us – not just young children. One practitioner in the LMU/NCB Well-being Project noted how after harvesting vegetables grown in the nursery garden, Maja (aged 2½ years) began to eat beetroot – a vegetable she had previously avoided. Now think about the opportunities you provide to widen the horizons of children in relation to the foods they eat, especially towards eating foods regarded as healthy.

Mealtimes: developing a sense of community and belonging

This final section examines mealtimes as events that are important for the well-being of young children and adults. Our focus here is on mealtimes engendering a sense of belonging and as a vehicle for children's collective participation in the 'life' of their early childhood setting.

Meal and snack times provide a temporal rhythm to the nursery day (Viruru 2001). Leavitt and Power (1997: 42) argue that 'the extent to which children experience predictability and security in daily routines and interpersonal relationships contributes to their sense of self and agency'. And it is this 'safe-because-same manner' associated with bodily routines such as mealtimes that is important in punctuating time and providing a sense of continuity (Crossley 2006: 109). If we consider young children who attend full day care – receiving breakfast, dinner, and tea as well as snacks – then meal and snack times are particularly significant in punctuating the day and should be considered as carefully as any other planned activity in the setting (Albon and Mukherji 2008; Manning-Morton and Thorp 2006).

Giovanni (2006) emphasizes the rituals associated with mealtimes and regards them as significant opportunities for young children to participate in the group life of the setting. She argues that developing a sense of group identity is important for children and suggests that mealtime rituals help to create an emotionally warm, calm environment in which communication can flourish between children and their peers and children and adults.

Kjorholt (2005: 158), writing about the Danish context, outlines a tendency to elevate 'the right [of the child] to be oneself'. Underpinning this, in the mealtime context, is the idea that children should be able to make individual choices over when to eat, which, she argues, negates the symbolic and relational importance of collective meal and snack times. Collective participation in events such as these, she argues, affirm and make 'visible everybody's belonging to a specific community of children' (Kjorholt 2005: 159). In terms of well-being, time and again relationships came up as of key importance in the LMU/NCB Well-being Project and it is this sense of connectedness and inter-dependence as opposed to separateness that we wish to foreground here. This, we feel, is especially important because food is regarded universally as a major source of sociality (Shilling 2005).

Friendships emerged as a central issue for children in many instances in the data from the LMU/NCB Well-being Project, and mealtimes are a key opportunity for children to interact with others and share companionship alongside the physical enjoyment of the food being eaten (Giovanni 2006). These data point to the need for practitioners to encourage and support children's peer relationships during mealtimes as well as during other parts of the nursery day and to ensure that conversation and playful interaction are encouraged. The corollary of this, of course, is the need to plan in adequate time for mealtime provision so as to avoid it being a task to get through as opposed to an enjoyable, relaxed time of the day (Albon and Mukherji 2008; Manning-Morton and Thorp 2006).

Reflective exercise

Take time to reflect further on the significance of food and mealtimes to the well-being of young children.

Reflect upon the mealtime provision in your setting in relation to the following questions: to what extent are peer relationships encouraged during mealtimes? Are children expected to sit quietly, not talking to others? Is there little time for playful interaction – indeed, is it positively discouraged? Can they sit with their friends?

Think of the things that make mealtimes an occasion that enhances your overall sense of well-being; for example, candles or flowers on the table; napkins and tablecloths; attractive crockery; time to talk; not feeling rushed; good quality food; the use of extra special items on celebratory occasions. Now think about the mealtime provision in your setting. How can mealtimes in your setting be improved so as to feel special? What might the children regard as special?

Conclusion

In this chapter, we have looked at how ideas about health are inextricably linked to well-being. Food plays an important role in our physical health and children's nutritional status has a profound effect on their life chances. However, inequalities of health persist and poverty impacts directly on families' access and ability to provide a healthy diet. Food also plays an important role in children's sense of identity, and through food events such as mealtimes, to their sense of belonging to a particular community. We suggest that early years practitioners need to consider the nutritional quality of the food on offer in their settings, but also attend closely to the mealtime experience – as a social event, imbued with meanings – as both shape the well-being of individuals.

References

Action for Children (2012) *UK Children will Go Hungry this Christmas.* Available at: http://www.actionforchildren.org.uk/news/archive/2012/november/uk-children-will-go-hungry-this-christmas [accessed 9 January 2013].

Albon, D. and Mukherji, P. (2008) *Food and Health in Early Childhood.* London: Sage.

Bell, D. and Valentine, G. (1997) *Consuming Geographies: We Are Where We Eat.* London: Routledge.

Bembreck, H. (2009) Children's 'becoming' in frontiering foodscapes, in A. James, A.T. Kjorholt and V. Tingstad (eds.) *Children, Food and Identity in Everyday Life.* London: Palgrave Macmillan.

Black, D., Morris, J., Smith, C. and Townsend, P. (1980) *Inequalities in Health: Report of a Research Working Group.* London: DHSS.

Blair, M. (2008) *Optimising Health in the Early Years.* Child Public Health Interest Group, Community Practitioners and Health Visitors Association, British Association of Community Child Health. London: Early Childhood Forum, National Children's Bureau.

Cameron, F., Weaver L., Wright, C. and Welbury, R. (2006) Dietary and social characteristics of children with severe tooth decay, *Scottish Medical Journal*, 51(3): 26–9.

Center on the Developing Child (2010) *The Foundations of Lifelong Health are Built in Early Childhood.* Cambridge, MA: Center on the Developing Child, Harvard University.

Child Poverty Action Group (CPAG) (2012) *Child Poverty Facts and Figures.* Available at: http://www.cpag.org.uk/child-poverty-facts-and-figures [accessed 18 July 2012].

Children's Food Trust (2012) *Eat Better, Start Better: Voluntary Food and Drink Guidelines for Early Years Settings in England – A Practical Guide.* Sheffield: Children's Food Trust.

Crossley, N. (2006) *Reflexive Embodiment in Contemporary Society*. Maidenhead: Open University Press.

Department of Health (DoH) (2003) *Tackling Health Inequalities: A Programme for Action*. Available at: http://webarchive.nationalarchives.gov.uk/+/www.dh.gov.uk/en/publicationsandstatistics/publications/publicationspolicyandguidance/dh_4008268 [accessed 18 July 2012].

Department of Health (DoH) (2010) *Healthy Child Programme*. Available at: http://webarchive.nationalarchives.gov.uk/20130107105354/http://www.dh.gov.uk/prod_consum_dh/groups/dh_digitalassets/@dh/@en/@ps/documents/digitalasset/dh_118525.pdf [accessed 17 July 2012].

Dinsdale, H., Rider, C. and Rutter, H. (2012) *National Child Measurement Programme: Changes in Children's Body Mass Index between 2006/07 and 2010/11*. Oxford: National Obesity Observatory.

Falk, P. (1991) The sweetness of forbidden fruit: towards an anthropology of taste, in E.L. Furst, M. Ekstrom, L. Holm and U. Kjaernes (eds.) *Palatable Worlds*. Oslo: SolumForlag.

Giovanni, D. (2006) The pleasure of eating, *Children in Europe*, 10: 10–11.

Howes, D. (2005) Introduction, in D. Howes (ed.) *Empire of the Senses: The Sensual Culture Reader*. Oxford: Berg.

Jonsson, I.M., Hallberg, L.R.-M. and Gustafsson, I.-B. (2002) Cultural foodways in Sweden: repeated focus group interviews with Somalian women, *International Journal of Consumer Studies*, 26(4): 328–39.

Keenan, J. and Stapleton, H. (2009) It depends what you mean by feeding 'on demand': mothers' accounts of babies' agency in infant–feeding relationships, in A. James, A.T. Kjorholt and V. Tingstad (eds.) *Children, Food and Identity in Everyday Life*. London: Palgrave Macmillan.

Kjorholt, A.T. (2005) The competent child and 'the right to be oneself': reflections on children as fellow citizens in an early childhood centre, in A. Clark, A.T. Kjorholt and P. Moss (eds.) *Beyond Listening: Children's Perspectives of Early Childhood Services*. Bristol: Policy Press.

Leavitt, R.L. and Power, M.B. (1997) Civilizing bodies: children in day care, in J. Tobin (ed.) *Making a Place for Pleasure in Early Childhood Education*. New Haven, CT: Yale University Press.

Lupton, D. (1996) *Food, the Body and the Self*. London: Sage.

Manning-Morton, J. and Thorp, M. (2006) *Key Times: A Framework for Developing High Quality Provision for Children from Birth to Three Years*. Maidenhead: Open University Press.

Marmot, M. (2010) *Fair Society, Healthy Lives: The Marmot Review. Strategic Review of Health Inequalities Post 2010. Executive Summary*. London: The Marmot Review.

Maslow, H. (1943) A theory of human motivation, *Psychological Review*, 50: 370–96.

National Children's Home (NCH) (2004) *Going Hungry: The Struggle to Eat Healthily on a Low Income*. Available at: http://www.actionforchildren.org.uk/media/146002/going_hungry.pdf [accessed 31 May 2013].

Newton, G. (2006) *The Aging Population*. London: Wellcome Trust.

Office for National Statistics (ONS) (2012) *What are the Chances of Surviving to Age 100?* Available at: http://www.ons.gov.uk/ons/dcp171776_260525.pdf [accessed 18 July 2012].

Ruxton, C. and Derbyshire, E. (2011) Diet adequacy in UK schoolchildren, *Nutrition and Food Science*, 41(1): 20–33.

Shilling, C. (2005) *The Body in Culture, Technology and Society*. London: Sage.

Sorhaindo, A. and Feinstein, L. (2006) *What is the Relationship between Child Nutrition and School Outcomes?* London: Centre for Research on the Wider Benefits of Learning, Institute of Education.

Stamatakis, E., Wardle, J. and Cole, T. (2010) Childhood obesity and overweight prevalence trends in England: evidence for growing socioeconomic disparities, *International Journal of Obesity*, 34: 41–7.

Valentine, G. (1999) Eating in: home consumption and identity, *The Sociological Review*, 47(3): 491–524.

Viruru, R. (2001) *Early Childhood Education: Postcolonial Perspectives from India*. London: Sage.

Waters, J. (2009) Well-being, in T. Waller (ed.) *An Introduction to Early Childhood* (2nd edn.). London: Sage.

World Health Organization (WHO) (1948) *WHO Definition of Health*. Available at: http://www.who.int/about/definition/en/print.html [accessed 17 July 2012].

World Health Organization (WHO) (1986) *The Ottawa Charter for Health Promotion*. Available at: http://www.who.int/healthpromotion/conferences/previous/ottawa/en/ [accessed 17 July 2012].

9 Supporting the well-being of children with disabilities and their families

Mary Dickins

Introduction

Evidence from parents of children with disabilities collected as part of the London Metropolitan University/National Children's Bureau Project 'Talking about Young Children's Well-being' (LMU/NCB Well-being Project) emphasizes the importance of the emotional health of their children in terms of their overall well-being. They argue that, first and foremost, disabled children's well-being is no different to any other child's well-being, but that once labelled, disabled children have an added difficulty, in that the 'medical' model of disability (Reiser and Mason 1992) has tended to attribute their emotional difficulties to their impairments and not their treatment at the hands of adults. Parental evidence also stresses the need for the emotional health of all children to take a higher priority and that the pressure for children to 'perform' in measurable ways represents a significant barrier to this. Findings from the LMU/NCB Well-being Project have highlighted the importance of these issues in relation to the overall well-being of all children and disabled children are, if anything, more vulnerable, since their progress towards set targets is often viewed from a deficit perspective and they are often under greater professional scrutiny.

Incorporating the view of well-being as a holistic, dynamic, and multi-dimensional concept, this chapter will explore the influence and relative impact of the medical and social models of disability in relation to the well-being of disabled children and their families. Inclusion in mainstream provision is also considered as a logical consequence of the adoption of the social model of disability in society as well as the ways in which early intervention can be used effectively as part of this process in settings.

This chapter is written against the backdrop of a shifting political and legislative landscape, in which the legislation and guidance that underpinned the policy for inclusion in the past have been absorbed by the Equality Act 2010 (Home Office 2010). The children and Families Bill, which is making its way through the parliamentary process, contains many of the recommendations set out in the Green Paper and consultation 'Support and Aspiration: A New Approach to Special Educational Needs and Disability', which was introduced to Parliament in early 2013 with implementation planned from spring 2014 (DfE 2012). A new code of Practice is currently being drafted. This Bill promises earlier identification and support and an increase in control and choice for parents regarding their child's provision. Worth noting is that these changes are proposed at a time when cuts in public spending have impacted negatively on the support and infrastructure previously in place in many local authority areas, with the resulting loss of knowledge, skills, and expertise on disability in mainstream provision.

Families with disabled children – the current context

Evidence from the campaigning charity Contact a Family (Bennett 2009: 5) found that negative attitudes towards disability and a lack of services are the main barriers preventing families from leading ordinary lives. Among the key findings were the following:

- Almost 70 per cent of respondents said that understanding and acceptance of disability from their community or society are poor or unsatisfactory.
- Over 60 per cent of families said they don't feel listened to by professionals.
- Over 60 per cent of families said they don't feel valued by society in their role as carers.
- Half of families with disabled children said the opportunity to enjoy play and leisure together is poor or unsatisfactory.

Another 2009 report (Slade et al. 2009) found that experiences of having to take a proactive role and in some cases fight to access services were felt to be time consuming and 'stressful' for parents and in some cases to lead to ill health. This was particularly the case in the early stages when parents were perhaps still coming to terms with a child's disability. Negotiating the diagnosis, assessment, and referral process was generally felt to be demanding, but particularly so if parents felt unsupported or obstructed by practitioners, when they described feeling 'demoralized' and 'disempowered'. Experiences of delays in diagnosing conditions and accessing services were felt to be detrimental in terms of their children's health, educational progress, and their emotional well-being. Less positive experiences of accessing services were also felt to place stress on family relationships, limiting the time and effort parents could give to partners and their other children.

In addition to these difficulties, a survey carried out by Contact a Family (2012: 3) asked over 2000 UK families caring for a disabled child about their current financial situation and found the following:

- 45 per cent of families with disabled children pay more for childcare than families with a non-disabled child.
- One in six (17 per cent) families is going without food.
- More than one in five (21 per cent) families is going without heating.

- Just over a quarter (26 per cent) of families are going without specialist equipment or adaptations.
- 86 per cent of families have gone without leisure and days out.
- One in five families had been threatened with court action because of non-payment of bills, including essentials such as utilities.

In addition, the survey highlighted considerable anxiety about benefit changes and the stigma associated with claiming them. A joint report from the Children's Society, Citizen's Advice, and Disability Rights UK (2012) estimates that up to 100,000 families with disabled children may see their incomes drop as a result of the introduction of the universal credit.

Support systems may also be harder to access; in 2010, almost half of local authorities in England and Wales had already reported insufficient childcare for disabled children. The isolation that families experience has a significant impact on their well-being. A survey of 1148 families by Contact a Family (2011) on the impact of isolation found that 72 per cent of those surveyed experienced mental ill-health such as anxiety, depression or breakdown due to isolation, and one in five said that isolation had led to the break-up of their family life.

The evidence of the LMU/NCB Well-being Project emphasized that a lack of parent-carer well-being can impact negatively on the well-being of the children. Depression, poor physical health, economic pressures, and isolation from community were all flagged up by participants as barriers to well-being.

Reflective exercise

List all of the terms, words, and phrases you have ever heard related to disability. Include those that are sometimes used as forms of abuse. DO NOT CENSOR. Include the terms that you use professionally as well.

- From this list, try to identify terms that might be considered positive.
- What does this list make you feel and what are the implications for disabled children and their families?

The next two sections will consider the extent to which these difficulties might be helped or exacerbated by the model of disability that underpins professionals' approaches to families and children.

What is the medical model of disability?

The medical model of disability is usually understood as an attitude of mind that pervades much of our current thinking and provision. At its heart is the idea that because disability is caused by physical or psychological impairment(s), the role of professionals is to cure and alleviate, thus making the child more 'normal'. Dickins with Denziloe state that:

> While there is nothing wrong at all with alleviating suffering or discomfort, the main problem with this model is that impairments are the sole focus of attention. The child becomes a set of problems rather than an individual with strengths and weaknesses to be welcomed into the world with joy and anticipation.
>
> (Dickins with Denziloe 2003: 6)

This overarching view of the child as 'faulty' means that they may also be regarded as failing if various treatments and interventions do not 'cure' the problem. As a consequence, at an early stage children may internalize negative messages that it may be their own 'fault' if they cannot be mobile, have full access to certain activities and places, have difficulties learning, communicating, and understanding, or look and behave differently. In this way, this model could be seen to reflect the 'instrumental' approach to well-being as identified in Chapter 1 of this book, as it focuses on the measurable medical aspects of a condition. Runswick-Cole explains how:

> A medical model framework emerges from models used in medicine in which practitioners think in terms of 'conditions', 'treatment', 'cure' and 'rehabilitation'. A medical model assumes that the disabled adult or child is deficient but, it is hoped, alterable; whereas society is fixed, with limited capacity for, or willingness to change.
>
> (Runswick-Cole 2008: 176)

While there is no doubt that some approaches can be very effective in alleviating suffering and helping children to achieve their potential, we need to remember that many disabilities are life-long and cannot be cured. Therefore, to support their well-being, children with disabling conditions need us to celebrate and accept them *as they are* and, in turn, to encourage self-acceptance and a positive self-image and identity in them. Taking these factors into account it seems, the medical model approach may serve to inhibit children's well-being rather than supporting its development.

What is the social model of disability?

In contrast to the medical model, the social model of disability (Reiser and Mason 1992) locates the 'problem' outside the province of disabled children and their families and back into the 'collective responsibility of society as a whole' (Dickins with Denziloe 2003: 6). In this model, it is the social and physical barriers that society creates that emerge as disabling factors and it has led to the view that many of the difficulties faced by disabled children and their families are caused by the attitudes of society and the barriers that these attitudes create.

For most protagonists, adopting the social model of disability necessitates the move towards inclusive mainstream provision and approaches (Reiser and Mason 1992). Segregated special schools are seen as barriers to acceptance, especially in the longer term, as it is harder for children to enter mainstream society as adults as they have been effectively kept away from their communities. These children are also seen as having been effectively segregated on the basis of their differences (Skrtic 1995).

Arguably, the social model approach is more effective in promoting overall well-being, as the centrality of the individual combined with the emphasis on society's responsibility to provide enabling social and environmental conditions means that requirements for both objective and subjective well-being are more likely to be met. It also reflects the emphasis that participants in the LMU/NCB Well-being Project put on the social aspects of well-being and the dynamic interaction between subjective well-being and the wider social context.

At the beginning – becoming the parent of a disabled child

> Babies lie there and are adored simply for being alive . . . but for many babies born with an impairment this welcome does not happen. The worry and fear, the medical interventions and the reaction from a world conditioned to think negatively about disabled people can instead surround the child with sadness, disappointment and anxiety. This will also produce an emotional response in the baby, but one in which very damaging messages can be internalized. Rather than feeling a source of joy to people, they can feel they are a source of pain, a burden, unwelcome.
>
> (Parents for Inclusion 2004: 1)

The impact of having a disabled child is as various and unique as each family, child, and set of particular circumstances. However, from the experiences that many parents describe, it is possible to discern certain patterns. Children who are born with a disability are not usually welcomed into the world with joy and acceptance. They are often greeted as 'bad news' by relatives and the general public and may be treated as a 'tragedy'. Many parents struggle to overcome the effects of negative interpretations of disability, which are all too often reinforced by the attitudes and assumptions of those around them. Yet as P. Russell (2003) observes, there are more disabled children surviving with complex multiple disabilities and rare conditions because of improvements in neonatal and medical care. In addition, there is a marked reported increase in the number of children with autistic spectrum disorders (ASD) and attention deficit hyperactive disorder (ADHD) across the UK (Baren-Cohen 2009).

Despite this, there is marked variation across the country in terms of the services available to support families. Understandably, some parents of disabled children are sad, angry, hostile, and confused, and this can affect how they perceive professionals and communicate with them. Encountering professionals who have a positive attitude and who are willing to understand, listen, and build trust can be an important step forward for families. Positive partnerships between practitioners and parents and carers were considered to be crucial in supporting children's well-being in the evidence gathered by the LMU/NCB Well-being Project. For parents who may have previously only encountered medical model attitudes, holistic social model approaches to their children, which focus on what they can rather than what they cannot achieve, can be especially valuable and affirmative.

The way in which parents are told of their child's disability may influence their capacity to respond positively to their child. Some parents may experience a grief process in the initial stages of diagnosis and/or prognosis of a disability, at whatever stage in the child's life this is taking place. This is known as the bereavement model of adjustment, which has been described by Küibler-Ross (1969), Hinton (1972), and Murray-Parkes (1972). They all observe that the grief process, whatever the situation, follows a generally predictable pattern of shock, denial, sorrow, and guilt, leading to eventual adaptation, reorientation, and learning to cope. There is no doubt that, through their own evidence, some parents' experiences seem to follow this pattern. However, individual parents will pass through these feelings in an individual way and not in any set order, sequence or within any given time frame. The length and the intensity of the process is determined by complex factors, including the reactions of immediate family and friends, and the level of practical and emotional support available in the early stages.

The grief model has been criticized as simplistic and leading to assumptions about parent's responses, which may in fact be positive as well as negative; it is an individual emotional journey. Carpenter and Egerton (2007) describe how some professionals find it more difficult to accept a positive reaction from parents, believing they must be in denial. 'Every time I expressed my joy to the staff at the hospital, they said, "She's denying reality." I understood the reality of my child's situation but, for me, there was another reality' (Kearney and Griffin 2001: 83).

Case study exercise

'When we were told at the hospital it was by this young house doctor. He just came marching into the ward, didn't take me into a side ward or anything and said "Yes, your daughter has Rett Syndrome, she will have epilepsy, sclerosis" and reeled off all the worst things. Didn't say she could have it or she will have it and I just walked out of the hospital thinking, "What on earth is going to happen?"'

(DfES 2004: 25)

'I think that the most significant thing that happened to me when I had my son was that my paediatrician was positive and the thing that he said to me that made me think more than anything was that he said "You have a lovely baby boy first".'

(DfES 2004: 30)

Consider the different experiences of the two parents quoted above. In the first scenario, the parent has had 'the news' presented negatively and insensitively from an entirely medical model perspective. In the second, the 'child first' principle of the social model has been adhered to.

What do you think are the likely consequences for these two families, especially in terms of their emotional adjustment to the news they have been given?

Models of disability and parental attitudes

Several writers have explored the relationship between the medical model and the choices that parents make in opting for special or mainstream placement for their child. The British Council of Disabled People (BCPD 2005) suggests that parents' demands for a special school placement may arise from their lack of experience of seeing children with special educational needs included in mainstream schools and the wider community. While Runswick-Cole (2008: 177) observes that, 'Parents who choose inclusive schooling for their children engage with a model of disability that focuses on the need to remove barriers to their children's learning and on their acceptance within mainstream settings.'

Runswick-Cole acknowledges though that all parents' perspectives can be inconsistent and that we should be wary of a simple typology. She cites Landsman (2005), who suggests that parents' choices are often driven not by ideology but pragmatism. Indeed, parents who initially opted for mainstream provision but then withdrew often did so because the needs of their children were not being met and many did so because of the effective exclusion that their children had experienced. In reality, even parents who campaign for inclusion sometimes have to select a special provision if the mainstream provision available cannot currently meet the needs of their child.

The social model of disability and inclusion

Any exploration into early years provision for disabled children is inextricably bound up with discussions about how and why we include children in mainstream provision and what the consequences might be of not doing this properly.

Jones (2004) describes how inclusion functions as an attitude or principle that is celebratory and appreciative of difference rather than seeking just to categorize, label, and segregate. But Runswick-Cole argues that the UK inclusion agenda has been compromised by:

> The attachment of successive governments to the view that inclusion is a response to the learning difficulties experienced by individual children and young people, rather than understanding inclusion as fundamentally being about equity and recognising and supporting the richness of social diversity.
>
> (Runswick-Cole 2011: 117)

From this perspective, the extent to which inclusion can be achieved is determined by the attitude adopted by society but also by the political will to make access to mainstream provision possible.

Dickins has argued from a social model perspective for an inclusive model of early years education that challenges us to review our principles, practices, policies, and procedures (Dickins with Denziloe 2003). From this perspective, inclusion in the early years offers potential benefits for everyone and supports the overall well-being of disabled children and their families. Disabled children benefit from contact with their non-disabled peers in terms of communication skills and social and emotional development. Importantly, parents of disabled children are able to become more active members of their local community, thereby suffering less from the isolation highlighted earlier. Good practice in the care and education of disabled children often improves practice for all children, as innovations and adaptations aimed at supporting the inclusion of disabled children often make learning more accessible and enjoyable for everybody. Inclusive practice should also mean that every child is able to experience success rather than failure, since play and learning have been made more accessible to them.

Reflective exercise

- Has your setting ever had to turn away a disabled child because it was not considered possible to meet their needs?
- What were the barriers and challenges that prevented admission?
- What kind of support and training would have made their inclusion possible?

Early intervention and well-being

For a disabled child the world can seem very strange indeed. Lots of adults paying attention to 'something' of which the child is completely unaware.

> The child's sense of self always includes what others call their 'impairment' as an integral part of their being. The only 'them' they have ever known. If they are in pain, they probably want it to stop. But apart from that, the child is like any other, driven to learn and become itself – a whole, new person with a body, mind and soul.
>
> (Mason 2000: 37)

Historically, early intervention has been regarded as a service targeting individual children, but from the 1970s onwards there has been an increasing recognition that high-quality family support is an essential element within any successful early intervention programme (Wolfendale 2000). The use of the general term 'early intervention' can itself be confusing and problematic unless we differentiate between early support for disabled children with life-long continuing conditions and intervention that is focused on children and families at risk of social exclusion or where special educational need may be pre-empted.

Early intervention has nevertheless become a byword for good practice in the UK (Allen 2011). The public and political message now enshrined in policy is that the earlier we can intervene, the more likely it is that the impact of disability, special educational needs, emotional and behavioural difficulties or speech and language impairment will automatically be diminished. While there are many examples of effective family and individual early interventions (C4EO 2011), it is still possible that inappropriate or unwelcome interventions might sometimes do more harm than good and even be positively detrimental to the well-being of disabled children and their families. Russell (2005) highlights the lack of hard evidence about the effectiveness of some interventions and recommends that the research agenda should include more longitudinal studies regarding what works and why.

In terms of early years practice with disabled children, most interventions will be relatively small scale and concerned with aspects of the learning and development of the individual child.

Case study 1

Jack is aged 4 and has been identified as being on the autistic spectrum. He was excluded from his previous nursery because they found his behaviour challenging and he was often in conflict with other children. According to his mother, the previous nursery had set targets for him around speech development and fine motor skills that he was unable to meet. A team decision is taken that the emotional and behavioural difficulties Jack is experiencing should take priority and in discussion with his parents an individual education plan (IEP) is drawn up that reflects these concerns. Initially, targets focus on turn-taking and sharing, and all staff agree consistent responses to behaviour that is considered unacceptable. Through observation it is established that Jack becomes agitated during noisy free play activities but responds well to one-to-one situations and smaller groups. Appropriate activities are built into his routine which reflect this. Staff and parents report an on-going improvement in behaviour now that his needs are better understood and he has experienced success rather than constant disapproval.

Case study 2

Rabina is a 3 year old with a slight learning disability who has been diagnosed with a speech delay. She is a sociable child and already uses non-verbal signals and gestures to communicate and take part in activities effectively. Her key worker meets with her parents and a decision is taken that the use of Makaton would help support her language development. At a team meeting it is decided that all staff and children should learn some Makaton alongside Rabina so that she does not feel isolated or stigmatized by the process.

Both these case studies reflect a social model approach and demonstrate the kind of intervention strategies that can help to support the well-being of disabled children rather than hinder it. Effective interventions that support well-being start with a positive focus that works from the child's existing strengths and there is sensitivity in terms of timing and ensuring interventions are appropriate. Effective communication and teamwork that includes parents and professionals are prerequisites, as are commitment and understanding of the issues raised for the child and family.

Conclusion

This chapter has highlighted some of the ways in which the medical and social models of disability impact on the well-being of disabled children and their families. By recognizing disability and special educational need as a 'complex combination of internal and external factors' (Jones 2004: 6), the conflict between the social and the medical model can be better understood. While early intervention can be tremendously helpful in supporting the well-being of disabled children and their families, inappropriate and intrusive interventions that do not take account of the social model can be damaging. The social model requires that we recognize that it is not only disabled children's impairments which determine quality of life and levels of well-being for them and their families, but also disabling attitudes and a disabling environment.

Arguably and despite considerable progress, the primary issues that have not yet been systematically addressed in the early years sector are negative attitudes and a lack of underpinning understanding about what it means to be disabled or to have a disabled child. The last word goes to Christine Lenehan, director of the Council for Disabled Children, who says:

> My view is disabled children are still seen as sub-species of child. There is definitely a perception in the early years sector that they know more about Martians than they do about disabled children. There is so much fear and ignorance about. Too many childcare workers see the disability first rather than the child, although there are some honorable exceptions.
>
> (Quarmby 2005)

This may seem harsh but it is the crux of the matter. I suggest that the most effective way of developing services that support the well-being of children with disabilities and their families is to take into account the pervasive effects of the medical model and to go beyond the rhetoric to ensure that the social model is properly understood in principle, policy, and practice. In this way, we can provide the acceptance that each family and child deserves in order to be full and valued members of society whatever their differences.

References

Allen, G. (2011) *Early Intervention: The Next Steps*. London: Cabinet Office.

Baren-Cohen, S. (2009) Prevalence of autistic spectrum conditions: UK school based population study, *British Journal of Psychiatry*, 194(6): 500–9.

Bennett, E. (2009) *What Makes My Family Stronger: A Report into What Makes Families with Disabled Children Stronger – Socially, Emotionally and Practically*. London: Contact a Family. Available at: http://www.cafamily.org.uk/media/392373/research_and_reportswhat_makesmyfamilystrongerwhatmakes_families_with_disabled_children_stronger_socially__emotionally_and_practically2009.pdf [accessed 8 June 2012].

British Council of Disabled People (BCDP) (2005) *British Council for Disabled People's Response to the Education and Skills Select Committee on Children with SEN*. Available at: http://www.publications.parliament.uk/pa/cm200506/cmselect/cmeduski/uc478-vii/uc11402.htm [accessed 7 January 2013].

Carpenter, B. and Egerton, J. (2007) *Early Support: Family Structures*. London: HMSO.

Centre for Excellence and Outcomes in Children and Young People's Services (C4EO) (2011) *Grasping the Nettle: Early Intervention for Children, Families and Communities*. Available at: http://www.c4eo.org.uk/themes/earlyintervention/files/early_intervention_grasping_the_nettle_full_report.pdf [accessed 8 January 2013].

Children's Society, Citizen's Advice, and Disability Rights UK (2012) *Holes in the Safety Net: The Impact of Universal Credit on Disabled People and Their Families.* Available at: http://www.disabilityrightsuk.org/holesinthesafetynet.pdf [accessed 8 January 2013].

Contact a Family (2011) *Forgotten Families: The Impact of Isolation on Families with Disabled Children.* Available at: http://www.cafamily.org.uk/media/381636/forgotten_isolation_report.pdf [accessed 7 January 2013].

Contact a Family (2012) *Counting the Costs 2012 – The Financial Reality for Families with Disabled Children Across the UK.* Available at: http://www.cafamily.org.uk/index.php?module=newsmodule&action=view&id=857&src=@random4864f-f40710ee [accessed 8 June 2012].

Department for Education (DfE) (2012) *Support and Aspiration: A New Approach to Special Educational Needs and Disability: Progress and Next Steps.* London: DfE.

Department for Education and Skills (DfES) (2004) *Early Support Professional Guidance.* London: DfES.

Dickins, M. with Denziloe, J. (2003) *All Together: How to Create Inclusive Services for Disabled Children and Their Families: A Practical Handbook for Early Years Workers.* London: National Children's Bureau.

Hinton, J. (1972) *Dying.* Harmondsworth: Pelican.

Home Office (2010) *Equality Act 2010.* Available at: http://www.legislation.gov.uk/ukpga/2010/15/contents/enacted [accessed 8 June 2012].

Jones, C.A. (2004) *Supporting Inclusion in the Early Years.* Maidenhead: Open University Press.

Kearney, P. and Griffin, T. (2001) Between joy and sorrow: being a parent of a child with developmental disability, *Journal of Advanced Nursing*, 34(5): 582–92.

Kübler-Ross, E. (1969) *On Death and Dying.* London: Tavistock.

Landsman, G. (2005) Mothers and models of disability, *Journal of Medical Humanities*, 26(2/3): 121–39.

Mason, M. (2000) *Incurably Human.* London: Working Press.

Murray-Parkes, C. (1972) *Bereavement: Studies of Grief in Adult Life.* Harmondsworth: Pelican.

Parents for Inclusion (2004) *Welcome Pack.* London: Parents for Inclusion.

Quarmby, K. (2005) Too much too young – are disabled children better off in mainstream care?, *The Guardian*, 23 February. Available at: http://www.guardian.co.uk/society/2005/feb/23/disability.childrensservices [accessed 18 February 2013].

Reiser, R. and Mason, M. (1992) *Disability Equality in the Classroom: A Human Rights Issue.* London: Disability Equality in Education.

Runswick-Cole, K. (2008) Between a rock and a hard place: parents' attitudes to the inclusion of children with special educational needs in mainstream and special schools, *British Journal of Special Education*, 35(3):173–80.

Runswick-Cole, K. (2011) Time to end the bias towards inclusive education?, *British Journal of Special Education*, 38(3): 112–19.

Russell, P. (2003) Access and achievement or social exclusion? Are the government's policies working for disabled children and their families?, *Children and Society*, 17: 215–25.

Russell, P. (2005) Getting it right from the start – policy development around early intervention in the UK, in B. Carpenter and J. Egerton (eds.) *Early Childhood Intervention: International Perspectives*. Coventry: West Midlands SEN Regional Partnership.

Skrtic, T. (1995) *Disability and Democracy: Reconstructing (Special) Education for Postmodernity*. New York: Teacher's College Press

Slade, Z., Coulter, A. and Joyce, L. (2009) *Parental Experiences of Services for Disabled Children*. London: DCSF.

Wolfendale, S. (2000) *Special Educational Needs in the Early Years: Snapshots of Practice*. London: RoutledgeFalmer.

Part 3

The well-being of adults living and working with babies and young children

10 The well-being of adults living with babies and young children

Penny Mukherji

Introduction

> Good parenting is at the heart of a child's well-being and development. And parents' and carers' well-being is key to their ability to raise their children. When mothers and fathers have poor well-being, they are less able to be good parents to their children.
>
> (Roberts et al. 2009: 11)

This chapter investigates how the well-being of babies and children is affected by the well-being of the adults with whom they live. Children's well-being is affected by factors such as social inequalities, poverty, discrimination, and the quality of their social relationships. For babies and young children, it is primarily within the context of the home, family, and community that these influences are mediated.

The findings from the London Metropolitan University/National Children's Bureau Project 'Talking about Young Children's Well-Being' (LMU/NCB Well-being Project) clearly indicated that participants saw the influence of children's families to be fundamental to their well-being. Children's well-being was seen to be conditional on them feeling a sense of connectedness to their family and community, experiencing positive attachment relationships within the family, and feeling included, valued, and accepted by the family. For these conditions to be met, participants were of the opinion that it was essential for parents themselves to have a positive sense of well-being. The children in the LMU/NCB Well-being Project also emphasized the importance of home and family for their well-being. Mothers, and to a lesser extent fathers, were seen by the children as central figures who influenced their happiness, and the well-being of their parents was seen as important to the children.

In this chapter, the influence of parental well-being on their children will be discussed. In particular, the effects of poverty and social inequality, and specific stressors such as discord within the family will be investigated in relation to the well-being of all family members. The effects upon children of parents who abuse drugs or alcohol will be discussed together with the impact upon children of mothers who are clinically depressed. The stresses imposed upon parents looking after children with disabilities will also be examined. Initiatives designed to support parents and promote their well-being will be discussed, together with the important role that early childhood practitioners can play.

How the well-being of adults affects the well-being of children

Case study exercise

In the LMU/NCB Well-being Project focus groups and seminars, parents and practitioners identified that children's well-being was dependent on the well-being of the whole family. One early childhood practitioner explained: 'If a family is emotionally well they can cope with issues and problems more. Children will feel happier and more resilient.' It was generally understood that the well-being of parents had a direct effect on the well-being of children; as one parent explained, 'my well-being will help me facilitate my children's well-being'.

Reflect upon the factors that may adversely affect parents' feelings of well-being and how this may, in turn, affect the well-being of the children within a family.

There are three main ways that parents' well-being may impact the well-being of their children.

Parents' well-being affects their attachment relationships with children

One of the strongest themes that emerged from the LMU/NCB Well-being Project is that to have a positive sense of well-being, children (and adults) need to experience close and loving relationships. This is the foundation upon which children's development is built (Osborne 2004) and is one of the key themes (positive relationships) in the Early Years Foundation Stage Curriculum (DfE 2012a). Close attachment relationships with their parents protect children and provide 'an important resource for navigating stressful life events' (Osborne 2004: 5).

However, not every parent is able to foster secure attachment relationships with their children. One of the factors that negatively affect the ability of parents to foster close relationships is stress (Jarvis and Creasey 1991). Later in the chapter, specific stressors that negatively affect parental well-being will be explored.

Parents' well-being affects their capacity to parent adequately

In addition, parents who are stressed may find it difficult to fulfil their parenting role effectively. Roberts et al. (2009: 13) explain that 'good parenting is at the heart of children's well-being and development. When mothers' and fathers' own well-being is under threat then their capacity to parent successfully diminishes.' If parents' well-being is compromised by factors such as being poor, out of work, or being unwell or otherwise disadvantaged, then not only may their internal capacity to support their children be limited, but they may also find it difficult to access external resources. Families may lack the support from their wider family and the local community (social capital) that would help them in their parenting role (Strategy Unit/DfES 2008).

Parents' emotional stress causes children to be stressed

In addition to parental stress having a negative impact on their ability to form close relationships with their children and to parent effectively, children can also be directly affected by the stress that the parent is experiencing. Young children are closely bound to their parents' emotions. From infancy babies 'read' their mothers' emotions, to see if a new situation is safe; this is known as social referencing (Robinson 2008). Early childhood practitioners will have had the experience of infants, new to a setting, looking at their mothers to see if it is safe to explore. Sometimes if a mother is anxious about leaving her child in an unfamiliar place, the child will experience her stress and may be reluctant to leave her. Because infants are so attuned to their parents' emotions, they will be affected by the stress parents are experiencing. The American Psychological Association is conducting a longitudinal study of stress in the American population. In 2010, it reported that although the majority of parents thought that they were shielding the children from the stress that they, as parents, were feeling, nearly all the children questioned knew their parents were stressed because of the way they behaved. Forty per cent of children reported that they felt sad and worried when they knew that their parents were stressed. In a review of the literature, Ruiz and Avant (2005) found that stress in infancy can have permanent, negative effects on children's health and development, while research findings from a longitudinal study undertaken by Essex et al. (2011) suggest that stress experienced by both mothers and fathers during their children's infancy can cause permanent changes in children's DNA.

Case study exercise

In the LMU/NCB Well-being Project, the following observation of children playing with jelly in an early childhood setting was recorded. The children were aged between 3 and 4 years.

For a while the children were quite contented in exploring the jelly. What happened next was quite unexpected. Child D picked up a few jelly cubes and was bashing them together. Child E noticed this and proceeded to tell me that the jelly bangs together just like her daddy's gall stones.

I listened and watched the expression on her face as she told me the tale of her daddy's gall stones. She said that he had three (pointing to three jelly cubes) gall stones in his tummy and they hurt. She said, 'did you know that my daddy has been to the doctor's and had blood taken out, it's this colour (pointing to the jelly) of his arm and the doctor put a plaster on it. Me and mummy have to look after daddy because he is sick and he has to stop drinking wine, it's this colour too' (pointing to the red jelly cubes).

Next she said that he has to go back to the doctor and have them 'shaken out'. She picked up the jelly cubes, shook them frantically between both hands and they fell out her hand onto the tray.

'I think they won't hurt daddy anymore and they will fall out just like this. You know Sharon, me and mummy can shake daddy if we were doctors to make the gall stones come out, my daddy has to drink water to get better because did you know water makes you healthy and his job makes him sick.'

This observation shows quite clearly that young children can, and do, absorb a lot of the stresses and worries that they encounter at home. This child is not only worried about her father's health, but has also picked up that there is an issue about his drinking and that his job is making him ill.

If you were the child's key person, how could you support both the child and the family?

There is extensive literature about the effects of specific parental stressors upon children. In 1991, the Department of Health identified that 'parenting capacity may be limited temporarily or permanently by poverty, racism, poor housing or unemployment or by personal or marital problems, sensory or physical disability, mental illness or past life experiences' (DoH 1991: 8).

The Department of Health (1991) identifies poverty as one of the main causes of stress that may negatively affect parenting capacity. This is a strongly held belief, supported by adult participants in the LMU/NCB Well-being Project. However, the evidence for this remains unclear. When Katz et al. (2007) reviewed the literature, they were unable to find a clear causal link between parenting and poverty. They found that individual parents react to poverty in different ways, depending on their temperament, their own experiences of being parented, and the degree to which they are supported by family and the community. Although there is a link between poverty, parental stress, and parenting skills, the direction of causality is not proven.

Marital problems and family breakdown are commonly cited as causes of stress that adversely affect children's well-being; however, a review of the literature by Stoll et al. (2012) identified that it is the conflict between parents that has the negative effect, rather than family breakdown *per se*. In a review of evidence for the Department for Children, Schools and Families, Mooney et al. (2009) identified that in cases of high levels of conflict and family violence, separation can actually be protective of children's well-being.

Children raised in families where there is domestic violence are especially vulnerable. Bird et al. (2011) report that children raised in families where there is domestic violence are between three and nine times as likely to be abused or injured as in non-violent households, and that in 60 per cent of cases where children have been abused, the mother will also have been a victim.

Domestic violence and child abuse are often fuelled by drug or alcohol misuse. In a study based on a London borough, Forester (2000) discovered that just over half the children on the child protection register had a parent who was misusing drugs or alcohol. As well as the increased possibility of violence within the home, parents who misuse substances are likely to be poor, inconsistent or neglectful parents. Children of such parents are at increased risk of developing social and emotional difficulties and often achieve less well at school than other children. Some children may be adversely affected in the womb by substances that their mothers have ingested during pregnancy (Vellman and Templeton 2007).

Maternal depression is another aspect of parental well-being that has a direct effect on outcomes for children. Barker et al. (2012) identified that children faced two sets of negative influences: depressed mothers are less likely than others to be able to provide a stable, safe, and consistent home environment for their children, and the very nature of their depression is likely to have direct effects on the child's development. Turney (2012) describes how depressed mothers' lack of energy may lead to them finding it difficult to parent effectively and consistently. In addition, depression can lead mothers to become unresponsive to their children, which can be particularly damaging to children's development if they are infants. Another aspect of maternal depression that Turney identifies is that mothers are less likely to be able to sustain relationships, either with their partners or with extended family or friends. This can lead to children being denied the very support and consistency from others that could protect their well-being.

As discussed in Chapter 9, parents who are looking after children with special educational needs and disabilities are another group whose well-being can be compromised (DfE 2011). Not only can parents be stressed over the identification and assessment of their children's needs, they may also find that they are materially less well off. Looking after a disabled child often means that one parent has to become a full-time carer and there are often additional costs involved. The stress of caring for a disabled child increases the likelihood of marital breakdown, further diminishing the well-being of parents (Joshi and Mukherji 2005).

Supporting the well-being of parents and families

It is clear from the LMU/NCB Well-being Project that practitioners often work with families where the parents' levels of well-being are compromised by some of the factors that have been identified in this chapter. Family stress may be transient and have little lasting effect upon children or parents may be facing more challenging situations that can have serious repercussions for children's well-being. Early childhood practitioners are part of a wider multi-disciplinary network, and training and experience are needed to know how to support families and how to handle suspicions of child abuse or neglect. Cleaver and colleagues emphasize that:

> Early identification and assessment are essential to ensure children and young people living with parental mental illness, learning disability, substance misuse and domestic violence, are not left in dangerous and abusive situations. Early identification depends on ensuring children and young people have opportunities to discuss their experiences with a trusted adult.
> (Cleaver et al. 2011: 208)

In the field of early childhood, the 'trusted adult' is likely to be the key person. The practitioner participants of the LMU/NCB Well-being Project discussed in detail the importance of the key person role and of the importance of working in a true partnership with parents.

Case study exercise

In the LMU/NCB Well-being Project, practitioners were asked what aspects of policy made positive contributions to children's well-being. It was acknowledged that the emphasis on parental partnership and the key person approach in the Early Years Foundation Stage (DCSF 2008) had had a beneficial effect. However, there were some concerns expressed. A strong theme was that there was not enough time to form close relationships with either the children or the parents. There was a generally held view that paperwork and other demands on staff were taking them away from the children. One practitioner said that there was 'not enough time to get to know the child and family as a practitioner'. Although positive parental partnerships were generally held to be important for children, parents and practitioners alike, there were concerns expressed about some of the perceived barriers to effective partnership.

One practitioner mentioned that one barrier was a 'fear of parents leading to lack of close relationships'. Another concern expressed was that there are sometimes 'different ideas between home and setting', which could lead to potentially difficult relationships with parents.

- Why do you think that there is sometimes a fear of parents?
- What is it that practitioners are afraid of?
- What are the issues about which parents and practitioners sometimes have different ideas?

The term 'parental partnership' is one that is often heard, although it means different things to different people. In the LMU/NCB Well-being Project, a variety of aspects of parental partnership were mentioned. MacNaughton and Hughes (2003) classified relationships with parents and the wider community according to inherent knowledge–power relationships. They identified three different sorts of parental partnerships:

1. There are those that conform to traditional power relationships, where the practitioner is held to be the professional expert and has the most power in the relationship. Parents are seen as knowing less than the professionals and so need directing. This is a deficit model, whereby parents are seen to be 'lacking' in some way and the role of the practitioner is to 'educate' parents, or to intervene to counteract the perceived deficits in parenting.
2. There are those that reform power relationships, where the relationship is more equal and power is shared between practitioner and parent. Parents and practitioners share information and the expertise of both is recognized.
3. There are those that transform power relationships, where parents hold the power and are involved in much of the important decision making in a setting. The practitioner's expertise is recognized, but the parents decide on policy, etc. This is an approach seen in parent cooperatives.

In the LMU/NCB Well-being Project, participants revealed that, for the most part, they hold a 'reforming' model of parental partnership. It was recognized that for children's well-being to be promoted, there needs to be a good relationship with parents. Participants talked about establishing a 'team ethos' between practitioner and parent, where parents are respected and individuality and difference are acknowledged. One early childhood practitioner commented that practitioners should 'find out what parents/families actually need . . . not make assumptions'. Another practitioner said, 'families are all different and have different values. We need to recognize this and ensure that we don't isolate individuals but work together as a community for the children's best interest.'

One aspect of parental partnership that was discussed by practitioners was the importance of parents feeling comfortable in the setting, as it was recognized that children would be reluctant to leave their parents if they detected that the parents were anxious about leaving them. If children see that their parents are happy and relaxed, they too are more likely to be relaxed.

Participants in the LMU/NCB Well-being Project identified that training is essential for early childhood practitioners if they are to work effectively with parents. Training programmes such as those developed by Pen Green (Whalley and the Penn Green Centre Team 2007) and the Parents, Early Years and Learning (PEAL) programme, developed by the Early Childhood Unit of the National Children's Bureau (PEAL 2012), are widely used. Both these programmes are based on the principle of mutual respect for parent and practitioner. Mitchell et al. (2006), who undertook research into parental partnerships in New Zealand, emphasize that mutual respect is a fundamental underpinning principle. Their findings showed that without mutual respect, divisions made relationships and communication with parents difficult.

Data from the LMU/NCB Well-being Project reveals that although practitioners profess a 'reforming' model of parental partnership, there remains an underlying critical view of parents who were seen to 'buy their children things instead of giving them time', 'have a child but still want the single life and the child is like an accessory', or are 'always working' and not spending time with their children. These views reveal the complex feelings that are aroused in the triangle of care between practitioner, parent, and child (Goldschmied and Selleck 1996), which if not effectively contained can result in difficult practitioner–parent relationships rather than mutually respectful ones. Therefore, the importance of promoting the kind of professional development opportunities as described above cannot be overemphasized.

Parenting support programmes

As well as arising from their feelings, the views revealed above also show that early childhood practitioners are influenced by the prevailing tendency for 'parent blaming' in the media and in policy statements. It is hard to look at a newspaper or watch the news on television without some comment being made about the 'problem' of poor parenting. There is a dominant view that many of the 'problems' in society are caused by parents who fail to discipline their children properly. The report into the August 2011 riots in the UK stated:

> We heard from many communities who felt that rioter behaviour could ultimately be ascribed to poor parenting. We need to consider what can be done to ensure that all children get the right support, control and guidance from parents and guardians.
>
> (Riots, Communities and Victims Panel 2012: 1)

However, as we have discussed previously, far from poor parenting causing social ills, the direction of causality flows the other way; social ills have a negative effect on parents' ability to parent effectively.

There is much research into what is the most appropriate, effective way to parent. In her research into American families, Baumrind (1966) concluded that parents who are caring, attentive, responsive, cooperative, and warm are able to provide the most effective parenting. When discipline is needed, child-friendly and age-appropriate methods are used. However, there is recognition that the concept of 'effective parenting' differs according to the cultural context of the family (Garcia and Garcia 2009). Most parenting support programmes in the UK are based on the 'authoritative' approach, sometimes known as 'positive parenting'. The three main programmes that are used in the UK for supporting parents are: Strengthening Families, Strengthening Communities; Triple P; and Webster Stratton.

Roberts et al. (2009) emphasize that supporting parental well-being should be an underpinning principle in any parenting support programme, and that improving parental well-being should be a key outcome of such programmes. They also recognize that parenting support programmes need to use a diversity of approaches, designed to meet the particular needs of the local community.

A multi-disciplinary approach to supporting families

Findings from the LMU/NCB Well-being Project suggest that practitioners clearly see that there is a need to support relationships that matter to children, and that parents are best supported by a multi-disciplinary approach. Participants talked about measures that the government could take to support parents with very young children, one suggestion being economic support to allow working mothers to stay at home for at least a year. At a local level, participants emphasized the value of perinatal parenting classes, baby massage courses, and support for parents in understanding how to promote children's well-being.

The acknowledgement that children's well-being can be improved by supporting the well-being of their parents is, of course, not new. The Children Act 2004 stated that 'a children's services authority in England must have regard to the importance of parents and other persons caring for children in improving the well-being of children' (Section 10(3) of the Children Act 2004). Current government initiatives, outlined in the Healthy Child Programme (DoH 2010), the Marmot Review (Marmot 2010), and *A New Approach to Child Poverty* (DWP and DfE 2011) reflect the concept that there should be targeted support for the most vulnerable families. At the present time, much of this support is delivered through the network of Sure Start children's centres, which have the remit of improving outcomes for young children and their families, focusing on the most disadvantaged (DfE 2012b).

As a response to the riots in 2011, the government set up the National Troubled Family Unit. A troubled family is defined as 'one that has serious problems, including parents not working and children not in school, and causes serious problems, such as youth crime and anti-social behaviour' (Communities and Local Government Website 2012). The government estimates that there are 1200 'troubled families' and has committed to 'turning around the lives' of these families by 2015 by joining up local services, dealing with each family's problems as a whole rather than individually, and appointing a single key worker to get to grips with their problems and work intensively to help them change for the long term. In July 2012, Louise Casey, who heads up the unit, interviewed sixteen families and concluded that, for these families, problems were complex, interrelated, and inter-generational. She suggests that supporting individual family members only has limited success and that problems can only really be understood 'by looking at the full cycle – and the full family. This requires services who work with families to take the long view; of what happened to the parents as children and of what has happened to the children since birth' (Casey 2012: 64).

Reflective exercise

Reflect upon your setting and evaluate the extent to which both policy and practice support the well-being of parents.

- How effective is the partnership between practitioners and parents?
- Is there a need for further training for the team in these aspects of working with families?

Conclusion

This chapter describes how the well-being of parents and adults living with children has a direct effect on their well-being. Parental stress can have negative effects on the formation of close attachment relationships with children and reduce adults' capacity to parent effectively. In addition, children are very aware of parental stress and this has been shown to negatively impact upon their development. Stressors such as 'poverty, racism, poor housing or unemployment or . . . personal or marital problems, sensory or physical disability, mental illness or past life experiences', all contribute to negative well-being in parents and ultimately that of their children (DoH 1991: 8). Early childhood settings, using a multi-disciplinary approach with other services, have an important role in supporting families and parents. This support should be based on mutual understanding and respect.

References

American Psychological Association (2010) *Stress in America Study: Key Findings.* Available at: http://www.apa.org/news/press/releases/stress/key-findings.pdf [accessed 13 July 2012].

Barker, E., Copeland, W., Maughn, B., Jaffee, S. and Uher, R. (2012) Relative impact of maternal depression and associated risk factors on offspring psychopathology, *British Journal of Psychiatry,* 200: 124–9.

Baumrind, D. (1966) Effects of authoritative parental control on child behaviour, *Child Development,* 37(4): 887–907.

Bird, W., Burton, E., Maryon-Davis, A., Murphy, M., Stewart-Brown, S., Weare, K. and Wilson, P. (2011) *Thinking Ahead: Why We Need to Improve Children's Mental Health and Well-being.* London: Faculty of Public Health.

Casey, L. (2012) *Listening to Troubled Families.* London: Department for Communities and Local Government. Available at: http://www.communities.gov.uk/communities/troubledfamilies/ [accessed 21 July 2012].

Cleaver, H., Unell, I. and Aldgate, J. (2011) *Children's Needs – Parenting Capacity. Child Abuse: Parental Mental Illness, Learning Disability, Substance Misuse and Domestic Violence* (2nd edn.). London: The Stationery Office.

Department for Children, Schools and Families (DCSF) (2008) *Statutory Framework for the Early Years Foundation Stage.* Nottingham: DCSF Publications.

Department for Education (DfE) (2011) *Support and Aspiration: A New Approach to Special Educational Needs and Disability: A Consultation.* London: The Stationery Office.

Department for Education (DfE) (2012a) *Statutory Framework for the Early Years Foundation Stage: Setting the Standards for Learning, Development and Care for Children from Birth to Five.* Available at: https://www.education.gov.uk/publications/standard/AllPublications/Page1/DFE-00023-2012.

Department for Education (DfE) (2012b) *Core Purpose of Sure Start Children's Centres.* Available at: http://www.education.gov.uk/childrenandyoungpeople/earlylearningandchildcare/a00191780/core-purpose-of-sure-start-childrens-centres [accessed 24 July 2012].

Department of Health (DoH) (1991) *The Care of Children: Principles and Practice in Guidance and Legislation.* London: HMSO.

Department of Health (DoH) (2010) *Healthy Child Programme.* Available at: http://www.dh.gov.uk/prod_consum_dh/groups/dh_digitalassets/@dh/@en/@ps/documents/digitalasset/dh_118525.pdf [accessed 17 July 2012].

Department of Work and Pensions and the Department for Education (DWP/DfE) (2011) *A New Approach to Child Poverty: Tackling the Causes of Disadvantage and Transforming Families' Lives.* London: TSO.

Essex, M.J., Thomas Boyce, W., Hertzman, C., Lam, L.L., Armstrong, J.M., Neumann, S.M.A. and Kobor, M.S. (2011) Epigenetic vestiges of early developmental adversity: childhood stress exposure and DNA methylation in adolescence, *Child Development*, 84(1): 58–75.

Forester, D. (2000) Parental substance misuse and child protection in a British sample: a survey of children on the child protection register in an inner London district office, *Child Abuse Review*, 9(4): 235–46.

Garcia, F. and Garcia, E. (2009) Is always authoritative the optimum parenting style? Evidence from Spanish families, *Adolescence*, 44(173): 101–31.

Goldschmied, E. and Selleck, D. (1996) *Communication Between Babies in their First Year*. London: National Children's Bureau.

Great Britain Parliament (2004) *The Children Act 2004*. London: The Stationery Office.

Jarvis, P. and Creasey, G. (1991) Parental stress, coping, and attachment in families with an 18-month-old infant, *Infant Behavior and Development*, 14(4): 383–95.

Joshi, U. and Mukherji, P. (2005) Special educational needs and inclusion, in L. Dryden, R. Forbes, P. Mukherji and L. Pound (eds.) *Essential Early Years*. London: Hodder Arnold.

Katz, I., Corlyon, J., La Placa, V. and Hunter, S. (2007) *The Relationship Between Parenting and Poverty*. York: The Joseph Rowntree Foundation.

MacNaughton, G. and Hughes, P. (2003) Curriculum contexts: parents and communities, in G. MacNaughton (ed.) *Shaping Early Childhood Learners, Curriculum and Contexts*. Maidenhead: Open University Press.

Marmot, M. (2010) *Fair Society, Healthy Lives: The Marmot Review. Strategic Review of Health Inequalities Post 2010. Executive Summary*. London: The Marmot Review.

Mitchell, L., Haggerty, M., Hampton, V. and Pairman, A. (2006) *Teachers, Parents, and Whānau Working Together in Early Childhood Education*. Wellington: New Zealand Council for Educational Research.

Mooney, A., Oliver, C. and Smith, M. (2009) *Impact of Family Breakdown on Children's Well-Being: Evidence Review*. London: Thomas Coram Research Unit, Institute of Education/DCSF.

Osborne, C. (2004) *Maternal Stress and Mothering Behaviors in Stable and Unstable Families*. Center for Research on Child Well-being Working Paper #03-08-FF. Available at: http://crcw.princeton.edu/workingpapers/WP03-08-FF-Osborne.pdf [accessed 13 July 2012].

PEAL (2012) *Welcome to Peal*. Available at: http://peal.org.uk/ [accessed 24 July 2012].

Riots, Communities and Victims Panel (2012) *After the Riots: The Final Report of the Riots, Communities and Victims Panel*. London: LCVP.

Roberts, Y., Brophy, M. and Bacon, N. (2009) *Parenting and Well-being: Knitting Families Together*. London: The Young Foundation.

Robinson, M. (2008) *Child Development From Birth to Eight: A Journey Through the Early Years*. Maidenhead: Open University Press.

Ruiz, R. and Avant, K. (2005) Effects of maternal prenatal stress on infant outcomes: a synthesis of the literature, *Advances in Nursing Science*, 28(4): 345–55.

Stoll, L., Michaelson, J. and Seaford, C. (2012) *Well-being Evidence for Policy*. London: New Economics Foundation.

Strategy Unit and Department for Education and Skills (DfES) (2008) *Families in Britain: An Evidence Paper*. London: Cabinet Office.

Turney, K. (2012) Pathways of disadvantage: explaining the relationship between maternal depression and children's problem behaviors, *Social Science Research*, 41(6): 1546–64.

Vellman, R. and Templeton, L. (2007) Understanding and modifying the impact of parents'substance misuse on children, *Advances in Psychiatric Treatment*, 13: 79–89.

Whalley, M. and the Pen Green Centre Team (2007) *Involving Parents in Their Children's Learning*. London: Paul Chapman.

11 The well-being of early childhood practitioners

Julia Manning-Morton

Introduction

In the London Metropolitan University/National Children's Bureau Project 'Talking about Young Children's Well-being' (LMU/NCB Well-being Project), the idea that practitioners' well-being is a pre-requisite for effectively supporting children's well-being was raised in every group discussion.

> Adults need to be resilient and have a good sense of well-being themselves.

> We need to think about the adults' self-worth and confidence and how that is transmitted to children.

In the project discussions, the idea of caring for themselves as practitioners really resonated with the groups but they were equally, if not more, aware of the impact of their own behaviours and attitudes on children's well-being, identifying a wide range of skills and knowledge that participants believe are essential to be an effective practitioner. Central to these discussions was the need to develop close, trusting relationships with children. Therefore, this chapter discusses the 'key person approach' as a central principle of early childhood practice and explores the implications of this for the concept of professionalism in the early childhood field.

Issues of training, qualifications, and professionalism will be discussed but the chapter will also consider other aspects of professional identity and how they relate to professional self-esteem. The chapter also considers the factors that inhibit the development of professional self-esteem in early childhood practitioners as well as how a sense of professional well-being is supported.

The key characteristics and skills of an early childhood practitioner

> People think I just sit around and play with children all day/change nappies and wipe noses.

This is the kind of sentiment often expressed by early childhood practitioners when asked how they think they are seen professionally, and it reveals several issues that relate to practitioners' well-being. One is that 'people', the wider society, do not appreciate or understand the full breadth and complexity of the early childhood practitioner's role or the skills and abilities that the role requires.

The Children's Workforce Development Council (CWDC 2010) identifies a broad range of understanding, skills, knowledge, and attributes required by those working with children and families, including:

- the ability to communicate and engage effectively
- knowledge and understanding of children's development
- the knowledge and skills to safeguard and promote the welfare of children
- the ability to support transitions
- multi-agency and integrated working
- information sharing.

The LMU/NCB Well-being Project identified each of the above as areas in which practitioners need to be proficient in order to support children's well-being. As well as encompassing this breadth of skills, however, participants also emphasized the complexity and interpersonal aspects of how practice is implemented, thereby focusing on practitioners' attributes such as:

> Being kind, understanding, attentive, approachable, nurturing, caring and affectionate, loving, tuned in, non-judgmental, and respectful.

These kinds of characteristics of practitioners have also been identified by others (Manning-Morton and Thorp 2003; Stonehouse 1988) as being especially necessary for practitioners working with 0–3 year olds but are also clearly necessary for practitioners working with older children. Manning-Morton and Thorp (2003, 2006) state that practitioners need to be able to 'act as guides and supporters to our youngest children' (2003: 14), be mature enough to feel positively challenged by children's needs and behaviours, be able to stay in touch with a child's feelings, and are people who show respect for children.

The emphasis on the subjective and emotional dimensions of practice here implies a focus on *how* things are done in settings as being significant in supporting children's well-being. This is in contrast to the Statutory Framework for the Early Years Foundation Stage (DfE 2012), which, except for one instruction that practitioners should guide children's development through 'warm, positive interaction', takes a more instrumental view of *what* practitioners must do, focusing principally on outlining practitioners' responsibilities in relation to planning and providing play and learning opportunities across the areas of learning and on assessing children's progress.

Observation as a key skill

An example of the dissonance between practitioners' thinking about practice that supports well-being and the outcomes-based approach underpinning the Early Years Foundation Stage (EYFS) is in relation to assessing children's development and learning. In the LMU/NCB Well-being Project discussions, 'observation' was identified as a key skill and essential practice as it enables practitioners to 'enter the child's world' and 'helps people to tune in', whereas the EYFS seems to emphasize the core purpose of observation and assessment as the need to identify where children are not meeting the specified early learning goals. The project discussions also indicated a broader and more holistic concept of observation that includes listening: 'Observing and listening to children to really get to know what they need'. As discussed in Chapter 1, adopting a holistic approach to well-being means thinking about children and their experiences in an integrated way, an approach that is made difficult when having to focus on separate areas when observing. Thus, to gather a more holistic picture of a child's development and learning, practitioners need to adopt an approach that recognizes the variety of ways that children show us what they know and can do, where all aspects of the child's development are recorded, and the way in which they interlink is made clear. This kind of integrated thinking is effectively developed through undertaking holistic observations based on the psychoanalytic approach to infant observation (Elfer 2005; Miller et al. 1989). Setting leaders who took part in the Emotional Well-being: Strong Teams project found that this approach 'has enabled staff to experience first-hand how it is for the child in our environment' and thereby to change practice more effectively (Manning-Morton and Wilson 2011). But practitioners also have to balance many demands, so need confirmation from colleagues and leaders that 'it's okay to spend time getting to know the children in your care'.

Reflective exercise

Make a note of the ways in which you get to know the children in your care. Then think about one child and note down the things you know about him/ her that immediately spring to mind. Then at the next available opportunity, spend fifteen minutes just watching that child, without writing anything down but noticing how you feel as well as what the child is doing.

As soon as possible afterwards, write down what you saw and felt as it comes to mind and, if possible, talk it through with a colleague.

- Have you learned anything new or different about this child?
- How did your feelings inform your understanding?

The key person approach and professionalism

Another aspect of practice identified in the LMU/NCB Well-being Project as being key to enabling children's well-being was valuing and promoting positive attachments with children. The EYFS also values relationships by requiring that 'Each child must be assigned a key person' (DfE 2012: 18). However, the discussion of the key person role in the framework is limited and, although it suggests that the key person 'offer a settled relationship for the child and build a relationship with their parents', the focus in the rest of the document again seems to be on administrative aspects and intervention where there may be concerns about a child's progress. This description seems more in keeping with the idea of 'key working' (allocating one practitioner to be the named person taking primary responsibility for a small group of children), which, in the 1990s, became more associated with organizational and administrative aspects rather than focusing on developing secure, trusting relationships with children. It was for this reason that Elfer et al. (2003) developed the concept of the 'key person approach' and why Manning-Morton and Thorp (2006) differentiate between these two ideas in the Key Times Framework.

In the LMU/NCB Well-being Project, it was clear that it was the detail of the interaction in relationships with children that was thought to be the most meaningful to children's well-being.

> We need to be approachable – tone of voice, mannerisms, and body language – to convey this.

> Real (authentic/interested/sustained) communication, including listening is very important as are non-verbal communications.

In this way, children would 'have a connection with genuine adults who form genuine relationships' that are 'trusting and comfortable, sensitive and professional'.

However, although the importance and qualities of attachment relationships (Bowlby 1988) were well defined in the LMU/NCB Well-being Project discussions, the key person approach (Elfer et al. 2003) itself was not often specifically cited as a practice that supports children's well-being. This may highlight perhaps a need for further clarity about the approach; certainly participants identified the need for further training and improved support in this respect. It may also reflect some conflict and discomfort with what forming close relationships with children in settings looks like and what they mean for practitioners' concept of themselves as professionals.

This discomfort may have its roots in a concept of professionalism that values knowledge over skills, a notion that has its roots in a Cartesian dualist philosophy that privileges the thinking mind, rationality, and knowledge over the physical body and the unpredictability of emotion (Manning-Morton 2006). In this view, then, practitioners who concern themselves with children's physical and emotional well-being (particularly those working with babies and toddlers, who are immersed daily in physical care) may be perceived as less professional. This may cause practitioners to want to distance themselves from such practices in order to gain professional recognition, hence the resistance on the part of some practitioners to the key person approach. However, given the huge emphasis in the LMU/ NCB Well-being Project on the centrality of nurturing relationships to children's well-being, it is imperative that practitioners embrace a professional identity that has at its core the skills to build and maintain such relationships and who recognize and value the physical and the emotional as well as the cognitive aspects of learning.

The reality of this professional approach, though, has both benefits and difficulties. As Manning-Morton (2006: 46) says:

> ...for the privilege of being seen as experts in children's learning and development, early years practitioners need to also engage with the darker side of children's learning and developing, with their distress, their defiance, their dependency and their inherent mess and chaos. This is a major professional challenge for early years practitioners, as engaging closely with young children touches deeply held personal values and often deeply buried personal experiences.

These difficult aspects can lead to a psychological defensive position, whereby practitioners may avoid getting emotionally close to children, asserting that it is not 'professional'. Or they may differentiate between love and relationships in the family context and 'professional love' (Page 2011) or 'professional relationships' in the setting, as revealed in the comment above and as discussed in the literature (Degotardi and Pearson 2009). However, accepting that relationships in the home may have different qualities to those in the setting, such as their longevity and cultural contexts, does not mean denying the feelings of love, trust, and care (and rivalry and anger) that arise in all close relationships. Parents in the LMU/NCB Well-being Project emphasized this as follows:

> In good schools you see great affection and caring for children, loving and affectionate staff whatever the age of the child.

> Showing love [supports well-being]. We are asking them [practitioners] to be like mothers and fathers because children are in a school environment from such an early age.

It should be noted here that these parents say 'like' mothers and fathers, which does not imply replicating or replacing parental love but rather embraces the notion of 'mother' as 'a person who takes on responsibility for children's lives and for whom providing child care is a significant part of her...working life' (Ruddick 1989, cited in Goldschmied and Selleck 1996: 6)

These parents go on to describe the physicality of a loving relationship: 'Loving is physical, lots of cuddles, kisses, nurturing. But they were equally aware of the level of anxiety that such a pedagogical approach provokes:

> Our fear in this country, in our culture means that you're not allowed to touch the children, means you can't show love.

The unnamed fear here is of the sexual abuse of children, the prevention of which must be a priority for all adults interested in children's well-being. However, ill-advised 'no touch' policies and disembodied practice (Johnson 2000; Tobin 1997) are no substitute for the thorough training and supervision of practitioners in safeguarding and child protection and may, instead, lead to the neglect of children's physical and emotional well-being. Therefore, to be able to engage with these more difficult aspects of children's learning and development, professional early childhood practitioners need to bring a high level of maturity and self-awareness to their job. They need to become experts in themselves too; able to look at their own motivations, values, and experiences, which will enable them to better understand and adjust their responses to children (Manning-Morton 2011).

This can only take place in an organizational context that values the emotional dimension of practice as a valid professional concern (Elfer 1996). Manning-Morton and Thorp (2003: 156) describe this as an 'emotionally intelligent cycle of practice' wherein the well-being of the children requires positive key person relationships, which in turn require the practitioner to have effective interpersonal and intrapersonal skills (Goleman 1996). If having such capabilities is accepted as potential lifelong learning rather than innate, practitioners must be offered opportunities to develop them. This requires training and supervision by skilled, knowledgeable leaders and facilitators who consider the process as well as the content of staff development, and where practitioners are enabled to make links between their personal experiences, values, theoretical knowledge, and their practice (Manning-Morton 2006).

Thinking about well-being in this way was illustrated in the project discussions by the image of a set of Russian dolls – with the child the smallest doll in the middle, safely contained by the parent, then the practitioner 'holding' the parent and child, then the manager or other leader supporting the practitioner. In this model, childminders who work mostly alone identified their support workers and the importance of a network as sources of support, while leaders of settings also identified networks of other leaders and a 'safe' group in which they can reflect on their practice.

Reflective exercise

- What opportunities do you have to reflect on your practice?
- Are their opportunities to discuss the emotional aspects of your practice, such as how difficult it is when a child finds it hard to settle or a parent rejects your offers of help?
- If you do not have this kind of support, how do you manage these difficult aspects of practice?

Professional support

Facilitating reflexive practice in an emotionally containing environment is the focus of the training approach described by Elfer and Dearnly (2007) and Manning-Morton and Wilson (2011) in the Emotional Well-being: Strong Teams Training. This training approach incorporates the ideas that personal attributes are an important part of the equation in work with very young children, that practitioners need to combine personal responsiveness with a professional perspective, and that the emotional well-being of children is critically dependent on the social and emotional well-being of early years practitioners. Therefore, the training sessions pay a lot of attention to the process of talking together in a group as well as exploring what is meant by emotional well-being and how it is nurtured or undermined in young children.

Without opportunities such as this for reflexive discussion, the various demands of the key person role, whether being too great and emotionally draining or repetitive and under-stimulating, can lead to stress and burnout. Together with other professionals in the 'helping' professions, early childhood practitioners may well see themselves as selfless people with an 'ambition to love and be of service to humanity' (Selleck and Griffin 1996: 168) but they also tend to be women with additional caring roles for young families or elderly relatives at home. The constant 'giving' that this entails means that their 'jug' of emotional resources can easily run dry, leading to self-protective measures that include disconnecting from work relationships, high levels of sickness, and staff turnover. With this in mind, paying attention to the well-being of practitioners has not only a positive impact on their immediate ability to respond positively to children, but also on the longer term context of continuity of experience for children, as practitioners who feel listened to and respected are less likely to be absent through sickness or leave their job.

A key way in which practitioners can be listened to is through effective, regular supervision sessions and team discussions in which skilled and knowledgeable leaders work together with teams to develop a shared vision that has an explicit value base and is guided by clear principles that will support the well-being of babies and young children. The psychological environment (Day et al. 1998) is shaped by the many daily interactions that children experience and was identified in the LMU/NCB Well-being Project as a key context for children's well-being. It is therefore necessary that practitioners, whether working individually in their homes or in teams in centres, prioritize thinking about *why* they do things in a particular way because the curriculum will be determined by and reflective of their preferences, values, and beliefs about how children learn and develop. This means reflecting on the personal experiences that have shaped your values (i.e. what you hold to be important in life).

Case study exercise

In a team exercise to develop a set of pedagogical guidelines, a group of practitioners responsible for advising settings not only drew on their knowledge of child development, but also reflected on their own early experiences to identify what were the personal values they brought to their professional practice. Once they had agreed some common values, they were able to identify the principles that related to them. A principle is a guide to action, so this enabled them to discuss what they saw as effective practice, or pedagogy that would reflect their values and principles.

Think about the values you hold – that is, something that you view to be important in life. It might be 'being respectful', 'being independent' or 'keeping things tidy', for example.

- Where did these values come from?
- How do they influence your practice and what you expect from children?
- Are your values similar or different to those of your co-workers or the children's parents?
- What are the implications of that?

Training and qualifications

The kind of training opportunities described above became more possible as the expansion policies of the last Labour government (1997–2007) made funds available to local authorities for the development of the early childhood workforce, funds that, under the current austerity measures, are being cut. Yet the EYFS is clear that, 'The daily experience of children in early years settings and the overall quality of provision depends on all practitioners having appropriate qualifications, training, skills and knowledge', and the review of early education and childcare qualifications, undertaken by Cathy Nutbrown on behalf of the Department for Education, agrees that increased graduate leadership has had 'huge positive impacts' on the quality of practice (Nutbrown 2012: 8). A current concern, expressed in the LMU/NCB Well-being Project, is that these cuts will be a further blow to practitioners' professional well-being and also to the quality of provision to children and families.

This concern is particularly acute since improvements such as Early Years Professional Status are still only recently introduced and have not yet had time to embed fully into the workforce. In addition, the criticisms of the calibre of early childhood practitioners, whether explicit in the media or implicit in organizational hierarchies, continue. Some of these criticisms were also raised by participants, with sections (not all) of the workforce being described as inexperienced and under-skilled. This problem was largely ascribed to the poor quality of qualification training and the low baseline of NVQ2 as an acceptable qualification standard: 'Childcare and education qualifications seem to have been watered down', 'Initial staff training is not fit for purpose.'

These concerns are reflected in the Nutbrown Report (2012) but the main thrust of the review's recommendations is on creating a single qualification route in the field to resolve confusion about the many and varied early childhood qualifications that exist.

The multiplicity of training routes and qualifications that early childhood practitioners currently hold has emerged from the gaps resulting from the historic split between 'care' and 'education' for young children in the UK. Nutbrown's solution to this is to recommend that early childhood practitioners all aim towards becoming teachers with an early years specialism on the basis that: 'Having qualified teachers leading early years practice will raise the status of the sector, increase professionalism and improve quality' (Nutbrown 2012: 8).

Although the views expressed in the project would have no argument with raising the status of the sector, the notion that quality is improved purely by practitioners having a teaching qualification would be contested, especially as the evidence that shows the positive impact of graduate practitioners relates more to practice with older children and not so much to practice with 0–3 year olds (Mathers et al. 2011).

The project discussions indicate problems with the panacea of qualified teacher status. One is that the content and focus of teacher training, as it currently exists for primary school children, has an instrumental focus by which practitioners are trained to narrowly follow curriculum guidelines and overvalue narrow skill sets of literacy and numeracy. In contrast, the participants in the LMU/NCB Well-being emphasized the need for training to include:

- respect for children and their rights
- understanding of attachment
- understanding of well-being
- understanding about the importance of quality and inclusive play (and engaging parents in the value of play).

These priorities are more reflective of the broader range of skills, knowledge, and abilities identified by the CWDC at the beginning of this chapter as required of the early childhood professional who is part of a multi-disciplinary team providing for the wide range of needs that young children and their families have. In this context, the 'professional boundary crossing' (Manning-Morton 2006) between education, social care, community work, and health that early childhood practitioners have to engage in practically, should also be reflected in their theoretical knowledge base and the skills they are trained to develop.

Professional self-esteem

Developing a professional identity that respects all aspects of practice and areas of knowledge remains an unresolved issue within the early childhood community. The historical context of provision that has been divided between 'care' and 'education' has still not been resolved into an intact field of practice and thereby a whole professional identity, despite the development of integrated children's centres. Therefore, the long identified disparity of value ascribed to some practitioners' areas of expertise and qualification over others continues and is still reflected in different pay and conditions of service between, for example, a practitioner with a teaching qualification and one with Early Years Professional Status.

It would appear, therefore, that the concept of the early childhood professional is still caught between the devil and the deep blue sea, not valued for being a carer and not trusted if seen as a teacher. Not being viewed as a 'proper' teacher or a 'real' social worker had previously been seen to impact negatively on practitioners' professional identity (Manning-Morton 2006). Yet, in the LMU/NCB Well-being Project, practitioners did not see themselves from this deficit viewpoint. There was a clarity and assurance in the project discussions of how highly skilled, demanding, and complex a job being an early childhood practitioner is, which conveyed a positive professional identity that is unique to itself rather than just a reflection of others. In addition, the assertion in discussions of the importance of practitioners' own well-being suggests a positive level of professional self-worth. This may arise from a gradually increasing level of professional recognition in society through the focus that has been on the early years for the past 15 years, allowing an acknowledgement within and perhaps also without the field, that working with very young children is an important job. However, this focus has also brought with it negative impacts on practitioners' well-being. Increased demands resulting from policy initiatives introduced in rapid succession, are cited in the project as a persistent source of stress in settings.

To exacerbate this, the increased recognition in policy has not brought with it better levels of pay or better working conditions. This was identified in some sectors in particular, where there are: 'young girls with low levels of knowledge and experience, they're run as a business first'; and where 'practitioners who are tired, undertake long hours, are put upon/bullied'. Such negative situations are only likely to get worse as the Coalition Government (2010–) pursues its ideology of de-regulation and plans to increase the ratios of children to staff permitted.

Another negative issue is that the expansion of provision has provoked the resurrection in some circles of the debate about whether young children should be cared for out of the home. Practitioners in the LMU/NCB Well-being Project complained that the mixed messages they get from research and policy makers and from the media leave them uncertain as to the validity of their work: 'The messages received are that we are not quite good enough as practitioners.' So, as the idea of early childhood being a critical time for development and learning and for future outcomes takes hold in the mind of society and policy makers, the important role that practitioners play in children's lives becomes recognized. But, as with parenting, teaching, and social work, this role might be lauded and appreciated on the one hand but on the other can be vilified when things go wrong and blamed for society's ills. In this scenario, well-being – whether it is of children, parents or practitioners – becomes reduced to being the individual's responsibility rather than a collective one.

Reflective exercise

Write down ten 'boasts' about your work. These might be things you think you do well personally or as part of a team; they might include personal attributes that you believe make you an effective practitioner or your particular professional skills. Try to use specific adjectives such as 'attentive listener' rather than 'good' or 'well'. This can also be done as a team exercise, where you each write one positive thing about every other team member, like a game of 'consequences' – remember, be specific!

Conclusion

'Professionalism' in the early years must be understood in terms of the day-to-day detail of practitioners' relationships with children, parents, and colleagues; relationships that demand high levels of physical, emotional, and personal knowledge and skill. Therefore, being an effective early childhood practitioner requires a professional approach that combines personal awareness with theoretical knowledge (Manning-Morton 2006). In the LMU/NCB Well-being Project, participants identified that this means that practitioners need to be well trained so that they can:

- value and promote positive attachments with children
- know how to meet children's needs
- understand risk and resilience factors underpinning children's well-being

- understand the importance of working in supportive partnerships with parents
- develop the ability to assess children's well-being through observation, including use of the Leuven Well-being and Involvement Scales (Laevers et al. 1997)
- understand research findings in the area of well-being.

As one participant said: 'We need more time and money; it's not that we're not capable, there is so much we could do.' But to do so much more than they already do, practitioners' well-being must also be recognized and attended to: 'The sector needs more opportunities to have a voice and be heard.' Therefore, practitioners need effective leadership support that includes opportunities to discuss the emotional impact of practice and opportunities to develop a shared team vision that puts children's well-being at the forefront of practice.

References

Bowlby, J. (1988) *A Secure Base: Clinical Applications of Attachment Theory*. London: Routledge.

Children's Workforce Development Council (CWDC) (2010) *The Common Core of Skills and Knowledge*. Available at: www.cwdcouncil.org.uk [accessed 29 January 2013].

Day, C., Hall, C. and Whitaker, P. (1998) *Developing Leadership in Primary Schools*. London: Paul Chapman.

Degotardi, S. and Pearson, E. (2009) Relationship theory in the nursery: attachment and beyond, *Contemporary Issues in Early Childhood*, 10(2): 144–55.

Department for Education (DfE) (2012) *Statutory Framework for the Early Years Foundation Stage: Setting the Standards for Learning, Development and Care for Children from Birth to Five*. London: DfE. Available at: https://www.education.gov.uk/publications/standard/AllPublications/Page1/DFE-00023-2012 [accessed 29 January 2013].

Elfer, P. (1996) Building intimacy in relationships with young children in nurseries, *Early Years*, 16(2): 30–4.

Elfer, P. (2005) Observation matters, in L. Abbott and A. Langston (eds.) *Birth to Three Matters: Supporting the Framework of Effective Practice*. Maidenhead: Open University Press.

Elfer, P. and Dearnley, D. (2007) Nurseries and emotional well-being: evaluating an emotionally containing model of professional development, *Early Years: An International Journal of Research and Development*, 27(3): 267–79.

Elfer, P., Goldschmied, E. and Selleck, D. (2003) *Key Persons in Nursery: Building Relationships for Quality Provision*. London: David Fulton.

Goldschmied, E. and Selleck, D. (1996) *Communication between Babies in Their First Year*. London: National Children's Bureau.

Goleman, D. (1996) *Emotional Intelligence: Why it Can Matter More Than IQ.* London: Bloomsbury.

Johnson, R.T. (2000) *Hands Off! The Disappearance of Touch in the Care of Children.* New York: Peter Lang.

Laevers, F., Vandenbussche, E., Kog, M. and Depondt, L. (1997) *A Process Oriented Child Monitoring System for Young Children.* Leuven: Centre for Experiential Education.

Manning-Morton, J. (2006) The personal is professional: professionalism and the birth to threes practitioner, *Contemporary Issues in Early Childhood,* 7(1): 42–52.

Manning-Morton, J. (2011) Not just the tip of the iceberg: psychoanalytic ideas and early years practice, in L. Miller and L. Pound (eds.) *Theories and Approaches to Learning in the Early Years.* London: Sage.

Manning-Morton, J. and Thorp, M. (2003) *Key Times for Play: The First Three Years.* Maidenhead: Open University Press.

Manning-Morton, J. and Thorp, M. (2006) *Key Times: A Framework for Developing High Quality Provision for Children From Birth to Three Years.* Maidenhead: Open University Press.

Manning-Morton, J. and Wilson, D. (2011) *Addressing emotional well-being for infants, toddlers and young children through the professional development of practitioners,* Presentation to the European Early Childhood Education Research Association, August.

Mathers, S., Ranns, H., Karemaker, A., Moody, A., Graham, J. and Siraj-Blatchford, I. (2011) *Evaluation of the Graduate Leader Fund: Final Report.* Research brief DfE-RB144. London: DfE.

Miller, L., Rustin, M., Rustin, M. and Shuttleworth, J. (eds.) (1989) *Closely Observed Infants.* London: Duckworth.

Nutbrown, C. (2012) Foundations for Quality: The Independent Review of Early Education and Childcare Qualifications: Final Report (Nutbrown Review). London: DfE. Available at: https://www.gov.uk/government/publications/nutbrown-review-foundations-for-quality [accessed 29 January 2013].

Page, J. (2011) Do mothers want professional carers to love their babies?, *Journal of Early Childhood Research,* 9(3): 310–23.

Selleck, D. and Griffin, S. (1996) Quality for the under threes, in G. Pugh (ed.) *Contemporary Issues in the Early Years: Working Collaboratively for Children* (2nd edn.). London: Paul Chapman.

Stonehouse, A. (ed.) (1988) *Trusting Toddlers: Programming for 1–3 Year Olds in Child Care Centres.* Melbourne, VIC: Australian Early Childhood Association.

Tobin, J.J. (ed.) (1997) *Making a Place for Pleasure in Early Childhood Education.* New Haven, CT: Yale University Press.

12 Leading the well-being of early years teams

Judy Stevenson

Chapter overview

It is clear from the discussions in previous chapters that leaders of early childhood settings are in a key position to influence the well-being of children and families, principally through supporting the well-being of practitioners. In the London Metropolitan University/National Children's Bureau Project 'Talking about Young Children's Well-being' (LMU/NCB Well-being Project) focus groups and seminars, practitioners recognized that their own well-being was essential if they are also to support children's well-being and be able to form bonds with children that are personal, yet still professional. Much is written about the need to leave our home lives with all their troubles and turmoil at the nursery door, but it is questionable how realistic this concept is in practice when engaging closely with children and their families raises issues and experiences that resonate with the lives of practitioners in so many ways. In addition, early years settings are complex organizations that call on us to interact and connect not only with children and families, but with colleagues in close-knit teams, where everything is done in close proximity to others and personal and professional values may conflict. This was highlighted as a concern during the focus groups and seminars when practitioners stated that disinterested or miserable adults and colleagues who aren't genuine inhibit well-being.

It is therefore the responsibility of those who are in a leadership and management position to address the well-being of the practitioners in the setting in a holistic way. This means more than the casual 'how are you' asked in passing in the corridor (although this is a valuable element), it is about regular support and supervision, encouraging reflective practice, building teams, and ensuring appropriate professional development. It is about the working environment, the culture and climate, and the spaces and silences offered for practitioners to pause and reflect on their experiences.

In this chapter, we will look at the implications of this for the leaders of early years settings, particularly during periods of change, and also consider how they can ensure their own well-being and develop their own support networks.

Supervision

An area discussed at the LMU/NCB Well-being Project seminars was the challenge of managing close emotional relationships with children while maintaining some professional distance. Participants recognized that although this ability improved with emotional maturity, it is very difficult to manage systematically over long periods and is, perhaps, unmanageable without organizational support. One way of a setting providing this support is through regular support and supervision meetings.

It is clear from discussions that the term 'supervision' has many different connotations and that experiences range from regular sessions externally facilitated, to weekly meetings with the manager, to no supervision at all. This is often dependent on practitioners' professional heritage or work setting and certainly many of those with an education heritage had minimal knowledge or understanding of supervision and linked the term to performance management or appraisal.

The Children's Workforce Development Council defines supervision as 'an accountable process which supports, assures and develops the knowledge, skills and values of an individual, group or team' (Skills for Care and the Children's Workforce Development Council 2007: 5). However, Whalley (2001) recognizes that supervision needs to address both personal and self-development issues as well as professional and team-building issues.

For the first time, the requirement for supervision is enshrined within early years policy. The *Statutory Framework for the Early Years Foundation Stage* (EYFS) states that: 'Providers must put appropriate arrangements in place for the supervision of staff who have contact with children and families' (DfE 2012: 3.19). It goes on to define their view that, 'Effective supervision provides support, coaching and training for the practitioner and promotes the interests of children. Supervision should foster a culture of mutual support, teamwork and continuous improvement which encourages the confidential discussion of sensitive issues.' The Tickell Review (2011: 5.17) goes slightly further and recognizes that 'supervision should be expressed in such a way that encourages reflective practice and moves away from the perception that it is merely a tick-box approach to check what practitioners are, or are not, doing'.

From these definitions, it is clear that the purpose of supervision is multifaceted, but may be summed up as needing two key elements: a way to support practitioners and continually enhance the quality of their work; and a forum for reflective dialogues that can improve the well-being of staff. Supervision needs to be recognized as a rigorous professional activity that is assigned regular time away from the children but should not be confused with counselling or therapy, which require specialized facilitators. As Rodd (2006) suggests, it may include how a situation at home or personal experience is impacting on a practitioner's work, but it would be inappropriate for this to become the main focus of supervision.

For some early years settings, establishing supervision in a manner that meets the requirements of the EYFS (DfE 2012) yet incorporates reflective practice will be a new experience. If supervision is to be successful and contribute to the well-being of the practitioners, it needs to be a dialogue that is open and receptive, offers praise balanced with new insights, and triggers a passion for continuing to travel on a journey with the children and their families.

It is clear that the supervisor needs to develop their own skills to facilitate these discussions, the principal one being their ability to communicate. In order to provide appropriate feedback, this incorporates not only asking open-ended questions, but also actively listening and hearing exactly what the practitioner has said – not what you think they have said (Whitaker 1995). It also involves really knowing every individual so that the supervisor can approach each staff member with respect, engaging with them in setting their own targets, preparing them for change, and identifying ways of maintaining their own well-being.

Case study

Naomi manages a small private nursery in North London. As a result of her studies, she introduced supervision for the first time. After the first year, staff highlighted the following benefits:

- help with practical day-to-day issues
- an objective view of difficult experiences and problems
- support in emotional issues which previously felt overwhelming
- an opportunity to discuss how professional development might change practice in one, three and five years' time.

One of the immediate changes Naomi identified was that staff relationships improved and a long-term change was that turnover and retention of staff was no longer an issue.

Encouraging reflective practice

The LMU/NCB Well-being Project participants were clear about the need for practitioners to have the time and mental space to think through their observations on the children in their care, their engagement with families, and their provision, all key factors in developing reflective practice. As one participant stated, 'staff are expected to engage in professional reflection, individually and in groups and managers have the responsibility to facilitate this'. While it is very easy to endorse the need for all practitioners to embrace reflective practice as a crucial element for their own well-being, it is not so easy to clarify exactly what is meant by reflective practice and the leadership role in establishing it as an accepted element of everyday work.

Reflective practice is the process by which we continually seek and achieve changes in our personal and professional work to improve the experiences we offer the children. There are many ways of achieving this, but if reflective practice is viewed as learning through and from experience, it involves challenging assumptions about everyday practice and being self-aware (Moon 1999). Everybody will have their preferred way of reflecting. Whether it is through keeping a written journal, critical incident analysis discussion with colleagues both inside and outside of the setting, or simply pausing and thinking through the day or the week (Bolton 2005), the important thing is to enter an experiential learning cycle (Kolb 1984), summarized as: Concrete Experience (doing or having an experience), Reflective Observation (reviewing/reflecting on the experience), Abstract Conceptualization (concluding/learning from the experience), and Active Experimentation (planning/trying out what you have learned). The process of reflection may lead to a change in the perspective of a situation or to undertake a different action if the situation re-occurs. Reflection will not always offer a solution but it can help to clarify a situation and think about how an issue might have been handled differently.

While much reflective practice is, by its very nature, personal, there is much to be gained if the manager of an early years setting can establish it as part of the setting ethos and culture, and providing the space for this to happen can do much to enhance the well-being of the practitioners, children, and their families. This means more than building in time for the weekly team meetings and the daily evaluation and planning cycle, although these are important in any setting. It is about encouraging a deeper level of thoughtfulness where practitioners feel valued and enabled to challenge themselves without risk of rebuke or retribution if an initiative fails and knowing that success will be celebrated and good practice shared.

Introducing reflective practice to a staff team is not an easy task. While a leader or manager can change their own stance to be willing to create a receptive ethos, embedding it as part of the culture needs the staff to recognize its value and to see how it can aid their personal well-being. This may need to begin as a formal element of staff meetings or training sessions, asking individuals to reflect by themselves or in teams on issue that is concerning them and respond to specific questions, such as: what happened? What do you think and feel? What was good or bad? What sense are you making of it? What else could you have done? What would you do differently if it happened again? This process may need to be repeated many times before it makes a genuine impact on individual and team well-being.

Building teams

The LMU/NCB Well-being Project identified that working with someone without a sense of personal well-being or someone who is emotionally needy impacts on and contributes to relationship difficulties in one's setting. All early years practitioners in group settings, regardless of the size of the setting, have to work in at least one team. The team may comprise the practitioners who work in a room or with a specific age group, or it may be several staff brought together to look at a specific area of policy or practice. Rarely does anyone have a choice over the team with which they are called upon to work. An unhappy team not only affects the well-being of the adults, it also affects the well-being of the children and their families. Thus the question for leaders and managers is how to build teams, maintain their professional effectiveness, and resolve the conflicts that inevitably arise from time to time.

Although many publications address theories on team dynamics and relationships, and we live in a culture in which an industry has developed to provide activities for team building, one theory continues to underpin why teams frequently have difficulties and can help practitioners to understand the process they are going through. In his 1965 article 'Developmental sequence in small groups', Tuckman suggests there are four stages in the development of any team:

1. *forming* – when everyone is trying to get to know each other and discovering their roles and responsibilities within the team
2. *storming* – when conflict occurs as the team members test each other
3. *norming* – as the team begins to gel
4. *performing* – when everyone is comfortable within the team, everyone knows their role and work alongside each other naturally

If leaders and managers, as well as the teams themselves, are able to understand and accept this basic theory, it can be easier to manage the process of building a team. Of course, teams run this course repeatedly as members leave or join, so teams regularly go through the fifth *mourning* stage too and then have to re-form and repeat the process. These changes bring different personalities together with different professional and personal values and therefore different pedagogical priorities; this can lead to differences of opinion and even conflict.

Conflict is very much part of human nature and ignoring the situation, hoping it will change or go away, is often the response in early years team, who have invested in a professional persona of being 'nice' (Manning-Morton and Wilson 2011). But this is not usually the best course of action for any leader or manager to take. It is important to distinguish here between conflict, with its connotations of fights and battles, and disagreements, which are differences of opinion. Many disagreements can be healthy, leading to greater creativity and innovation, but still need to be managed in a supportive manner where everyone is encouraged to express their views openly, where everyone is listened to, and where everyone can then agree a way forward (Smith and Langston 1999). Indeed, there are times where the leader or manager needs to raise issues that may be controversial, knowing that there will be disagreements, but knowing that such debates are necessary to move policy and practice forward. Conflicts are in their very nature more destructive and can destroy the well-being of all involved. Dealing with a member of staff who is behaving destructively can take a long time – as employment legislation runs its course – so it is far better for everyone if issues can be resolved quickly and promptly in the early stages of difficulty. Any action is dependent on the nature of the conflict, but it is important to identify the exact issues, gather information from as many sources as possible without being influenced by gossip, and then consider a range of possible solutions. This may be through a meeting where everyone can voice their feelings, clear the air, and move forward, or through a greater level of arbitration.

One of the hardest issues in building teams is how to maintain motivation and avoid the complacency that can set in when groups have been together for a long period of time. Sometimes, the temptation might be to move individuals around as the first strategy and this can be useful in distributing expertise and creating climates for innovation. But this is not always possible and should only be undertaken with great forethought and consideration of the needs of children and families, which must come first. It might also be a way of avoiding dealing with a negative dynamic directly. Leaders need to support staff to enable them to take on new challenges, which may initially be stressful, but in the long term can stimulate and refresh them and provide that missing motivation.

A culture and climate that supports well-being

Every early years setting has its own atmosphere and environment, and we would all acknowledge that in some we immediately feel comfortable and 'at home', whereas others we like less and they make us feel uncomfortable. This is less about buildings, decoration, and displays, although they make their own impact, but more about the culture which reflects and impacts on the well-being of everyone in the setting.

Hall and Hord (2001: 94) define organizational culture as: 'the individually and socially constructed values, norms and beliefs about an organization and how it should behave that can be measured only by observation of the setting using qualitative methods'. The idea of culture can best be seen in the routines adopted by the practitioners, such as whether everyone helps tidy up or whether rituals used for celebrations are shared by all. The impact of the leader and manager on the culture of a setting cannot be underestimated. It begins with establishing shared values, principles, and visions that underpin the ethos of the way practitioners work with children, families, and each other, and infiltrate every aspect of working lives and well-being, such as whether staff have the time and space for both professional debate and personal storytelling. We work within a caring profession, which needs to begin with the way a leader cares for the staff team and encourages interpersonal relationships within the team. While practitioners may not choose work colleagues to be their best friends outside of work, friendliness and politeness create a positive environment and caring about each other helps to build resilience in times of stress and difficulty.

Maintaining well-being throughout periods of change

One of the elements identified in the LMU/NCB Well-being Project focus groups and seminars as affecting staff and individual well-being was the experience of having been through a period of unprecedented change in policy and practice since the mid-1990s. Such major changes are in addition to the individual changes in personnel and ways of working that are unique to each setting. Although change can be a positive stimulus and can increase motivation and create new opportunities, it is also associated with a feeling of loss, a grieving for the past, denial, anger, and uncertainty as it runs its course, all of which take their toll on personal and group well-being (Kearney and Hyle 2003). A leader, therefore, needs to be skilful in the way any change is introduced so as to minimize stress and unhappiness for a staff team. It is also important to avoid overloading everyone and causing disequilibrium unnecessarily. Sometimes, it is better to live a little longer with a situation to maintain the health of everyone.

Fullan (2007: 66) writes about three broad phases in the change process:

- *initiation* – making the decision to change something;
- *implementation* – putting the change into place; and
- *institutionalization* – where the change is embedded in the setting.

The leader needs to judge the timing of each phase with great care, continuously balancing the needs of the staff with the imperative to progress with change. Throughout, communication and realistic consultation are at the heart of the process. There is no point consulting people if there is no real choice, as this only leads to frustration, but there is a purpose if they can influence either the decision or the timing. It is essential for the leader to ensure that everyone has the physical and emotional space and time for discussion, recognizing that sometimes this is best done individually rather than as a group.

Understanding why people are resistant to change is important in overcoming negative emotions, and it often helps to think about who might resist new initiatives and why before even beginning to make changes. Careful advance planning can influence the way people react throughout the change process. Kotter (1988) suggests that when faced with resistance, the leader needs to communicate, educate, involve, facilitate, negotiate, manipulate, and if all else fails, use explicit and implicit coercion. Certainly, coercion will do little for the well-being of the individual, but if speed is essential and it is clear that nothing else will work, it may be the only option to safeguard the well-being of the team as a whole. One member of staff can make others frightened, angry or resistant and gossip can infiltrate and undermine many initiatives that initially seem straightforward and uncontroversial.

Kurt Lewin developed the idea of 'forcefield analysis' (Lewin 1943) as a way of distinguishing between forces that support a proposed change and those that work against it. This theory suggests that the usual emphasis on the forces driving the change forward can have a negative impact on motivation and commitment. In contrast, giving a team the opportunity to explore and express their anxieties and concerns about the change can reduce the strength of resistance or even overcome it completely.

The emotionally literate leader

Being able to support a team through change in the way described above requires well-developed interpersonal skills on the part of the leader. There are many correlations between the emotional needs of the children and families and those of the practitioners, and a good leader will always bear this in mind. Much has been written about leadership styles, traits, and characteristics (see, for example, Rodd 2006), and the need for anyone in a senior position to have a repertoire of responses that they can call on depending on the situation. However, to ensure the well-being of others, it is important that a high level of emotional literacy underpins a leadership style (Goleman 1998). This may be recognized by the ability to harness all of oneself – feelings, hunches, gut reactions, intuitions, alongside knowledge, experience, thoughts, and logic – to make sense of situations and inform decision making. To do this means developing self-awareness, self-regulation, and empathy.

Self-awareness is knowing how you feel and understanding how your emotions and actions impact on those around you. This can be observed in its simplest form by noticing how, when the leader smiles and chats happily to everyone, the whole atmosphere is raised. Self-awareness can be developed by keeping a reflective journal (Bolton 2005) and after a period of time analysing your reactions to people and situations to identify common themes. It can also help simply to slow down and think about your emotional reaction before responding to someone or something. There is no harm in telling someone you need to think and will respond later. Leaders who were part of the Emotional Well-being: Strong Teams training in a London borough identified that keeping a journal 'helps me get a perspective so I no longer take work home with me in my head so much. I also have more focus so things are dealt with; journaling helps with this' (Manning-Morton and Wilson 2011).

Rodd (2006) highlights that leaders who are skilful in self-regulation rarely attack others or make rushed and emotional decisions; they focus on their values and what is important to them and concentrate on staying emotionally in control. To develop these skills, it is necessary to think about your values and exactly what you will not compromise because it is at the core of yourself. Knowing this means you will not have to think twice about moral or ethical decisions. Practise being calm and try to challenge your own reactions to people and situations. Taking deep breaths, slowing down your thinking and again, stalling for time, can help. It can also be worthwhile to write down your negative thoughts, then tear them up and throwing them away.

Reflective exercise

Consider a situation you faced at work that challenged you. Make some notes about what was difficult about that situation for you.

- How did it make you feel?
- Which of your values was it challenging?
- What did you want to come out of the situation for you and for the other person/people?
- Would any of the suggestions above have helped?

For leaders, having empathy is critical to managing a successful team or organization. Leaders with empathy have the ability to put themselves in someone else's shoes. They help develop the people on their team, challenge others who are acting unfairly, give constructive feedback, and listen to those who need it.

If you want to earn the respect and loyalty of your team, then show them you care by being empathic. The best way to develop this skill is to put yourself in someone else's position. Again, pause and take the time to look at the situation from the other person's perspective. Pay careful attention to the body language you use – do you cross your arms, shuffle your feet or bite your lip? – and to the body language those around you are using. Noticing this can help you identify how someone really feels (Cournoyer 2011).

Finally, develop your social and communication skills. Leaders who have good social skills are also good at managing change and resolving conflicts diplomatically. Think about how you talk to others, your tone of voice, and your facial expressions. Again, slow yourself down, and always think before you speak or press the send button on an e-mail.

The well-being of the leader

This chapter has focused on how the attitude and practice of the leader underpins the well-being of the practitioners in every area of practice within the setting, how supervision can open doorways, and how teams need developing and supporting through change. Of equal importance, however, is who provides such support for the leader or manager.

In the Emotional Well-being: Strong Teams training (Elfer and Dearnley 2007; Manning-Morton and Wilson 2011), it is recognized that leaders of settings need to be able to contain personal distress and maintain perspective when working with social disadvantage, challenging behaviours, intimate family issues, and family or staff distress. Therefore, as well as group training on supporting the emotional well-being of practitioners and children, the training also offered small group supervision in which the centre leaders could have time and space to reflect on work issues and their responses to them. These leaders reported that these sessions filled a previously unmet need for support and mutual sharing and as a result they gave their staff more time to talk, they reflected more, and looked at situations from different perspectives.

Unfortunately, the need for this kind of support has yet to be fully recognized and few early years settings provide a budget for external supervision. Similarly, local authority budgets have been cut to the extent where inspectors, advisors, and improvement partners no longer fulfil this role. Some settings may have a chair of a governing body or a management committee who are happy to take on this role, but of course they may not have been recruited to this post with this role in mind.

It therefore falls to the leader or manager to develop their own support systems. In examining the support for children's centre leaders, Sharp et al. (2012: 60) identify that 'Children's Centre leaders should make the most of the networks and links that already exist in the early years to support each other in this time of change and uncertainty.' They assert that 'leaders should consider their own health and welfare and identify strategies and support to help manage stress'. These points are true for all who work in the sector.

We are all used to pouring out our hearts to friends and families, but this may not be the best way forward in finding the emotional and professional support that leaders and managers need. Working with other settings and developing relationships of interdependence and trust is a new role for many early years leaders that is not always comfortable, particularly in environments still dominated by competition, but such relationships may provide the best form of mutual support.

Reflective exercise

Think about the setting you work in, or one which you are very familiar with, and make a list of all the positive things that happen to make you feel supported and contained in your work.

- Who takes the responsibility for this and what is your role in caring for your colleagues?
- Are there any aspects that could be improved, and how could you take these ideas forward and make them happen?
- Everyone working in a setting has a leadership role; how are you going to develop your skills in maintaining adult well-being?

Conclusion

In this chapter, we have considered the responsibilities of the leader or manager for ensuring the well-being of the staff team and how, through giving this a high priority, individuals and teams are better able to concentrate on the well-being of the children and families they work with. This is not an easy task for an individual leader and although any of the elements highlighted may make a difference, it is the overall approach and attitude to being a leader and how these are disseminated through the setting that will underpin the well-being of the staff team. However, in the same way that children have to learn that they are responsible for their own actions, it may take time to change the perceptions of individuals and the entire staff team.

References

Bolton, G. (2005) *Reflective Practice*. London: Sage.

Cournoyer, B.R. (2011) *The Social Work Skills Workbook*. Belmont, CA: Brooks/Cole, Cengage Learning.

Department for Education (DfE) (2012) *Statutory Framework for the Early Years Foundation Stage: Setting the Standards for Learning, Development and Care for Children from Birth to Five*. London: DfE.

Elfer, P. and Dearnley, D. (2007) Nurseries and emotional well-being: evaluating an emotionally containing model of professional development, *Early Years: An International Journal of Research and Development*, 27(3): 267–79.

Fullan, M. (2007) *The New Meaning of Educational Change* (4th edn.). New York: Teachers College Press.

Goleman, D. (1998) What makes a leader?, *Harvard Business Review*, November–December: 93–102.

Hall, G. and Hord, S. (2001) *Implementing Change: Patterns, Principles and Potholes*. Needham Heights, MA: Allyn & Bacon.

Kearney, K. and Hyle, A. (2003) The grief cycle and educational change, *Planning and Changing*, 34: 32–57.

Kolb, D.A. (1984) *Experiential Learning Experience as a Source of Learning and Development*. Englewood Cliffs, NJ: Prentice-Hall.

Kotter, J. (1988) *The Leadership Factor*. New York: Collier Macmillan.

Lewin, K. (1943) Defining the 'field at a given time', *Psychological Review*, 50: 292–310. Republished in *Resolving Social Conflicts and Field Theory in Social Science* (1997). Washington, DC: American Psychological Association.

Manning-Morton, J. and Wilson, D. (2011) *Addressing emotional well-being for infants, toddlers and young children through the professional development of practitioners*, Presentation to the European Early Childhood Education Research Association, August.

Moon, J. (1999) *Reflection in Learning and Professional Development: Theory and Practice*. Abingdon: RoutledgeFalmer.

Rodd, J. (2006) *Leadership in Early Childhood Education*. Maidenhead: Open University Press.

Sharp, C., Lord, P., Handscomb, G., Macleod, S., Southcott, C., George, N. and Jeffes, J. (2012) *Highly Effective Leadership in Children's Centres*. Nottingham: NCSL.

Skills for Care and the Children's Workforce Development Council (2007) *Providing Effective Supervision*. London: TSO.

Smith, A. and Langston, A. (1999) *Managing Staff in Early Years Settings*. London: Routledge.

Tickell, C. (2011) *The Early Years: Foundations for Life, Health and Learning*. London: DfE.

Tuckman, B. (1965) Developmental sequence in small groups, *Psychological Bulletin*, 63: 384–99. Reprinted in *Group Facilitation: A Research and Applications Journal*, 3(spring): 66–81.

Whalley, M. (2001) Working as a team, in G. Pugh (ed.) *Contemporary Issues in the Early Years*. London: Paul Chapman.

Whitaker, P. (1995) *Managing to Learn*. London: Cassell.

Conclusion: supporting well-being in early years practice

Julia Manning-Morton

Introduction

This final chapter considers the concept of well-being arising from the London Metropolitan University/National Children's Bureau Project 'Talking about Young Children's Well-being' (LMU/NCB Well-being Project) and the implications of this for observing and assessing children's well-being and for the approach taken to the curriculum in early childhood settings.

How do we identify well-being in babies and young children?

As discussed at the beginning of this book, there are several problems in identifying and measuring well-being in babies and young children. First, measures usually used in research are based on objective proxies such as educational attainment, health/immunization rates or family economic well-being, as used in the UNICEF research on child well-being in rich countries (UNICEF 2007) or the Child and Youth Well-being Index used by the Foundation for Child Development in the USA (Ben-Arieh 2008). This means that children's issues are then identified according to adults' priorities rather than their own. Second, even where children's subjective experiences of well-being are included, the indicators arise from consultations with older children and young adults; the voices of babies and young children are not included. Third, without a refined understanding and definition of the concept of well-being, the validity of any indicators used is weakened (Ben-Arieh 2008).

The LMU/NCB Well-being Project set out to address each of these issues by canvassing the views of children, parents, and practitioners on how they understood babies and young children's well-being. The project did not concern itself directly with how well-being might be measured but at the same time part of the process of the project was to identify what constitutes well-being for babies and young children so that we can develop practice and provision accordingly. This implies that practitioners have to be able to understand the different components of well-being and all the factors that contribute to children's potential for experiencing well-being. It also implies that we have to be able to identify and agree what *ill-being* is, which means being able to confront the difficulties and adversities inherent in society, children's lives, and early childhood settings. This does not, however, mean adopting a deficit approach to thinking about children and about well-being. One of the issues identified in research with young people such as that carried out by the Children's Society (Rees et al. 2012) is that although adult-driven research includes negative indicators such as 'risky behaviours', young people emphasize more positive aspects of well-being instead. Mayr and Ulich (2009) agree that we should move away from a deficit approach and instead develop tools to gather empirical evidence about children's well-being. But there are two issues we have to address in order to do this: first, we have to agree what we mean by well-being and what we think it looks like; and second, we have to accept that measuring this most slippery and complex of concepts cannot be accomplished by ticking a set of boxes.

Generally, writings on well-being use a broad definition as a basis for their discussions, such as 'Wellbeing is generally understood as the quality of people's lives ' (Statham and Chase 2010: 2), or 'people's satisfaction or happiness with their lives as a whole and with particular aspects of their lives' (Rees et al. 2012: 6). These kinds of definitions are helpful in as much as they set out the parameters of the thinking and approach of those offering the definition. In this way, the LMU/NCB Well-being Project emergent definition of well-being represents the thinking and discussions across the project.

The London Metropolitan University/National Children's Bureau Project 'Talking about Young Children's Well-Being': the project's conception of well-being

Well-being is a state that is dynamic and mutable and for which predisposing factors and experiences are necessary. These factors interact, combine and accumulate to enable or preclude experiencing states of well-being. In this way factors that are internal/subjective may be enhanced or exacerbated by external social, economic and policy factors and our interpretation and engagement with social factors are influenced by our inner well-being.

But for early childhood practitioners wanting to evaluate the effectiveness of their practice and provision, more detail of what being in a state of well-being might look like in young children is required.

Grappling with these issues and considering young children's well-being is not a new focus for early childhood practitioners and thinkers. In 1997, Ferre Laevers and his colleagues in Belgium developed 'A process oriented child monitoring system' which identifies two indicators of quality early education: children's well-being and involvement (Laevers et al. 1997). They suggest well-being means 'feeling at home', 'being oneself', and/or 'feeling happy' (p. 5), the first two of which participants in the LMU/NCB Well-being Project would agree with. However, they considered that well-being constituted more than happiness, although Laevers' and colleagues' description of children who are in a state of well-being as feeling like 'fish in water' (p. 15) was generally thought to encapsulate a feeling of well-being.

This kind of detailed 'lived' definition of well-being is helpful in thinking about measuring well-being in early childhood settings. Laevers et al. (1997) identify eight signs of well-being:

- Openness and receptivity
- Flexibility
- Self-confidence and self-esteem
- Being able to defend oneself, assertiveness
- Vitality
- Relaxation and inner peace
- Enjoyment without restraints
- Being in touch with one's self.

(Laevers et al. 1997: 16–19)

All of these signs chime with the manifestations of children's well-being suggested in the LMU/NCB Well-being Project, the key points of which are listed below:

- Appearance, such as:
  - Looking healthy and well cared for
  - Facial expressions, such as: smiling, bright sparkling eyes
  - Body language, such as: eye contact, relaxed open body stance
  - Body movement, such as: running, jumping, dancing, clapping hands, being 'bouncy', moving about happily with purposeful movements
  - Vibrancy
- Behaviours, such as:
  - Being curious, wanting to explore
  - Happily interacting with adults, peers, and the environment
  - Being enthusiastic about people, play, and food
  - Confident expression of thoughts and feelings
  - Successfully regulating emotions
  - Showing friendliness, empathy, and caring
  - Showing pride in achievements and recovery from mistakes and disappointments
  - Showing trust and affection
  - A sense of belonging
  - Eager and keen to try new things and join in
  - Persistence, engagement, and involvement
  - Able to take risks.

However, measuring these things immediately involves making judgements about the degree to which the presence or absence of an indicator means that a child's well-being is compromised or grading the child's level of well-being. The inherent difficulty here is that the observer's values and own perspective then influence their interpretation of what they see; what I consider to look 'healthy and well cared for' will probably be different to that of someone else. To make these values explicit and therefore useful to interpretation requires that assessment of well-being, like all assessments in early childhood practice, be based on regular and frequent, open observations that are interpreted in consultation with colleagues and parents. Practitioners also need to have been through a process of discussion that results in an agreed perspective on well-being and an understanding of the complexity of the concept. Laevers and colleagues' focus on well-being as a 'process variable' (Laevers et al. 1997: 6) is helpful here as it suggests that making these observations is an on-going activity, which can then prompt 'instant action and... successful short-term adjustments'. This reflects the dynamic and mutable quality of well-being put forward in the project's definition and avoids looking at well-being as an outcome.

Another issue that practitioners need to guard against is applying criteria such as those above in a blanket fashion to all children. In the same way as we have complained that well-being indicators devised for older children are used inappropriately with young children, so too must we consider that the Leuven Well-being Scales and to an extent the LMU/NCB Well-being Project indicators have been identified mostly with 3–6 year olds in mind. For example, 'successfully regulating emotions' or 'assertiveness' look very different in most 2 year olds to what you might look for in a 4 year old and different again in a 4 year old with a particular disability or learning need. A useful way of avoiding these pitfalls is to ask not 'Does this child show trust and affection?', for example, but to ask 'In what way...?' or 'What examples have I seen of...?' (Manning-Morton and Thorp 2006).

Although Manning-Morton and Thorp (2006) provide many examples of practices that support the development and learning of 0–3 year olds, further consideration of specific indicators for babies' and toddlers' well-being would be useful. Rosie Roberts's ideas of 'companionable learning' (Roberts 2010) are helpful in this regard, as they emphasize the centrality of relationships in all aspects of well-being for babies, which she says is manifested through:

- *Agency*: a state of well-being that is indicated through being able to make a difference, how a person learns, how confident they are, their self-esteem.
- *Belonging-and-boundaries*: also a state of well-being that is indicated through how safe someone feels, feeling special and wanted, being part of what is going on around them.
- *Communication*: a central process of well-being that relies on talking, listening, understanding, and communicating with other people.

- *Physical well-being*: which, together with communication, Roberts says is a determinant of well-being and forms the basis of the other aspects (Roberts 2010: 32).

In this way, Roberts indicates that there are determinants of well-being (Physical and Communication) that underpin states of well-being (Agency and Belonging) (Roberts 2010: 29). Laevers and colleagues also identify pre-requisites for reaching a state of well-being, including having basic needs met: physical needs; the need for affection, warmth, and tenderness; the need for safety, clarity, and continuity; the need for recognition; the need to experience oneself as competent; and the need to be morally 'correct' and to give life a meaning (Laevers et al. 1997: 16). These points very much reflect Maslow's (1943) Hierarchy of Needs, although neither Roberts nor Laevers imply a hierarchy and in fact emphasize the integrated, holistic nature of well-being.

Practice contexts that support children's well-being

The focus on contexts that facilitate and enhance children's well-being is a strong feature of each of these pieces of work and the 'conversation' we had across the early childhood community in the LMU/NCB Well-being Project suggests that we think young children's potential to experience well-being is enhanced when the following are in place:

Their emotions are understood in the context of secure, close, consistent relationships
The emphasis in the LMU/NCB Well-being Project on the centrality of nurturing relationships to children's well-being means that the Key Person Approach (Elfer et al. 2003) must be at the core of daily practice in early childhood settings. As Manning-Morton and Thorp (2003, 2006) point out, for babies and young children to develop a positive sense of self that is integrated and continuous, they need high levels of continuity, consistency, and constancy in their experiences and relationships. This means that practitioners need to be both physically and emotionally available, thereby providing for the child's need for a 'secure base' from which they can go out and explore (Bowlby 1988). In practice, as Goldschmied and Jackson (2004) make clear, being consistent in the physical and emotional care of children from birth to 3 years old means that for the times that the key person and child are together in the setting, the key person should:

- settle their key children as they arrive each day
- eat with their key children in small key groups and hold key children who are bottle-fed to feed
- change and toilet key children, using sensitive handling and familiar words
- dress and wash key children, offering help as needed but also supporting their growing skills.

For older children, these things remain important but may have a slightly different emphasis. Grenier et al. (2008) suggest that practitioners in nursery and reception classes ask themselves the following:

- How do parents/carers and practitioners work together during the settling-in period?
- How do staff make sure that children feel secure when the time comes to say goodbye and stay in the nursery or reception class without the parent or carer?
- How are care routines like toileting, getting dressed or changed, eating or resting managed for children so that they feel personalized, rather than in an institutional and uncaring system?
- Are children comforted by their key person when they feel distressed or tired?
- If a child's behaviour is challenging, how do you ensure that a limited number of staff who have a trusting relationship with the child manage difficult incidents?

A key concept in the Key Person Approach is that to become healthily independent, a baby or young child needs first to be able to depend on having their needs met reliably and sensitively. So within these relationships children must be given time to express their feelings and feel supported. In so doing, practitioners are positively contributing to young children's present well-being and future resilience.

Their experiences are congruent with their idea of who they are; so their unique selves are reflected back to them in relationships and the environment and their interests and learning styles are valued

A central aspect of well-being is a positive sense of being someone who is respected and valued. This means thinking carefully about how children are given choices and are involved in the organization of their day and their environment. It also means paying careful attention to how children's home cultures are recognized and valued in the setting, and ensuring that prejudice and bias are challenged. Siraj-Blatchford and Clarke (2000: 14–17) identify six stages of equity-oriented practice, which offer practitioners a useful tool for monitoring an anti-bias approach.

To be successful in this, practitioners need to know each child and their family well: their likes and dislikes, the way they communicate, and any changes or special events in their lives. Time and space to talk are required for this to happen, for both children and parents.

The LMU/NCB Well-being Project identified that observation is a key skill for the early childhood professional and a key aspect of practice for getting to know children well. Important aspects of this practice include developing observation and any resulting assessment as a shared dialogue in which children's and parents' voices are prominent, and using a holistic approach to undertaking observations in order to understand the whole child and their context.

By undertaking such observations, practitioners can tune in to children's particular styles of play and learning and devise play opportunities that follow the child's interests and are a good match to their abilities. They can then also develop a play environment that is not only interesting, stimulating, challenging, and fun, but also relevant and meaningful to the child.

Their friendships are nurtured and valued from birth enhancing their sense of group belonging

Participants in the LMU/NCB Well-being Project recognized the importance of supporting young children's friendships in general terms but there was little detail of what that might look like in practice. This is an aspect for further exploration and future training it seems for early childhood practitioners in the UK, where we need to explore the balance between our support for the 'Unique Child' (DfES 2007) and how we help children be part of a social group.

One aspect that was addressed though was group size and structure. In the same way that we must develop continuity and consistency in key person relationships with children by reducing the number of changes and transitions that children make within and between settings, so too must we consider the disruption that such changes cause to young children's friendships. In addition, we need to think about how the size and age range in a group will impact on children's ability to make friends. Young children communicate with each other better in small groups and can then get to know each other well. In these circumstances, negotiating different agendas and conflict is more manageable for children. In research into quality in settings in the USA, Howes et al. (1992) identified that children are more likely to experience developmentally appropriate activities and adults spend more time interacting with them when they are in groups of:

- 6 or fewer for babies
- 12 or fewer for toddlers
- 18 or fewer for 3–5 year olds.

They found that as a consequence children cared for in smaller groups perform better in tests of language and learning and are more socially competent with their peers. As these group sizes are often exceeded in settings in the UK, this level of quality seems to be something to aim for.

They have free access to interesting and challenging play materials and spaces indoors and outdoors, in the setting, and in the community

Children, parents, and practitioners in the LMU/NCB Well-being Project addressed this in different ways but the need to be able to take risks and have space to run, climb and explore, both indoors and out, was prioritized overall. This highlights the need to make movement play a priority in settings. In addition, practitioners emphasized the importance of open-ended and sensory materials that enable children's creativity and imagination to flourish, while parents identified that a play-based curriculum that supports creativity should be adopted in the first years of school too. Above all, it was clear that children need practitioners who take an interest, are fun and are a participant in their play, not just a provider and observer.

Their families, whatever form they take, are supported and valued

Respectful and communicative partnerships between parents and practitioners were identified in the LMU/NCB Well-being Project as a key contributory factor to supporting young children's well-being in early childhood settings. This takes three forms:

1. Involving parents in their children's learning through sharing knowledge and understanding of assessment and planning processes and information sessions, and through including parents' expertise and skills in the group and in decision making through management and parent committees.
2. Support for inexperienced parents or parents facing particular difficulties through peer support groups, information and training sessions, and one-to-one consultancy sessions.
3. Multi-disciplinary working through which practitioners can signpost families to relevant information and services that support their wider social context, such as financial or employment information.

The LMU/NCB Well-being Project also identified that wider social policy must address issues of work–life balance for parents through more generous parental leave and family-friendly employment policies, giving parents and children the opportunity to spend time together and to reduce family stress.

Their professional carers are supported and valued for all their skills, knowledge, and attributes

Working with babies and young children, in whatever capacity or setting, is a complex and demanding job that requires a deep understanding and broad knowledge of children's development and learning, a mature self-knowledge, good interpersonal and intrapersonal skills, and physical strength and resilience (Manning-Morton 2006).

To maintain the kind of effective practice identified in this chapter and throughout this book, practitioners need regular and effective support and supervision from knowledgeable and skilled leaders. They also need regular opportunities to talk and listen to colleagues about children and their practice in order to develop a shared vision, and like the children, time to play and have fun.

The importance of this work cannot rely on supposed 'natural' caring attributes; caring abilities need to be nurtured through training also. The knowledge and experience of practitioners is a key feature in providing effective provision that supports children's well-being, thus the quality, as well as the level, of training must be second to none. As one participant in the LMU/NCB Well-being Project said, what is required is 'highly qualified staff in high-quality provision with no one below excellent!'

They have a strong sense of belonging to their setting and local community, where they are listened to, acknowledged, and affirmed, and their contribution is sought and valued

The process of listening to children, integral to the LMU/NCB Well-being Project, was successful because some of the settings that took part were already involved in the Young Children's Voices Network (YCVN) based at the National Children's Bureau or had received training in 'Listening' or the 'Mosaic Approach' (Clark and Moss 2011). The network aims to embed a listening culture in early childhood settings so that children's views are incorporated into organizational processes. It would be meaningless if the practice of consulting children in this way had only been practised during the project. As Moss says:

> Listening is not only a complex concept, but it goes to the heart of the theories, relationships and practice that shape early childhood work. It should not be an add-on, to meet some external requirement . . . if we choose to listen to young children, it should be because listening is part of our beliefs about learning, relationships, democracy and ethics. It is an integral part of how we think life should be lived.
>
> (Moss 2001, cited in Dickins 2011: 6)

In the YCVN leaflet *Why and How We Listen to Young Children*, Alison Clark points out the many benefits to children in a setting where there is a listening culture. She suggests that when young children feel that their views are valued, they become more confident. In turn, this confidence can support them in gaining social and practical skills and the process of having time and space to be listened to can enhance cognitive skills as they process and reflect on their understandings (Clark 2008). In this way, we can see how developing a listening culture can contribute to children's potential for experiencing well-being.

They are taken into account in society as a whole, so national and local policies ensure that all children's needs can be met by their families and communities – because it takes a village to raise a child

Well-being not just well-becoming. A fundamental way in which babies and young children must be treated is to take account of their well-being *now* rather than treat it as a resource in which to invest for the future.

Being consulted. One of the aims of the Young Children's Voices Network is to support local authorities to meet their statutory requirement under the Childcare Act 2006. In this way, it is hoped that those responsible for planning and commissioning services will be better informed about what works for children, families, and communities. *Raising Standards – Improving Outcomes* (Statutory Guidance: Early Years Outcomes Duty, Childcare Act 2006) states that:

> For services to be successful and have a positive impact on young children's lives, the voices of young children themselves need to be listened to and actively taken into account. Undertaking consultations with young children as the primary users of early years services, can inform not only frontline practitioners and managers of their needs but also reveal barriers to development which can inform more strategic planning to improve outcomes and opportunities for all young children.
>
> (cited in Williams 2009: 8)

However, as discussed in Part 1 of this book, there are many instances in research and policy making where the needs and views of young children and their families are not considered or included. The most recent of these, which will have a direct negative impact on the well-being of children, families, and practitioners, is the proposal to increase the ratio of children to adults permitted in settings (DfE 2013). This proposal is made in direct opposition to both research that shows that quality of caregiving is generally lower when more children are being cared for (Howes et al. 1992) and the professional opinions of practitioners and the preferences of parents.

Participants in the LMU/NCB Well-being Project identified that ratios of children to practitioners should in fact be *reduced* from current figures, suggesting that a 1:1 ratio for babies and a 1:2 ratio for 2 year olds (rather than the 1:6 ratio proposed by government) are more likely to enable them to meet children's needs. They were also clear that it should be government funding that provides more affordable childcare, not parents' fees, and expressed concern that the economy is being prioritized over children's and families' well-being.

A 'connections' curriculum

The perspective that emerges from the discussions in the LMU/NCB Well-being Project not only suggests *what* our practice should include but *how* we should be approaching it. Making connections between the many parts of a whole has been the central theme of the project both in the process and in the findings. The emphasis on the interconnectedness and interdependence of all aspects of well-being in the project discussions gave rise to the holistic concept of well-being adopted here.

Our interpretation of 'holistic' is something that is multi-dimensional, with all the different dimensions being interrelated, emphasizing that attention must be paid to the whole as well as to each dimension. This perspective is reflective of a dynamic systems perspective (Schaffer 2006) and an ecological systems (Bronfenbrenner 1979) theoretical approach to human development, which hopefully enables us to move away from the compartmentalization of children's development and learning inherent to the Early Years Foundation Stage curriculum framework (DfE 2012).

So, rather than a focus on outcomes, the approach suggested here is one where together, children, parents, and practitioners seek to make connections in all aspects of practice and provision:

- connections between people in the setting (key persons, parent partnership, teamwork, and leadership support);
- connections between each individual child and the group (interests, playthings, languages, and cultures);
- connections with places and things (at home, in the community, with the natural world, across the globe);
- connections between thinking, feeling, playing, and learning (exploring, imagining, moving, being);
- connections in our theoretical thinking and practices (across disciplines, between practitioners);
- connections to our own childhoods and to children's current experience (between personal experience, personal and professional values and practice);
- connections between settings (networking, training, sharing, collective action).

These are important because no one is an island; we are all dependent on each other and on the planet. The image that conveys this interconnectedness and dynamic flow of well-being is the mandala, which represents the relationship between the internal and the external, the individual and the cosmos to form an indistinguishable whole (see Figure 3).

Final thoughts

Well-being is not about just being okay, coping or surviving. Well-being is about thriving, blossoming, and flourishing. Our wish is that this book will contribute to the early childhood community's ability to enhance children's potential to flourish and experience well-being.

However, it is of grave concern in the early childhood community that, in the context of the current economic recession, the window of opportunity for a

Figure 3   A drawing of a Mandala.

positive focus on well-being that existed briefly at the beginning of the twenty-first century has passed. As the focus in policy and financial support moves away from the provision of universal services for young children and returns to looking at only what must be done for the most 'in need', we ask ourselves: 'In the context of targeted services, is looking after the well-being of all our youngest citizens a luxury the UK is no longer willing to pay for?'

Which, in turn, gives rise to the question of whether, in the early childhood community when services are being reduced and many parents' and practitioners' employment security is uncertain, this is the time to be talking about well-being. And the answer is: 'If not now, then when?'

References

Ben-Arieh, A. (2008) Indicators and indices of children's well-being: towards a more policy-oriented perspective, *European Journal of Education*, 43(1): 37–50.

Bowlby, J. (1988) *A Secure Base: Clinical Applications of Attachment Theory*. London: Routledge.

Bronfenbrenner, U. (1979) *The Ecology of Human Development: Experiments by Nature and Design*. Cambridge, MA: Harvard University Press.

Clark, A. (2008) *Why and How We Listen to Young Children*. London: The Young Children's Voices Network, National Children's Bureau. Available at: http://www.ncb.org.uk/ycvn/about-ycvn [accessed 15 February 2013].

Clark, A. and Moss, P. (2011) *Listening to Young Children: The Mosaic Approach* (2nd edn.). London: National Children's Bureau.

Department for Education (DfE) (2012) *Statutory Framework for the Early Years Foundation Stage: Setting the Standards for Learning, Development and Care for Children from Birth to Five*. London: DfE.

Department for Education (DfE) (2013) *More Great Childcare*. London: DfE. Available at: http://www.education.gov.uk/childrenandyoungpeople/earlylearningandchildcare/a00220847/more-great-childcare [accessed 28 February 2013].

Department for Education and Skills (DfES) (2007) *The Early Years Foundation Stage: Setting the Standards for Learning, Development and Care for Children from Birth to Five*. Nottingham: DfES Publications. Available at: http://archive.defra.gov.uk/sustainable/government/publications/uk-strategy/ [accessed 28 February 2013].

Dickins, M. (2011) *Leadership for Listening*. London: The Young Children's Voices Network, National Children's Bureau. Available at: http://www.ncb.org.uk/ycvn/about-ycvn [accessed 15 February 2013].

Elfer, P., Goldschmied, E. and Selleck, D. (2003) *Key Persons in Nursery: Building Relationships for Quality Provision*. London: David Fulton.

Goldschmied, E. and Jackson, S. (2004) *People Under Three: Young Children in Day Care* (2nd edn.). London: Routledge.

Grenier, J., Manning-Morton, J., Elfer, P., Dearnley, K. and Wilson, D. (2008) *The Key Person in Reception Classes and Small Nursery Settings, Social and Emotional Aspects of Development: Guidance for Practitioners Working in the Early Years Foundation Stage*. London: DCSF.

Howes, C., Phillips, D.A. and Whitebook, M. (1992) Thresholds of quality: implications for the social development of children in centre-based childcare, *Child Development*, 63: 449–60.

Laevers, F., Vandenbussche, E., Kog, M. and Depondt, L. (1997) *A Process Oriented Child Monitoring System for Young Children*. Leuven: Centre for Experiential Education.

Manning-Morton, J. (2006) The personal is professional: professionalism and the birth to threes practitioner, *Contemporary Issues in Early Childhood*, 7(1): 42–52.

Manning-Morton, J. and Thorp, M. (2003) *Key Times for Play: The First Three Years.* Maidenhead: Open University Press.

Manning-Morton, J. and Thorp, M. (2006) *Key Times: A Framework for Developing High Quality Provision for Children from Birth to Three Years.* Maidenhead: Open University Press.

Maslow, H. (1943) A theory of human motivation, *Psychological Review*, 50: 370–96.

Mayr, T. and Ulich, M. (2009) Social-emotional well-being and resilience of children in early childhood settings – PERIK: an empirically based observation scale for practitioners, *Early Years*, 29(1): 45–57.

Rees, G., Bradshaw, J., Goswami, H., Keung, A., Pople, L. and Main, G. (2012) *The Good Childhood Report 2012: A Review of Our Children's Well-being.* London: The Children's Society.

Roberts, R. (2010) *Well-Being from Birth.* London: Sage.

Schaffer, H.R. (2006) *Key Concepts in Developmental Psychology.* London: Sage.

Siraj-Blatchford, I. and Clarke, P. (2000) *Supporting Identity, Diversity and Language in the Early Years.* Buckingham: Open University Press.

Statham, J. and Chase, E. (2010) *Childhood Wellbeing: A Brief Overview.* Childhood Wellbeing Research Centre Briefing Paper 1. London: TCRU.

United Nations Children's Fund (UNICEF) (2007) *Child Poverty in Perspective: An Overview of Child Well-being in Rich Countries. A Comprehensive Assessment of the Lives and Well-being of Children and Adolescents in the Economically Advanced Nations.* Innocenti Report Card 7. Florence: UNICEF Innocenti Research Centre.

Williams, L. (2009) *Listening as a Way of Life.* London: The Young Children's Voices Network, National Children's Bureau. Available at: http://www.ncb.org.uk/ycvn/about-ycvn [accessed 15 February 2013].

Index

Locators shown in *italics* refer to figures, tables, examples and case studies.

International Perspectives on Early Childhood Education and Care

Jan Georgeson and Jane Payler

9780335245918 (Paperback)
February 2013

eBook also available

There is a growing interest in understanding how early years care and education is organised and experienced internationally. This book examines key influential approaches to early years care as well as some less well-known systems from around the world.

Key features:

- Informs those studying early years about perspectives in other countries
- Encourages critical thinking about issues, influences and the complexities of early years provision around the world
- Promotes critical reflection on students' own provision and the current context of that provision

www.openup.co.uk

CHARACTERISTICS OF EFFECTIVE EARLY LEARNING
Helping young children become learners for life

Helen Moylett

9780335263264 (Paperback)
October 2013

eBook also available

The key argument of *The Characteristics of Effective Early Learning* is that how children learn is as important as what they learn. This book helps you understand how to support the learning and development of young children through promoting the characteristics of effective early learning: play and exploring, active learning, and creating and thinking critically.

Key features:

- Investigates how children engage in learning through playing and exploring, and are motivated through active learning
- Explores how children become creative and critical thinkers able to review their own learning and thinking, imaginatively solving problems and excited by their own
- Examines appropriate approaches to observation, assessment and planning

www.openup.co.uk

RETHINKING SUPERHERO AND WEAPON PLAY
Superheroes and Children's Moral
Development

Steven Popper

9780335247066 (Paperback)
April 2013

eBook also available

This book explores children's war, weapon and superhero play with a view to examining its potential (positive) impact on developing moral values and sensibilities, and to the many moral themes available for children's exploration during their engagement with such play, and the traditional and continuing need for children to receive a good moral education, with reference to many ideas from educational philosophy.

Key features:

- It links examples of children's real-life play and perspectives to theories about play, moral development and narrative psychology
- It explores the continuing attraction of classical dualism (i.e. good versus evil) for children and various educational perspectives about this
- Contains a wealth of learning opportunities and suggestions of ways to use superheroes to advance children's moral, philosophical and emotional thinking

www.**openup**.co.uk